THE POETRY OF THE NEGRO
1746-1949

THE POETRY OF THE NEGRO 1746-1949

AN ANTHOLOGY EDITED BY

LANGSTON HUGHES

AND

ARNA BONTEMPS

DOUBLEDAY & COMPANY, INC.

GARDEN CITY, NEW YORK

ACKNOWLEDGMENTS

The editors of this anthology are deeply indebted to the following persons for advice, guidance, research, or discovery: in regard to the poetry of the Caribbean, particularly are we grateful to Vivian L. Virtue and Wycliffe S. Bennett of the Poetry League of Jamaica, and to Edna Manley; for invaluable assistance in assembling the biographies of the Haitian poets, to René Piquion, Clovis Charlot, and Dr. Mercer Cook; for careful research and help with the many details of checking and preparing the manuscript, to Dr. Hugh S. Smythe, Rosamond Johnson, Minnie Redmond Bowles, Nathaniel V. White, and Marjorie Greene; for aid in securing certain poems to Ralph Ellison and Cedric Dover; and to Arthur Spingarn for sharing with us his vast knowledge of the Negro literature of this hemisphere.

PREFACE

The title of this volume has somewhat more reference to a theme and a point of view than to the racial identity of some of its contributors. But this does not mean it has none at all. A number of the poems were chosen because the writers belonged to the group which is defined in the United States as Negro, even though the sum of such inclusions may be smaller than the number of selections made on other grounds.

If the compilers had sought for a racial idiom in verse form among Negroes, they should have concerned themselves with the words of Negro spirituals, with folk rhymes, with blues, and other spontaneous lyrics. These song materials, no doubt, suggest a kind of poetry that is racially distinctive, that lies essentially outside the literary traditions of the language which it employs. But the present anthology consists of poems written within that tradition, by Negroes as well as others.

The common thread, of course, is the Negro's experience in the Western world. Where the author is a Negro, any comment on any subject is considered within this limit. Poems by others are included only when they touch the subject directly, except in the case of the Caribbean countries, where a departure from this principle seemed necessary in a few cases in order to make representative selections.

Another factor, too, blurred this logic a little. Racial distinctions vary from country to country. Any effort to apply the yardstick of the United States to the other Americas is likely to confuse more than it clarifies. No such attempt was made by the compilers. Moreover, in the pre-

dominantly Negro countries around the Caribbean, selections of representative poems were made sometimes without respect either to racial
implications in the verses or to the identity of the poets. This point was
explained to those contributors to whom it was not clear.

The arrangement of the poems was influenced by other considera-
tions. In the major section, containing the work of Negro poets of the
United States, a chronological order was followed, based on the date
of the poet's birth, or the closest estimate that could be made of it. The
poems in the other two sections follow sequences which seemed gen-
erally appropriate for reading purposes, the deciding element being
sometimes historical, sometimes dramatic.

On the whole the aim was to assemble selections which would be at
once representative of the Negro's own poetic expression and of the
poetry he inspired others to write. The Long Island slave Jupiter Hammon's "An Evening Thought: Salvation by Christ, with Penitential
Cries" (1760) was the first well-known literary work by a Negro published in the United States. Evidence of an earlier Negro poet has been
found in references to a Lucy Terry, to whom a verse account of an
Indian raid on Deerfield in 1746 is credited. But the original version of
this literary work appears to have been lost. The one used by George
A. Sheldon in his *Negro Slavery in Old Deerfield* and quoted in this
volume is rather enigmatically described as "secondary."

Hammon was followed by Phillis Wheatley, a delicate girl who not
only produced a larger amount of poetry but also won the attention of
George Washington and Thomas Jefferson as well as a number of
prominent people in London. Somewhat later another slave, who was
permitted to hire himself out, found employment in the home of the
president of the University of North Carolina and in this atmosphere
composed poems that were published in Raleigh in 1829.

These articulate slaves belonged to a tradition of writers in bondage
which goes back to Aesop and Terence. While Aesop's writing appears
to have won him rewards of a sort, there is no sure indication that he
succeeded in writing himself out of servitude. Terence did, however,
and so did Phillis Wheatley of West Africa and Boston. Hammon became a pamphleteer for freedom, but his final years are obscure. George
Moses Horton, the slave poet of North Carolina, waited for his deliverance till the Northern armies invaded the South.

Meanwhile in Louisiana free men of color became an important
element of the population, gained wealth, sent their youth to Paris to

study drama, music, and fencing, and to hobnob with the friends of
Alexandre Dumas; to Rome to devote themselves to sculpture and singing. Many of these young people were not inclined to return to their
native state, with its oppressive racial attitudes, but some were drawn
again by the bittersweet allurements of home in New Orleans. Enough
trained musicians came back, for example, to bring about the organiza-
tion of a symphony orchestra of one hundred members among this
group at one time. Their influence in literature was strong enough to
produce an anthology of poetry in 1845. The volume was called *Les
Cenelles*, and it contained verse by a dozen of the younger French-
speaking poets among the free Negroes writing at that time, including
Victor Séjour, who was later to become a popular playwright in Paris.
Oddly, the members of this group had not been taught to link themselves personally with the condition of the slaves, and their poetry
scarcely touched racial feeling.

So the traditions of Negro poetry derive from influences and sources
as far apart as those that inspired Jupiter Hammon's "An Address to
Negroes in the State of New York" (1787) and Horton's book of verse,
The Hope of Liberty, on the one hand, and Phillis Wheatley's refined
and tempered *Poems on Various Subjects, Religious and Moral* (1773)
and *Les Cenelles* on the other. The lines from these to Dunbar and
Braithwaite, to Hughes and Cullen and Donald Jeffrey Hayes, to Margaret Walker and Gwendolyn Brooks are not hard to draw.

The Negro in Western civilization has been exposed to overwhelming
historical and sociological pressures that are bound to be reflected in
the verse he has written and inspired. The fact that he has used poetry
as a form of expression has also brought him into contact with literary
trends and influences. How one of these forces or the other has pre-
dominated and how the results may be weighed and appraised are
among the questions to which the poetry itself contains answers.

LANGSTON HUGHES
ARNA BONTEMPS

CONTENTS

1. NEGRO POETS OF THE U. S. A.

2. TRIBUTARY POEMS BY NON-NEGROES

3. THE CARIBBEAN

JAMAICA

BIOGRAPHICAL NOTES

TRANSLATORS

AUTHOR INDEX

FIRST LINE INDEX

1 NEGRO POETS OF THE U.S.A.

BARS FIGHT
by Lucy Terry

August 'twas the twenty fifth
Seventeen hundred forty-six
The Indians did in ambush lay
Some very valient men to slay
The names of whom I'll not leave out
Samuel Allen like a hero fout
And though he was so brave and bold
His face no more shall we behold.
Eleazer Hawks was killed outright
Before he had time to fight
Before he did the Indians see
Was shot and killed immediately.
Oliver Amsden he was slain
Which caused his friends much grief and pain.
Samuel Amsden they found dead
Not many rods off from his head.
Adonijah Gillet we do hear
Did lose his life which was so dear.
John Saddler fled across the water
And so excaped the dreadful slaughter.
Eunice Allen see the Indians comeing
And hoped to save herself by running
And had not her petticoats stopt her
The awful creatures had not cotched her
And tommyhawked her on the head
And left her on the ground for dead.
Young Samuel Allen, Oh! lack a-day
Was taken and carried to Canada.

AN EVENING THOUGHT
Salvation by Christ, With Penitential Cries
by Jupiter Hammon

Salvation comes by Christ alone,
The only Son of God;
Redemption now to every one,
That love his holy Word.
Dear Jesus we would fly to Thee,
And leave off every Sin,
Thy tender Mercy well agree;
Salvation from our King;
Salvation comes now from the Lord,
Our victorious King.
His holy Name be well ador'd,
Salvation surely bring.
Dear Jesus give thy Spirit now,
Thy Grace to every Nation,
That han't the Lord to whom we bow,
The Author of Salvation.
Dear Jesus unto Thee we cry,
Give us the Preparation;
Turn not away thy tender Eye;
We see thy true Salvation.
Salvation comes from God we know,
The true and only One;
It's well agreed and certain true,
He gave his only Son.
Lord hear our penitential Cry:
Salvation from above;
It is the Lord that doth supply,
With his Redeeming Love.
Dear Jesus by thy precious Blood,
The World Redemption have:
Salvation now comes from the Lord,
He being thy captive slave.
Dear Jesus let the Nations cry,

And all the People say,
Salvation comes from Christ on high,
Haste on Tribunal Day.
We cry as Sinners to the Lord,
Salvation to obtain;
It is firmly fixt his holy Word,
Ye shall not cry in vain.
Dear Jesus unto Thee we cry,
And make our Lamentation:
O let our Prayers ascend on high;
We felt thy Salvation.
Lord turn our dark benighted Souls;
Give us a true Motion,
And let the Hearts of all the World,
Make Christ their Salvation.
Ten Thousand Angels cry to Thee,
Yea louder than the Ocean.
Thou art the Lord, we plainly see;
Thou art the true Salvation.
Now is the Day, excepted Time;
The Day of Salvation;
Increase your Faith, do not repine:
Awake ye every Nation.
Lord unto whom now shall we go,
Or see a safe Abode;
Thou hast the Word Salvation too
The only Son of God.
Ho! every one that hunger hath,
Or pineth after me,
Salvation be thy leading Staff,
To set the Sinner free.
Dear Jesus unto Thee we fly;
Depart, depart from Sin,
Salvation doth at length supply,
The Glory of our King.
Come ye Blessed of the Lord,
Salvation greatly given;
O turn your Hearts, accept the Word,
Your souls are fit for Heaven.

Dear Jesus we now turn to Thee,
Salvation to obtain;
Our Hearts and Souls do meet again,
To magnify thy Name.
Come holy Spirit, Heavenly Dove,
The Object of our Care;
Salvation doth increase our Love;
Our Hearts hath felt thy fear.
Now Glory be to God on High,
Salvation high and low;
And thus the Soul on Christ rely,
To Heaven surely go.
Come Blessed Jesus, Heavenly Dove,
Accept Repentance here;
Salvation give, with tender Love;
Let us with Angels share. Finis.

HIS EXCELLENCY GENERAL WASHINGTON
by Phillis Wheatley

Celestial choir! enthron'd in realms of light,
Columbia's scenes of glorious toils I write.
While freedom's cause her anxious breast alarms,
She flashes dreadful in refulgent arms.
See mother earth her offspring's fate bemoan,
And nations gaze at scenes before unknown!
See the bright beams of heaven's revolving light
Involved in sorrows and the veil of night!
  The goddess comes, she moves divinely fair,
Olive and laurel binds her golden hair:
Wherever shines this native of the skies,
Unnumber'd charms and recent graces rise.
Muse! how propitious while my pen relates
How pour her armies through a thousand gates,
As when *Eolus* heaven's fair face deforms,
Enwrapp'd in tempest and a night of storms;
Astonish'd ocean feels the wild uproar,

The refluent surges beat the sounding shore;
Or thick as leaves in Autumn's golden reign,
Such, and so many, moves the warrior's train.
In bright array they seek the work of war,
Where high unfurl'd the ensign waves in air.
Shall I go to Washington their praise recite?
Enough thou know'st them in the fields of fight.
Thee, first in peace and honours,—we demand
The grace and glory of thy martial band.
Fam'd for thy valour, for thy virtues more,
Hear every tongue thy guardian and implore!
   One century scarce perform'd its destined round,
When *Gallic* powers *Columbia's* fury found;
And so may you, whoever dares disgrace
The land of freedom's heaven defended race!
Fir'd are the eyes of nations on the scales,
For in their hopes *Columbia's* arm prevails.
Anon *Britannia* droops the pensive head,
While round increase the rising hills of dead.
Ah! cruel blindness to *Columbia's* state!
Lament thy thirst of boundless power too late.
   Proceed, great chief, with virtue on thy side,
Thy ev'ry action let the goddess guide.
A crown, a mansion, and a throne that shine,
With gold unfading, *Washington!* be thine.

ON IMAGINATION
by Phillis Wheatley

Thy various works, imperial queen, we see,
How bright their forms! how deck'd with pomp by thee!
Thy wond'rous acts in beauteous order stand,
And all attest how potent is thine hand.
   From *Helicon's* refulgent heights attend
Ye sacred choir, and my attempts befriend:
To tell her glories with a faithful tongue,
Ye blooming graces, triumph in my song.

Now here, now there, the roving *Fancy* flies,
Till some lov'd object strikes her wand'ring eyes
Whose silken fetters all the senses bind,
And soft captivity involves the mind.
    Imagination! who can sing thy force?
Or who describe the swiftness of thy course?
Soaring through air to find the bright abode?
Th' empyreal palace of the thund'ring God,
We on thy pinions can surpass the wind,
And leave the rolling universe behind:
From star to star the mental optics rove,
Measure the skies, and range the realms above.
There in one view we grasp the mighty whole,
Or with new worlds amaze th' unbounded soul.
    Though *Winter* frowns to *Fancy's* raptur'd eyes
The fields may flourish, and gay scenes arise;
The frozen deeps may break their iron bands,
And bid their waters murmur o'er the sands.
Fair *Flora* may resume her fragrant reign,
And with her flow'ry riches deck the plain;
Sylvanus may diffuse his honors round,
And all the forest may with leaves be crown'd:
Show'rs may descend, and dews their gems disclose,
And nectar sparkle on the blooming rose.
    Such is thy pow'r, nor are thine orders vain,
O thou the leader of the mental train:
In full perfection all thy works are wrought,
And thine the sceptre o'er the realms of thought.
Before thy throne the subject-passions bow,
Of subject-passions sov'reign ruler thou:
At thy command joy rushes on the heart,
And through the glowing veins the spirits dart.
    Fancy might now her silken pinions try
To rise from earth, and sweep th' expanse on high;
From *Tithon's* bed now might *Aurora* rise,
Her cheeks all glowing with celestial dyes,
While a pure stream of light o'erflows the skies.
The monarch of the day I might behold,
And all the mountains tipt with radiant gold,

But I reluctant leave the pleasing views,
Which *Fancy* dresses to delight the *Muse;*
Winter austere forbids me to aspire,
And northern tempests damp the rising fire;
They chill the tides of *Fancy's* flowing sea,
Cease then, my song, cease the unequal lay.

ON LIBERTY AND SLAVERY[1]
by George Moses Horton

Alas! and am I born for this,
    To wear this slavish chain?
Deprived of all created bliss,
    Through hardship, toil and pain!

How long have I in bondage lain,
    And languished to be free!
Alas! and must I still complain—
    Deprived of liberty.

Oh, Heaven! and is there no relief
    This side the silent grave—
To soothe the pain—to quell the grief
    And anguish of a slave?

Come, Liberty, thou cheerful sound,
    Roll through my ravished ears!
Come, let my grief in joys be drowned,
    And drive away my fears.

Say unto foul oppression, Cease:
    Ye tyrants rage no more,
And let the joyful trump of peace,
    Now bid the vassal soar.

[1]From *Poems of an Exile,* by George M. Horton, copyright, 1931. Reprinted by permission of the Bobbs-Merrill Company.

Soar on the pinions of that dove
  Which long has cooed for thee,
And breathed her notes from Afric's grove,
  The sound of Liberty.

Oh, Liberty! thou golden prize,
  So often sought by blood—
We crave thy sacred sun to rise,
  The gift of nature's God!

Bid Slavery hide her haggard face,
  And barbarism fly:
I scorn to see the sad disgrace
  In which enslaved I lie.

Dear Liberty! upon thy breast,
  I languish to respire;
And like the Swan unto her nest,
  I'd to thy smiles retire.

Oh, blest asylum—heavenly balm!
  Unto thy boughs I flee—
And in thy shades the storm shall calm,
  With songs of Liberty!

THE SLAVE AUCTION
by Frances E. W. Harper

The sale began—young girls were there,
  Defenceless in their wretchedness,
Whose stifled sobs of deep despair
  Revealed their anguish and distress.

And mothers stood with streaming eyes,
  And saw their dearest children sold;
Unheeded rose their bitter cries,
  While tyrants bartered them for gold.

And woman, with her love and truth—
 For these in sable forms may dwell—
Gaz'd on the husband of her youth,
 With anguish none may paint or tell.

And men, whose sole crime was their hue,
 The impress of their Maker's hand,
And frail and shrinking children, too,
 Were gathered in that mournful band.

Ye who have laid your love to rest,
 And wept above their lifeless clay,
Know not the anguish of that breast,
 Whose lov'd are rudely torn away.

Ye may not know how desolate
 Are bosoms rudely forced to part,
And how a dull and heavy weight
 Will press the life-drops from the heart.

LET THE LIGHT ENTER
by Frances E. W. Harper

"Light! more light! the shadows deepen
 And my life is ebbing low,
Throw the windows widely open:
 Light! more light! before I go.

"Softly let the balmy sunshine
 Play around my dying bed,
E'er the dimly lighted valley
 I with lonely feet must tread.

"Light! more light! for Death is weaving
 Shadows 'round my waning sight,
And I fain would gaze upon him
 Through a stream of earthly light."

Not for greater gifts of genius;
  Not for thoughts more grandly bright,
All the dying poet whispers
  Is a prayer for light, more light.

Heeds he not the gathered laurels,
  Fading slowly from his sight;
All the poet's aspirations
  Center in that prayer for light.

Gracious Saviour, when life's day-dreams
  Melt and vanish from the sight,
May our dim and longing vision
  Then be blessed with light, more light.

EPIGRAM[2]
by Armand Lanusse

"Do you not wish to renounce the Devil?"
Asked a good priest of a woman of evil
Who had so many sins that every year
They cost her endless remorse and fear.
"I wish to renounce him forever," she said,
"But that I may lose every urge to be bad,
Before pure grace takes me in hand,
Shouldn't I show my daughter how to get a man?"

                                            L. H.

VERSE WRITTEN IN THE ALBUM OF MADEMOISELLE ———[3]
by Pierre Dalcour

The evening star that in the vaulted skies
  Sweetly sparkles, gently flashes,
To me is less lovely than a glance of your eyes
  Beneath their brown lashes.

                                            L. H.

[2,3]Translated by Langston Hughes.

THE FEET OF JUDAS
by George Marion McClellan

Christ washed the feet of Judas!
The dark and evil passions of his soul,
His secret plot, and sordidness complete,
His hate, his purposing, Christ knew the whole,
And still in love he stooped and washed his feet.

Christ washed the feet of Judas!
Yet all his lurking sin was bare to him,
His bargain with the priest, and more than this,
In Olivet, beneath the moonlight dim,
Aforehand knew and felt his treacherous kiss.

Christ washed the feet of Judas!
And so ineffable his love 'twas meet,
That pity fill his great forgiving heart,
And tenderly to wash the traitor's feet,
Who in his Lord had basely sold his part.

Christ washed the feet of Judas!
And thus a girded servant, self-abased,
Taught that no wrong this side the gate of heaven
Was ever too great to wholly be effaced,
And though unasked, in spirit be forgiven.

And so if we have ever felt the wrong
Of trampled rights, of caste, it matters not,
What e'er the soul has felt or suffered long,
Oh, heart! this one thing should not be forgot:
Christ washed the feet of Judas.

THE WAY-SIDE WELL[4]
by Joseph S. Cotter, Sr.

A Fancy halts my feet at the way-side well.
It is not to drink, for they say the water is brackish.
It is not to tryst, for a heart at the mile's end beckons me on.
It is not to rest, for what feet could be weary when a heart at the mile's
    end keeps time with their tread?
It is not to muse, for the heart at the mile's end is food for my being.
I will question the well for my secret by dropping a pebble into it.
Ah, it is dry.
Strike lightning to the road, my feet, for hearts are like wells. You may
    not know they are dry 'til you question their depths.
Fancies clog the way to Heaven, and saints miss their crown.

THE TRAGEDY OF PETE[5]
by Joseph S. Cotter, Sr.

> There was a man
>   Whose name was Pete,
> And he was a buck
>   From his head to his feet.
>
> He loved a dollar,
>   But hated a dime;
> And so was poor
>   Nine-tenths of the time.
>
> The Judge said "Pete,
>   What of your wife?"
> And Pete replied
>   "She lost her life."

[4],[5]From *Caroling Dusk,* by Countee Cullen, copyright, 1927, by Harper &
Brothers.

"Pete," said the Judge,
    "Was it lost in a row?
Tell me quick,
    And tell me how."

Pete straightened up
    With a hic and a sigh,
Then looked the Judge
    Full in the eye.

"O, Judge, my wife
    Would never go
To a Sunday dance
    Or a movie show.

"But I went, Judge,
    Both day and night,
And came home broke
    And also tight.

"The moon was up,
    My purse was down,
And I was the bully
    Of the bootleg town.

"I was crooning a lilt
    To corn and rye
For the loop in my legs
    And the fight in my eye.

"I met my wife;
    She was wearing a frown,
And catechising
    Her Sunday gown.

" 'O Pete, O Pete'
    She cried aloud,
'The Devil is falling
    Right out of a cloud.'

"I looked straight up
And fell flat down
And a Ford machine
Pinned my head to the ground.

"The Ford moved on,
And my wife was in it;
And I was sober,
That very minute.

"For my head was bleeding,
My heart was a-flutter;
And the moonshine within me
Was tipping the gutter.

"The Ford, it faster
And faster sped
Till it dipped and swerved
And my wife was dead.

"Two bruised men lay
In a hospital ward—
One seeking vengeance,
The other the Lord.

"He said to me:
'Your wife was drunk,
You are crazy,
And my Ford is junk.'

"I raised my knife
And drove it in
At the top of his head
And the point of his chin.

"O Judge, O Judge,
If the State has a chair,
Please bind me in it
And roast me there."

There was a man
   Whose name was Pete,
And he welcomed death
   From his head to his feet.

MISS MELERLEE
by John Wesley Holloway

Hello dar, Miss Melerlee!
Oh, you're pretty sight to see!
Sof' brown cheek, an' smilin' face,
An' willowy form chuck full o' grace—
De sweetes' gal Ah evah see,
An' Ah wush dat you would marry me!
   Hello, Miss Melerlee!

Hello dar, Miss Melerlee!
You're de berry gal fo' me!
Pearly teef, an' shinin' hair,
An' silky arm so plump an' bare!
Ah lak yo' walk, Ah lak yo' clothes,
An' de way Ah love you—goodness knows!
   Hello, Miss Melerlee!

Hello dar, Miss Melerlee!
Dat's not yo' name, but it ought to be!
Ah nevah seed yo' face befo'
An' lakly won't again no mo';
But yo' sweet smile will follow me
Cl'ar into eternity!
   Farewell, Miss Melerlee!

A LITANY AT ATLANTA[6]
Done at Atlanta,
in the Day of Death, 1906
By William Edward Burghardt DuBois

O Silent God, Thou whose voice afar in mist and mystery hath left our ears an-hungered in these fearful days—
Hear us, good Lord!

Listen to us, Thy children: our faces dark with doubt are made a mockery in Thy sanctuary. With uplifted hands we front Thy heaven, O God crying:
We beseech Thee to hear us, good Lord!

We are not better than our fellows, Lord, we are but weak and human men. When our devils do deviltry, curse Thou the doer and the deed: curse them as we curse them, do to them all and more than ever they have done to innocence and weakness, to womanhood and home.
Have mercy upon us, miserable sinners!

And yet whose is the deeper guilt? Who made these devils? Who nursed them in crime and fed them on injustice? Who ravished and debauched their mothers and their grandmothers? Who bought and sold their crime, and waxed fat and rich on public iniquity?
Thou knowest, good God!

Is this Thy Justice, O Father, that guile be easier than innocence, and the innocent crucified for the guilt of the untouched guilty?
Justice, O Judge of men!

Wherefore do we pray? Is not the God of the fathers dead? Have not seers seen in Heaven's halls Thine hearsed and lifeless form stark amidst the black and rolling smoke of sin, where all along bow bitter forms of endless dead?
Awake, Thou that sleepest!

[6]From *Darkwater*, by W. E. Burghardt DuBois, copyright, 1920, by Harcourt, Brace and Company, Inc.

Thou are not dead, but flown afar, up hills of endless light, thru blazing corridors of suns, where worlds do swing of good and gentle men, of women strong and free——far from the cozenage, black hypocrisy and chaste prostitution of this shameful speck of dust!

Turn again, O Lord, leave us not to perish in our sin!

From lust of body and lust of blood
Great God, deliver us!

From lust of power and lust of gold,
Great God, deliver us!

From the leagued lying of despot and of brute,
Great God, deliver us!

A city lay in travail, God our Lord, and from her loins sprang twin Murder and Black Hate. Red was the midnight; clang, crack and cry of death and fury filled the air and trembled underneath the stars when church spires pointed silently to Thee. And all this was to sate the greed of greedy men who hide behind the veil of vengeance!

Bend us Thine ear, O Lord!

In the pale, still morning we looked upon the deed. We stopped our ears and held our leaping hands, but they—did they not wag their heads and leer and cry with bloody jaws: *Cease from Crime!* The word was mockery, for thus they train a hundred crimes while we do cure one.

Turn again our captivity, O Lord!

Behold this maimed and broken thing; dear God, it was an humble black man who toiled and sweat to save a bit from the pittance paid him. They told him: *Work and Rise.* He worked. Did this man sin? Nay, but some one told how some one said another did—one whom he had never seen nor known. Yet for that man's crime this man lieth maimed and murdered, his wife naked to shame, his children, to poverty and evil.

Hear us, O Heavenly Father!

Doth not this justice of hell stink in Thy nostrils, O God? How long shall the mounting flood of innocent blood roar in Thine ears and pound in our hearts for vengeance? Pile the pale frenzy of blood-crazed brutes who do such deeds high on Thine altar, Jehovah Jireh, and burn it in hell forever and forever!

Forgive us, good Lord; we know not what we say!

Bewildered we are, and passion-tost, mad with the madness of a mobbed and mocked and murdered people; straining at the armposts of Thy Throne, we raise our shackled hands and charge Thee, God, by the bones of our stolen fathers, by the tears of our dead mothers, by the very blood of Thy crucified Christ: *What meaneth this?* Tell us the Plan; give us the Sign!

Keep not Thou silence, O God!

Sit no longer blind, Lord God, deaf to our prayer and dumb to our dumb suffering. Surely, Thou too art not white, O Lord, a pale, bloodless, heartless thing?

Ah! Christ of all the Pities!

Forgive the thought! Forgive these wild, blasphemous words. Thou art still the God of our black fathers, and in Thy soul's soul sit some soft darkenings of the evening, some shadowings of the velvet night.

But whisper—speak—call, great God, for Thy silence is white terror to our hearts! The way, O God, show us the way and point us the path.

Whither? North is greed and South is blood; within, the coward, and without the liar. Whither? To death?

Amen! Welcome dark sleep!

Whither? To life? But not this life, dear God, not this. Let the cup pass from us, tempt us not beyond our strength, for there is that clamoring and clawing within, to whose voice we would not listen, yet shudder lest we must, and it is red, Ah! God! It is a red and awful shape.

Selah!

In yonder East trembles a star.

Vengeance is mine; I will repay, saith the Lord!

Thy will, O Lord, be done!

Kyrie Eleison!

Lord, we have done these pleading, wavering words.
We beseech Thee to hear us, good Lord!

We bow our heads and hearken soft to the sobbing of women and
little children.
We beseech Thee to hear us, good Lord!

Our voices sink in silence and in night.
Hear us, good Lord!

In night, O God of a godless land!
Amen!

In silence, O Silent God.
Selah!

PAUL LAURENCE DUNBAR
by James David Corrothers

He came, a youth, singing in the dawn
Of a new freedom, glowing o'er his lyre,
Refining, as with great Apollo's fire,
His people's gift of song. And thereupon,
This Negro singer, come to Helicon,
Constrained the masters, listening to admire,
And roused a race to wonder and aspire,
Gazing which way their honest voice was gone,
With ebon face uplit of glory's crest.
Men marveled at the singer, strong and sweet,
Who brought the cabin's mirth, the tuneful night,
But faced the morning, beautiful with light,
To die while shadows yet fell toward the west,
And leave his laurels at his people's feet.

Dunbar, no poet wears your laurels now;
None rises, singing, from your race like you.
Dark melodist, immortal, though the dew
Fell early on the bays upon your brow,

And tinged with pathos every halcyon vow
   And brave endeavor. Silence o'er you threw
   Flowerets of love. Or, if an envious few
Of your own people brought no garlands, how
Could malice smite him whom the gods had crowned?
   If, like the meadow-lark, your flight was low,
   Your flooded lyrics half the hilltops drowned;
A wide world heard you, and it loved you so,
   It stilled its heart to list the strains you sang,
   And o'er your happy songs its plaudits rang.

AN INDIGNATION DINNER[7]
by James David Corrothers

Dey was hard times jes fo' Christmas round our neighborhood one year;
So we held a secret meetin', whah de white folks couldn't hear,
To 'scuss de situation, an' to see what could be done
Towa'd a fust-class Christmas dinneh an' a little Christmas fun.

Rufus Green, who called de meetin', ris an' said: "In dis here town,
An' throughout de land, de white folks is a'tryin' to keep us down."
S' 'e: "Dey bought us, sold us, beat us; now dey 'buse us 'ca'se we's free;
But when dey tetch my stomach, dey's done gone too fur foh me!

"Is I right?" "You sho is, Rufus!" roared a dozen hungry throats.
"Ef you'd keep a mule a-wo'kin', don't you tamper wid his oats.
Dat's sense," continued Rufus. "But dese white folks nowadays
Has done got so close and stingy you can't live on what dey pays.

"Here 'tis Christmas-time, an', folkses, I's indignant 'nough to choke.
Whah's our Christmas dinneh comin' when we's mos' completely broke?
I can't hahdly 'fo'd a toothpick an' a glass o' water. Mad?
Say, I'm desp'ret! Dey jes better treat me nice, dese white folks had!"

Well, dey 'bused de white folks scan'lous, till old Pappy Simmons ris,
Leanin' on his cane to s'pote him, on account his rheumatis',
An' s' 'e: "Chillun, whut's dat wintry wind a-sighin' th'ough de street
'Bout yo' wasted summeh wages? But, no matter, we mus' eat.

"Now, I seed a beau'ful tuhkey on a certain gemmun's fahm.
He's a-growin' fat an' sassy, an' a-struttin' to a chahm.
Chickens, sheeps, hogs, sweet pertaters—all de craps is fine dis year;
All we needs is a committee foh to tote de goodies here."

Well, we lit right in an' voted dat it was a gran' idee,
An' de dinneh we had Christmas was worth trabblin' miles to see;
An' we eat a full an' plenty, big an' little, great an' small,
Not beca'se we was dishonest, but indignant, sah. Dat's all.

O BLACK AND UNKNOWN BARDS[8]
by James Weldon Johnson

O black and unknown bards of long ago,
How came your lips to touch the sacred fire?
How, in your darkness, did you come to know
The power and beauty of the minstrels' lyre?
Who first from midst his bonds lifted his eyes?
Who first from out the still watch, lone and long,
Feeling the ancient faith of prophets rise
Within his dark-kept soul, burst into song?

Heart of what slave poured out such melody
As "Steal away to Jesus"? On its strains
His spirit must have nightly floated free,
Though still about his hands he felt his chains.
Who heard great "Jordan roll"? Whose starward eye
Saw chariot "swing low"? And who was he
That breathed that comforting, melodic sigh,
"Nobody knows de trouble I see"?

[8]From *St. Peter Relates an Incident*, by James Weldon Johnson, copyright, 1917, 1921, and 1935, by James Weldon Johnson. Reprinted by permission of The Viking Press, Inc., New York.

What merely living clod, what captive thing,
Could up toward God through all its darkness grope,
And find within its deadened heart to sing
These songs of sorrow, love and faith, and hope?
How did it catch that subtle undertone,
That note in music heard not with the ears?
How sound the elusive reed so seldom blown,
Which stirs the soul or melts the heart to tears.

Not that great German master in his dream
Of harmonies that thundered amongst the stars
At the creation, ever heard a theme
Nobler than "Go down, Moses." Mark its bars
How like a mighty trumpet-call they stir
The blood. Such are the notes that men have sung
Going to valorous deeds; such tones there were
That helped make history when Time was young.

There is a wide, wide wonder in it all,
That from degraded rest and servile toil
The fiery spirit of the seer should call
These simple children of the sun and soil.
O black slave singers, gone, forgot, unfamed,
You—you alone, of all the long, long line
Of those who've sung untaught, unknown, unnamed,
Have stretched out upward, seeking the divine.

You sang not deeds of heroes or of kings;
No chant of bloody war, no exulting paean
No arms-won triumphs; but your humble strings
You touched in chord with music empyrean.
You sang far better than you knew; the songs
That for your listeners' hungry hearts sufficed
Still live—but more than this to you belongs:
You sang a race from wood and stone to Christ.

FIFTY YEARS[9]
1863–1913
by James Weldon Johnson

On the Fiftieth Anniversary
of the Signing
of the Emancipation Proclamation

O brothers mine, today we stand
    Where half a century sweeps our ken,
Since God, through Lincoln's ready hand,
    Struck off our bonds and made us men.

Just fifty years—a winter's day—
    As runs the history of a race;
Yet, as we look back o'er the way,
    How distant seems our starting place!

Look farther back! Three centuries!
    To where a naked, shivering score,
Snatched from their haunts across the seas,
    Stood, wild-eyed, on Virginia's shore.

.   .   .

For never let the thought arise
    That we are here on sufferance bare;
Outcasts, asylumed 'neath these skies,
    And aliens without part or share.

This land is ours by right of birth,
    This land is ours by right of toil;
We helped to turn its virgin earth,
    Our sweat is in its fruitful soil.

Where once the tangled forest stood—
  Where flourished once rank weed and thorn—
Behold the path-traced, peaceful wood,
  The cotton white, the yellow corn.

To gain these fruits that have been earned,
  To hold these fields that have been won,
Our arms have strained, our backs have burned,
  Bent bare beneath a ruthless sun.

That Banner which is now the type
  Of victory on field and flood—
Remember, its first crimson stripe
  Was dyed by Attucks' willing blood.

And never yet has come the cry—
  When that fair flag has been assailed—
For men to do, for men to die,
  That we have faltered or have failed.

We've helped to bear it, rent and torn,
  Through many a hot-breath'd battle breeze
Held in our hands, it has been borne
  And planted far across the seas.

And never yet—O haughty Land,
  Let us, at least, for this be praised—
Has one black, treason-guided hand
  Ever against that flag been raised.

Then should we speak but servile words,
  Or shall we hang our heads in shame?
Stand back of new-come foreign hordes,
  And fear our heritage to claim?

No! stand erect and without fear,
  And for our foes let this suffice—
We've bought a rightful sonship here,
  And we have more than paid the price.

And yet, my brothers, well I know
   The tethered feet, the pinioned wings,
The spirit bowed beneath the blow,
   The heart grown faint from wounds and stings;

The staggering force of brutish might,
   That strikes and leaves us stunned and dazed;
The long, vain waiting through the night
   To hear some voice for justice raised.

Full well I know the hour when hope
   Sinks dead, and round us everywhere
Hangs stifling darkness, and we grope
   With hands uplifted in despair.

Courage! Look out, beyond, and see
   The far horizon's beckoning span!
Faith in your God-known destiny!
   We are a part of some great plan.

Because the tongues of Garrison
   And Phillips now are cold in death,
Think you their work can be undone?
   Or quenched the fires lit by their breath?

Think you that John Brown's spirit stops?
   That Lovejoy was but idly slain?
Or do you think those precious drops
   From Lincoln's heart were shed in vain?

That for which millions prayed and sighed,
   That for which tens of thousands fought,
For which so many freely died,
   God cannot let it come to naught.

THE CREATION[10]
by James Weldon Johnson

And God stepped out on space,
And he looked around and said:
I'm lonely—
I'll make me a world.

And far as the eye of God could see
Darkness covered everything,
Blacker than a hundred midnights
Down in a cypress swamp.

Then God smiled,
And the light broke,
And the darkness rolled up on one side,
And the light stood shining on the other,
And God said: That's good!

Then God reached out and took the light in His hands,
And God rolled the light around in His hands
Until He made the sun;
And He set that sun a-blazing in the heavens.
And the light that was left from making the sun
God gathered up in a shining ball
And flung against the darkness,
Spangling the night with the moon and stars.
Then down between
The darkness and the light
He hurled the world;
And God said: That's good!

Then God himself stepped down—
And the sun was on His right hand,
And the moon was on His left;
The stars were clustered about His head,

And the earth was under His feet.
And God walked, and where He trod
His footsteps hollowed the valleys out
And bulged the mountains up.

Then He stopped and looked and saw
That the earth was hot and barren.
So God stepped over to the edge of the world
And He spat out the seven seas—
He batted His eyes, and the lightnings flashed—
He clapped His hands, and the thunders rolled—
And the waters above the earth came down,
The cooling waters came down.

Then the green grass sprouted,
And the little red flowers blossomed,
The pine tree pointed his finger to the sky,
And the oak spread out his arms,
The lakes cuddled down in the hollows of the ground,
And the rivers ran down to the sea;
And God smiled again,
And the rainbow appeared,
And curled itself around His shoulder.

Then God raised His arm and He waved His hand
Over the sea and over the land,
And He said: Bring forth! Bring forth!
And quicker than God could drop His hand,
Fishes and fowls
And beasts and birds
Swam the rivers and the seas,
Roamed the forests and the woods,
And split the air with their wings.
And God said: That's good!

Then God walked around,
And God looked around
On all that He had made.
He looked on His world

With all its living things,
And God said: I'm lonely still.

Then God sat down—
On the side of a hill where He could think;
By a deep, wide river He sat down;
With His head in His hands,
God thought and thought,
Till He thought: I'll make me a man!

Up from the bed of the river
God scooped the clay;
And by the bank of the river
He kneeled Him down;
And there the great God Almighty
Who lit the sun and fixed it in the sky,
Who flung the stars to the most far corner of the night,
Who rounded the earth in the middle of His hand;
This Great God,
Like a mammy bending over her baby,
Kneeled down in the dust
Toiling over a lump of clay
Till He shaped it in His own image;

Then into it He blew the breath of life,
And man became a living soul.
Amen. Amen.

THE GLORY OF THE DAY WAS IN HER FACE[11]
by James Weldon Johnson

The glory of the day was in her face,
The beauty of the night was in her eyes.
And over all her loveliness, the grace
Of Morning blushing in the early skies.

[11]From *St. Peter Relates an Incident*, by James Weldon Johnson, copyright, 1917, 1921, and 1935, by James Weldon Johnson. Reprinted by permission of The Viking Press, Inc., New York.

And in her voice, the calling of the dove;
Like music of a sweet, melodious part.
And in her smile, the breaking light of love;
And all the gentle virtues in her heart.

And now the glorious day, the beauteous night,
The birds that signal to their mates at dawn,
To my dull ears, to my tear-blinded sight
Are one with all the dead, since she is gone.

SENCE YOU WENT AWAY[12]
by James Weldon Johnson

Seems lak to me de stars don't shine so bright,
Seems lak to me de sun done loss his light,
Seems lak to me der's nothin' goin' right,
    Sence you went away.

Seems lak to me de sky ain't half so blue,
Seems lak to me dat ev'ything wants you,
Seems lak to me I don't know what to do,
    Sence you went away.

Seems lak to me dat ev'ything is wrong,
Seems lak to me de day's jes twice as long,
Seems lak to me de bird's forgot his song,
    Sence you went away.

Seems lak to me I jes can't he'p but sigh,
Seems lak to me ma th'oat keeps gittin' dry,
Seems lak to me a tear stays in my eye,
    Sence you went away.

MY CITY[13]
by James Weldon Johnson

When I come down to sleep death's endless night,
The threshold of the unknown dark to cross,
What to me then will be the keenest loss,
When this bright world blurs on my fading sight?
Will it be that no more I shall see the trees
Or smell the flowers or hear the singing birds
Or watch the flashing streams or patient herds?
No, I am sure it will be none of these.

But, ah! Manhattan's sights and sounds, her smells,
Her crowds, her throbbing force, the thrill that comes
From being of her a part, her subtle spells,
Her shining towers, her avenues, her slums——
O God! the stark, unutterable pity,
To be dead, and never again behold my city!

LIFT EVERY VOICE AND SING[14]
by James Weldon Johnson

Lift every voice and sing
Till earth and heaven ring,
Ring with the harmonies of Liberty;
Let our rejoicing rise
High as the listening skies,
Let it resound loud as the rolling sea.
Sing a song full of the faith that the dark past has taught us,
Sing a song full of the hope that the present has brought us,
Facing the rising sun of our new day begun
Let us march on till victory is won.

Stony the road we trod,
Bitter the chastening rod,
Felt in the days when hope unborn had died;
Yet with a steady beat,
Have not our weary feet
Come to the place for which our fathers sighed?
We have come over a way that with tears has been watered,
We have come, treading our path through the blood of the slaughtered,
Out from the gloomy past,
Till now we stand at last
Where the white gleam of our bright star is cast.

God of our weary years,
God of our silent tears,
Thou who has brought us thus far on the way;
Thou who has by Thy might
Led us into the light,
Keep us forever in the path, we pray.
Lest our feet stray from the places, our God, where we met Thee,
Lest, our hearts drunk with the wine of the world, we forget Thee;
Shadowed beneath Thy hand,
May we forever stand.
True to our God,
True to our native land.

SYMPATHY[15]
by Paul Laurence Dunbar

I know what the caged bird feels, alas!
When the sun is bright on the upland slopes;
When the wind stirs soft through the springing grass,
And the river flows like a stream of glass;
When the first bird sings and the first bud opes,
And the faint perfume from its chalice steals—
I know what the caged bird feels!

[15]From *The Complete Poems of Paul Laurence Dunbar*, copyright, 1896, 1899, 1905, 1913, by Dodd, Mead & Company, Inc.

I know why the caged bird beats his wing
Till its blood is red on the cruel bars;
For he must fly back to his perch and cling
When he fain would be on the bough a-swing;
And a pain still throbs in the old, old scars
And they pulse again with a keener sting—
I know why he beats his wing!

I know why the caged bird sings, ah me,
When his wing is bruised and his bosom sore,—
When he beats his bars and he would be free;
It is not a carol of joy or glee,
But a prayer that he sends from his heart's deep core,
But a plea, that upward to Heaven he flings—
I know why the caged bird sings!

DAWN[16]
by Paul Laurence Dunbar

An angel, robed in spotless white,
Bent down and kissed the sleeping Night.
Night woke to blush; the sprite was gone.
Men saw the blush and called it Dawn.

A NEGRO LOVE SONG[17]
by Paul Laurence Dunbar

Seen my lady home las' night,
    Jump back, honey, jump back.
Hel' huh han' an' sque'z it tight,
    Jump back, honey, jump back.
Hyeahd huh sigh a little sigh,
Seen a light gleam f'om huh eye,

[16,17]From *The Complete Poems of Paul Laurence Dunbar*, copyright, 1896, 1899, 1905, 1913, by Dodd, Mead & Company, Inc.

An' a smile go flittin' by——
    Jump back, honey, jump back.

Hyeahd de win' blow thoo de pine,
    Jump back, honey, jump back.
Mockin'-bird was singin' fine,
    Jump back, honey, jump back.
An' my hea't was beatin' so,
When I reached my lady's do',
Dat I couldn't ba' to go——
    Jump back, honey, jump back.

Put my ahm aroun' huh wais',
    Jump back, honey, jump back.
Raised huh lips an' took a tase,
    Jump back, honey, jump back.
Love me, honey, love me true?
Love me well ez I love you?
An' she answe'd, " 'Cose I do"——
    Jump back, honey, jump back.

WHEN MALINDY SINGS[18]
by Paul Laurence Dunbar

G'way an' quit dat noise, Miss Lucy——
    Put dat music book away;
What's de use to keep on tryin'?
    Ef you practise twell you're gray,
You cain't sta't no notes a-flyin'
    Lak de ones dat rants and rings
F'om de kitchen to de big woods
    When Malindy sings.

You ain't got de nachel o'gans
    Fu' to make de soun' come right,
You ain't got de tu'ns an' twistin's
    Fu' to make it sweet an' light.

[18]From *The Complete Poems of Paul Laurence Dunbar*, copyright, 1896, 1899
1905, 1913, by Dodd, Mead & Company, Inc.

Tell you one thing now, Miss Lucy,
  An' I'm tellin' you fu' true,
When hit comes to raal right singin',
  'T ain't no easy thing to do.

Easy 'nough fu' folks to hollah,
  Lookin' at de lines an' dots,
When dey ain't no one kin sence it,
  An' de chune comes in, in spots;
But fu' real melojous music,
  Dat jes' strikes yo' hea't and clings,
Jes' you stan' an' listen wif me
  When Malindy sings.

Ain't you nevah hyeahd Malindy?
  Blessed soul, tek up de cross!
Look hyeah, ain't you jokin', honey?
  Well, you don't know whut you los'.
Y' ought to hyeah dat gal a-wa'blin',
  Robins, la'ks, an' all dem things,
Heish dey moufs an' hides dey faces
  When Malindy sings.

Fiddlin' man jes' stop his fiddlin',
  Lay his fiddle on de she'f;
Mockin'-bird quit tryin' to whistle,
  'Cause he jes' so shamed hisse'f.
Folks a-playin' on de banjo
  Draps dey fingahs on de strings——
Bless yo' soul——fu'gits to move em,
  When Malindy sings.

She jes' spreads huh mouf and hollahs,
  "Come to Jesus," twell you hyeah
Sinnahs' tremblin' steps and voices,
  Timid-lak a-drawin' neah;
Den she tu'ns to "Rock of Ages,"
  Simply to de cross she clings,
An' you fin' yo' teahs a-drappin'
  When Malindy sings.

Who dat says dat humble praises
    Wif de Master nevah counts?
Heish yo' mouf, I hyeah dat music,
    Ez hit rises up an' mounts—
Floatin' by de hills an' valleys,
    Way above dis buryin' sod,
Ez hit makes its way in glory
    To de very gates of God!

Oh, hit's sweetah dan de music
    Of an edicated band;
An' hit's dearah dan de battle's
    Song o' triumph in de lan'.
It seems holier dan evenin'
    When de solemn chu'ch bell rings,
Ez I sit an' ca'mly listen
    While Malindy sings.

Towsah, stop dat ba'kin', hyeah me!
    Mandy, mek dat chile keep still;
Don't you hyeah de echoes callin'
    F'om de valley to de hill?
Let me listen, I can hyeah it,
    Th'oo de bresh of angels' wings,
Sof' an' sweet, "Swing Low, Sweet Chariot,"
    Ez Malindy sings.

LITTLE BROWN BABY[19]
by Paul Laurence Dunbar

Little brown baby wif spa'klin' eyes,
    Come to yo' pappy an' set on his knee.
What you been doin', suh—makin' san' pies?
    Look at dat bib—you's ez du'ty ez me.

Look at dat mouf—dat's merlasses, I bet;
  Come hyeah, Maria, an' wipe off his han's.
Bees gwine to ketch you an' eat you up yit,
  Bein' so sticky an' sweet—goodness lan's!

Little brown baby wif spa'klin' eyes,
  Who's pappy's darlin' an' who's pappy's chile?
Who is it all de day nevah once tries
  Fu' to be cross, er once loses dat smile?
Whah did you git dem teef? My, you's a scamp!
  Whah did dat dimple come f'om in yo' chin?
Pappy do' know you—I b'lieves you's a tramp;
  Mammy, dis hyeah's some ol' straggler got in!

Let's th'ow him outen de do' in de san',
  We do' want stragglers a-layin' 'roun' hyeah;
Let's gin him 'way to de big buggah-man;
  I know he's hidin' erroun' hyeah right neah.
Buggah-man, buggah-man, come in de do',
  Hyeah's a bad boy you kin have fu' to eat.
Mammy an' pappy do' want him no mo',
  Swaller him down f'om his haid to his feet!

Dah, now, I t'ought dat you'd hug me up close.
  Go back, ol' buggah, you sha'n't have dis boy.
He ain't no tramp, ner no straggler, of co'se;
  He's pappy's pa'dner an' playmate an' joy.
Come to you' pallet now—go to yo' res';
  Wisht you could allus know ease an' cleah skies;
Wisht you could stay jes' a chile on my breas'—
  Little brown baby wif spa'klin' eyes!

A DEATH SONG[20]
by Paul Laurence Dunbar

Lay me down beneaf de willers in de grass,
Whah de branch 'll go a-singin' as it pass.
 An' w'en I's a-layin' low,
 I kin hyeah it as it go
Singin', "Sleep, my honey, tek yo' res' at las'."

Lay me nigh to whah hit meks a little pool,
An' de watah stan's so quiet lak an' cool,
 Whah de little birds in spring,
 Ust to come an' drink an' sing,
An' de chillen waded on dey way to school.

Let me settle w'en my shouldahs draps dey load
Nigh enough to hyeah de noises in de road;
 Fu' I t'ink de las' long res'
 Gwine to soothe my sperrit bes'
Ef I's layin' 'mong de t'ings I's allus knowed.

ERE SLEEP COMES DOWN TO SOOTHE THE WEARY EYES[21]
by Paul Laurence Dunbar

Ere sleep comes down to soothe the weary eyes,
 Which all the day with ceaseless care have sought
The magic gold which from the seeker flies;
 Ere dreams put on the gown and cap of thought,
And make the waking world a world of lies,——
 Of lies most palpable, uncouth, forlorn,
That say life's full of aches and tears and sighs,——
 Oh, how with more than dreams the soul is torn,
Ere sleep comes down to soothe the weary eyes.

[20,21]From *The Complete Poems of Paul Laurence Dunbar*, copyright, 1896, 1899, 1905, 1913, by Dodd, Mead & Company, Inc.

Ere sleep comes down to soothe the weary eyes,
   How all the griefs and heartaches we have known
Come up like pois'nous vapors that arise
   From some base witch's caldron, when the crone,
To work some potent spell, her magic plies.
   The past which held its share of bitter pain,
Whose ghost we prayed that Time might exorcise,
   Comes up, is lived and suffered o'er again,
Ere sleep comes down to soothe the weary eyes.

Ere sleep comes down to soothe the weary eyes,
   What phantoms fill the dimly lighted room;
What ghostly shades in awe-creating guise
   Are bodied forth within the teeming gloom.
What echoes faint of sad and soul-sick cries,
   And pangs of vague inexplicable pain
That pay the spirit's ceaseless enterprise,
   Come thronging through the chambers of the brain,
Ere sleep comes down to soothe the weary eyes.

Ere sleep comes down to soothe the weary eyes,
   Where ranges forth the spirit far and free?
Through what strange realms and unfamiliar skies
   Tends her far course to lands of mystery?
To lands unspeakable—beyond surmise,
   Where shapes unknowable to being spring,
Till, faint of wing, the Fancy fails and dies
   Much wearied with the spirit's journeying,
Ere sleep comes down to soothe the weary eyes.

Ere sleep comes down to soothe the weary eyes,
   How questioneth the soul that other soul,
The inner sense which neither cheats nor lies,
   But self exposes unto self, a scroll
Full writ with all life's acts unwise or wise,
   In characters indelible and known;
So, trembling with the shock of sad surprise,
   The soul doth view its awful self alone,
Ere sleep comes down to soothe the weary eyes.

When sleep comes down to seal the weary eyes,
    The last dear sleep whose soft embrace is balm,
And whom sad sorrow teaches us to prize
    For kissing all our passions into calm,
Ah, then, no more we heed the sad world's cries,
    Or seek to probe th' eternal mystery,
Or fret our souls at long-withheld replies,
    At glooms through which our visions cannot see,
When sleep comes down to seal the weary eyes.

COMPENSATION[22]
by Paul Laurence Dunbar

Because I had loved so deeply,
    Because I had loved so long,
God in His great compassion
    Gave me the gift of song.

Because I have loved so vainly,
    And sung with such faltering breath,
The Master, in infinite mercy,
    Offers the boon of death.

SONNET
by Alice Dunbar Nelson

I had no thought of violets of late,
The wild, shy kind that spring beneath your feet
In wistful April days, when lovers mate
And wander through the fields in raptures sweet.
The thought of violets meant florists' shops,
And bows and pins, and perfumed papers fine;
And garish lights, and mincing little fops
And cabarets and songs, and deadening wine.

So far from sweet real things my thoughts had strayed,
I had forgot wide fields, and clear brown streams;
The perfect loveliness that God has made,—
Wild violets shy and Heaven-mounting dreams.
And now—unwittingly, you've made me dream
Of violets, and my soul's forgotten gleam.

THE HOUSE OF FALLING LEAVES
by William Stanley Braithwaite

The House of Falling Leaves we entered in—
He and I—we entered in and found it fair;
At midnight some one called him up the stair,
And closed him in the Room I could not win.
Now must I go alone out in the din
Of hurrying days: for forth he cannot fare;
I must go on with Time, and leave him there
In Autumn's house where dreams will soon grow thin.

When Time shall close the door unto the house
And open that of Winter's soon to be,
And dreams go moving through the ruined boughs—
He who went in comes out a Memory.
From his deep sleep no sound may e'er arouse,—
The moaning rain, nor wind-embattled sea.

THE WATCHERS[23]
by William Stanley Braithwaite

Two women on the lone wet strand
        (*The wind's out with a will to roam*)
The waves wage war on rocks and sand,
        (*And a ship is long due home.*)

[23]From *Selected Poems*, by William Stanley Braithwaite, Coward-McCann, Inc., publishers.

The sea sprays in the women's eyes—
    (*Hearts can writhe like the sea's wild foam*)
Lower descend the tempestuous skies,
    (*For the wind's out with a will to roam.*)

"O daughter, thine eyes be better than mine,"
    (*The waves ascend high as yonder dome*)
"North or south is there never a sign?"
    (*And a ship is long due home.*)

They watched there all the long night through—
    (*The wind's out with a will to roam*)
Wind and rain and sorrow for two,—
    (*And heaven on the long reach home.*)

WHITE MAGIC: AN ODE
by William Stanley Braithwaite

Read at the Centenary Celebration
of the Birth of John Greenleaf Whittier
at Faneuil Hall, December 17, 1907

White magic of the silences of snow!
Over the Northern fields and hills, the moon
Spreads her veil o'er the wizardry below;
Amongst the ruined tree-tops is a croon
Of the long-vanished populace of Spring;
    There is a glory here
Where the lone farmhouse windows, glimmering
Across the snow-fields, warm the chilly air.
Peace is upon the valley like a dream
    By Merrimac's swift stream,
Where his pure presence made the earth so fair.

Time cannot tarnish the glory of the hills:
Tides cannot wear the immaterial winds
To outworn voids where no loud echo fills
The long beach-comber which the sea unbinds;

The moon shall light the sun ere these things be;
    But sooner our glad hearts
Know not darkness from sunlight on the sea
Ere from the lips of Memory departs
Thought or speech unpraiseful of Whittier's life,
    White magic of song and strife—
Strife for the right—Song for a sake not art's.

In the rough farmhouse of his lowly birth
The spirit of poetry fired his youthful years;
No palace was more radiant on earth,
Than the rude home where simple joys and tears
Filled the boy's soul with the human chronicle
    Of lives that touched the soil.
He heard about him voices—and he fell
To dreams, of the dim past, 'midst his daily toil;
Romance and legend claimed his Muse's voice
    Till the heroic choice
Of duty led him to the battle's broil.

Song then became a trumpet-blast; he smote
The arrogance of evil in the State;
The indignation of his music wrote
A flaming wrath in councils of debate.
'Twas passion for the justice of God's word—
    Man's common heritage
Fulfilled in the high name of Brotherhood.
The oracle and prophet of his age,
He led men doubtful between wrong and right
    Through Song to see the light,
And smite the evil power with their rage.

He helped to seal the doom. His hope was peace
With the great and attained. Beyond his will
Fate shaped his aims to awful destinies
Of vengeful justice—now valley and hill
Groaned with the roar of onset; near and far
    The terrible, sad cries
Of slaughtered men pierced into sun and star;

Beyond his will the violence—but the prize
Of Freedom, blood had purchased, won to God
      His praise that all men trod
Erect, and clothed in Freedom, 'neath the skies.

Let thanks be ours for this great passion in him;
And praise be our remembrance of his trust;
Blessings that no compromise could win him,
Like Ichabod, to soil his glory in the dust.
Let ours be, too, his spirit of forgiving:
      We can but master fate
By the sure knowledge of our brother's living—
Won by matching his virtues, not his hate.
Let the white radiance of his Inward Light
      Be to us, step and sight
Up the steep road of life to Heaven's gate.

THE ARSENAL OF THE LORD[24]
by William Stanley Braithwaite

Against this wrong of the Teutonic might
From lease-lend stores we give the Nations aid
Who stand embattled, but are unafraid;
Our wealth and labor visioned to a height
Undreamed of, bulwarked are for Freedom's right.
Thus making planes, munitions, it is said
We are the arsenal—by hopes repaid—
Of Democracies, to sustain their fight.
But this is not enough. O my dear Land!
Engirt your Spirit with the dreams of those
Who cleared the Wilderness with Cross in hand.
To Britain, China, Russia, and their foes
Be bounteous with the Faith within you stored,
And stand for all, Arsenal of the Lord!

[24]From *Selected Poems,* by William Stanley Braithwaite. Coward-McCann, Inc., publishers.

THE TEACHER
by Leslie Pinckney Hill

Lord, who am I to teach the way
To little children day by day,
So prone myself to go astray?

I teach them KNOWLEDGE, but I know
How faint they flicker and how low
The candles of my knowledge glow.

I teach them POWER to will and do,
But only now to learn anew
My own great weakness through and through.

I teach them LOVE for all mankind
And all God's creatures, but I find
My love comes lagging far behind.

Lord, if their guide I still must be,
Oh, let the little children see
The teacher leaning hard on Thee.

TUSKEGEE
by Leslie Pinckney Hill

Wherefore this busy labor without rest?
Is it an idle dream to which we cling,
Here where a thousand dusky toilers sing
Unto the world their hope? "Build we our best.
By hand and thought," they cry, "although unblessed."
So the great engines throb, and anvils ring,
And so the thought is wedded to the thing;
But what shall be the end, and what the test?

Dear God, we dare not answer, we can see
Not many steps ahead, but this we know—
If all our toilsome building is in vain,
Availing not to set our manhood free,
If envious hate roots out the seed we sow,
The South will wear eternally a stain.

A WINTER TWILIGHT
by Angelina W. Grimké

A silence slipping around like death,
Yet chased by a whisper, a sigh, a breath;
One group of trees, lean, naked and cold,
Inking their crest 'gainst a sky green-gold;
One path that knows where the corn flowers were;
Lonely, apart, unyielding, one fir;
And over it softly leaning down,
One star that I loved ere the fields went brown

FOR THE CANDLE LIGHT
by Angelina W. Grimké

The sky was blue, so blue, that day,
And each daisy white, so white;
Oh! I knew that no more could rains fall gray,
And night again be night.

I knew! I knew! Well, if night is night,
And the gray skies grayly cry,
I have in a book, for the candle light,
A daisy, dead and dry.

WHEN THE GREEN LIES OVER THE EARTH
by Angelina W. Grimké

When the green lies over the earth, my dear,
A mantle of witching grace,
When the smile and the tear of the young child year
Dimple across its face,
And then flee, when the wind all day is sweet
With the breath of growing things,
When the wooing bird lights on restless feet
And chirrups and trills and sings
    To his lady-love
    In the green above,
Then oh! my dear, when the youth's in the year,
Yours is the face that I long to have near,
    Yours is the face, my dear.

But the green is hiding your curls, my dear,
Your curls so shining and sweet;
And the gold-hearted daisies this many a year
Have bloomed and bloomed at your feet,
And the little birds just above your head
With their voices hushed, my dear,
For you have sung and have prayed and have pled
    This many, many a year.
    And the blossoms fall,
    On the garden wall,
And drift like snow on the green below.
    But the sharp thorn grows
    On the budding rose,
And my heart no more leaps at the sunset glow,
For oh! my dear, when the youth's in the year,
Yours is the face that I long to have near,
Yours is the face, my dear.

TENEBRIS
by Angelina W. Grimké

There is a tree, by day,
That, at night,
Has a shadow,
A hand huge and black,
With fingers long and black.
          All through the dark,
Against the white man's house,
          In the little wind,
The black hand plucks and plucks
          At the bricks.
The bricks are the color of blood and very small.
          Is it a black hand,
          Or is it a shadow?

THE BLACK FINGER
by Angelina W. Grimké

I have just seen a beautiful thing
          Slim and still,
Against a gold, gold sky,
          A straight cypress,
          Sensitive
          Exquisite,
A black finger
Pointing upwards.
Why, beautiful, still finger are you black?
And why are you pointing upwards?

MY HERO
To Robert Gould Shaw
by Benjamin Brawley

Flushed with the hope of high desire,
   He buckled on his sword,
To dare the rampart ranged with fire,
   Or where the thunder roared;
Into the smoke and flame he went,
   For God's great cause to die—
A youth of heaven's element,
   The flower of chivalry.

This was the gallant faith, I trow,
   Of which the sages tell;
On such devotion long ago
   The benediction fell;
And never nobler martyr burned,
   Or braver hero died,
Than he who worldly honor spurned
   To serve the Crucified.

And Lancelot and Sir Bedivere
   May pass beyond the pale,
And wander over moor and mere
   To find the Holy Grail;
But ever yet the prize forsooth
   My hero holds in fee;
And he is Blameless Knight in truth,
   And Galahad to me.

LIFE-LONG, POOR BROWNING . . .
by Anne Spencer

Life-long, poor Browning never knew Virginia,
Or he'd not grieved in Florence for April sallies
Back to English gardens after Euclid's linear:
Clipt yews, Pomander Walks, and pleached alleys;

Primroses, prim indeed, in quiet ordered hedges,
Waterways, soberly, sedately enchanneled,
No thin riotous blade even among the sedges,
All the wild country-side tamely impaneled . . .

Dead, now, dear Browning, lives on in heaven,—
(Heaven's Virginia when the year's at its Spring)
He's haunting the byways of wine-aired leaven
And throating the notes of the wildings on wing;

Here canopied reaches of dogwood and hazel,
Beech tree and redbud fine-laced in vines,
Fleet clapping rills by lush fern and basil,
Drain blue hills to lowlands scented with pines . . .

Think you he meets in this tender green sweetness
Shade that was Elizabeth . . . immortal completeness!

LETTER TO MY SISTER
by Anne Spencer

It is dangerous for a woman to defy the gods;
To taunt them with the tongue's thin tip,
Or strut in the weakness of mere humanity,
Or draw a line daring them to cross;
The gods own the searing lightning,
The drowning waters, tormenting fears
And anger of red sins.

Oh, but worse still if you mince timidly—
Dodge this way or that, or kneel or pray,
Be kind, or sweat agony drops
Or lay your quick body over your feeble young;
If you have beauty or none, if celibate
Or vowed—the gods are Juggernaut,
Passing over . . . over . . .

This you may do:
Lock your heart, then, quietly,
And lest they peer within,
Light no lamp when dark comes down
Raise no shade for sun;
Breathless must your breath come through
If you'd die and dare deny
The gods their god-like fun.

AT THE CARNIVAL
by Anne Spencer

Gay little Girl-of-the-Diving-Tank,
I desire a name for you,
Nice, as a right glove fits;
For you—who amid the malodorous
Mechanics of this unlovely thing,
Are darling of spirit and form.
I know you—a glance, and what you are
Sits-by-the-fire in my heart.
My Limousine-Lady knows you, or
Why does the slant-envy of her eye mark
Your straight air and radiant inclusive smile?
Guilt pins a fig-leaf; Innocence is its own adorning.
The bull-necked man knows you—this first time
His itching flesh sees from divine and vibrant health,
And thinks not of his avocation.
I came incuriously—
Set on no diversion save that my mind
Might safely nurse its brood of misdeeds
In the presence of a blind crowd.
The color of life was gray.
Everywhere the setting seemed right
For my mood!

Here the sausage and garlic booth
Sent unholy incense skyward;
There a quivering female-thing
Gestured assignations, and lied
To call it dancing;
There, too, were games of chance
With chances for none;
But oh! the Girl-of-the-Tank, at last!
Gleaming Girl, how intimately pure and free
The gaze you send the crowd,
As though you know the dearth of beauty
In its sordid life.
We need you—my Limousine-Lady,
The bull-necked man, and I.
Seeing you here brave and water-clean,
Leaven for the heavy ones of earth,
I am swift to feel that what makes
The plodder glad is good; and
Whatever is good is God.
The wonder is that you are here;
I have seen the queer in queer places,
But never before a heaven-fed
Naiad of the Carnival-Tank!
Little Diver, Destiny for you,
Like as for me, is shod in silence;
Years may seep into your soul
The bacilli of the usual and the expedient;
I implore Neptune to claim his child to-day!

LINES TO A NASTURTIUM
A lover muses
by Anne Spencer

Flame-flower, Day-torch, Mauna Loa,
I saw a daring bee, today, pause, and soar,
    Into your flaming heart;
Then did I hear crisp crinkled laughter
As the furies after tore him apart?

A bird, next, small and humming,
Looked into your startled depths and fled. . . .
Surely, some dread sight, and dafter
Than human eyes as mine can see,
Set the stricken air waves drumming
In his flight.

Day-torch, Flame-flower, cool-hot Beauty,
I cannot see, I cannot hear your fluty
Voice lure your loving swain,
But I know one other to whom you are in beauty
Born in vain;
Hair like the setting sun,
Her eyes a rising star,
Motions gracious as reeds by Babylon, bar
All your competing;
Hands like, how like, brown lilies sweet,
Cloth of gold were fair enough to touch her feet. . . .
Ah, how the senses flood at my repeating,
As once in her fire-lit heart I felt the furies
Beating, beating.

FOR JIM, EASTER EVE
by Anne Spencer

If ever a garden was Gethsemane,
with old tombs set high against
the crumpled olive tree—and lichen,
this, my garden, has been to me.
For such as I none other is so sweet:
Lacking old tombs, here stands my grief,
and certainly its ancient tree.

Peace is here and in every season
a quiet beauty.
The sky falling about me
evenly to the compass . . .

What is sorrow but tenderness now
in this earth-close frame of land and sky
falling constantly into horizons
of east and west, north and south;
what is pain but happiness here
amid these green and wordless patterns,—
indefinite texture of blade and leaf:

Beauty of an old, old tree,
last comfort in Gethsemane.

MORNING LIGHT
The Dew-Drier
by Effie Lee Newsome

In Africa little black boys,
"human brooms," are sent before the explorers
into jungle grasses that tower many feet
to tread down a path
and meet sometimes
the lurking leopard or hyena.
They are called Dew-Driers.

Brother to the firefly——
For as the firefly lights the night,
So lights he the morning——
Bathed in the dank dews as he goes forth
Through heavy menace and mystery
Of half-waking tropic dawn,
Behold a little black boy,
A naked black boy,
Sweeping aside with his slight frame
Night's pregnant tears,
And making a morning path to the light
For the tropic traveler!

ARCTIC TERN IN A MUSEUM
by Effie Lee Newsome

I see you in the silver
Of moons that shine in the morning,
Swung in an argent west,
Before dim autumn dawns.
I see your slim, long wings,
Stayed speed and boundless power
And miles and miles and miles,
From arctic to antarctic,
From antarctic to arctic
On through the leagueless skies.
And while you swing, still,
In the museum's habitat,
You bring the bleak heart of tundras.
Your pallid, still plumage
In silver and white
To me seems but one message—
One single symbol—
Flight.

LITTLE BIRCHES
by Effie Lee Newsome

The little birches haunt the hills
In silent, silver masses,
Their violet velvet shadow robes
Beside them on the grasses.

THE HEART OF A WOMAN
by Georgia Douglas Johnson

The heart of a woman goes forth with the dawn,
As a lone bird, soft winging, so restlessly on,
Afar o'er life's turrets and vales does it roam
In the wake of those echoes the heart calls home.

The heart of a woman falls back with the night,
And enters some alien cage in its plight,
And tries to forget it has dreamed of the stars,
While it breaks, breaks, breaks on the sheltering bars.

YOUTH
by Georgia Douglas Johnson

The dew is on the grasses, dear,
    The blush is on the rose,
And swift across our dial-youth,
    A shifting shadow goes.

The primrose moments, lush with bliss,
    Exhale and fade away,
Life may renew the Autumn time,
    But nevermore the May!

REMEMBER
by Georgia Douglas Johnson

When love's brief dream is done
Pass on. Nor hope to see again
The burnished glow of yesterday
Gone with its setting sun.

Know this, the little while of love
Is fleeting as a cloud,
As lissom as a zephyr's breath,
As fickle as a crowd.

Its gleaming rainbow flames the sky—
Enthralls—then fades from sight:
Love for a day, an hour and then—
Remember through the night.

THE SUPPLIANT
by Georgia Douglas Johnson

Long have I beat with timid hands upon life's leaden door,
Praying the patient, futile prayer my fathers prayed before,
Yet I remain without the close, unheeded and unheard,
And never to my listening ear is borne the waited word.

Soft o'er the threshold of the years there comes this counsel cool:
The strong demand, contend, prevail; the beggar is a fool!

OLD BLACK MEN
by Georgia Douglas Johnson

They have dreamed as young men dream
Of glory, love and power;
They have hoped as youth will hope
Of life's sun-minted hour.

They have seen as others saw
Their bubbles burst in air,
And they have learned to live it down
As though they did not care.

INTERRACIAL
by Georgia Douglas Johnson

Let's build bridges here and there
Or sometimes, just a spiral stair
That we may come somewhat abreast
And sense what cannot be exprest,
And by these measures can be found
A meeting place—a common ground
Nearer the reaches of the heart
Where truth revealed, stands clear, apart;
With understanding come to know
What laughing lips will never show:
How tears and torturing distress
May masquerade as happiness:
Then you will know when my heart's aching
And I when yours is slowly breaking.
Commune—The altars will reveal . . .
We then shall be impulsed to kneel
And send a prayer upon its way
For those who wear the thorns today.

Oh, let's build bridges everywhere
And span the gulf of challenge there.

I CLOSED MY SHUTTERS FAST LAST NIGHT
by Georgia Douglas Johnson

I closed my shutters fast last night,
Reluctantly and slow,
So pleading was the purple sky
With all the lights hung low;
I left my lagging heart outside
Within the dark alone,
I heard it singing through the gloom
A wordless, anguished tone.

Upon my sleepless couch I lay
Until the tranquil morn
Came through the silver silences
To bring my heart forlorn,
Restoring it with calm caress
Unto its sheltered bower,
While whispering: "Await, await
Your golden, perfect hour."

RECESSIONAL
by Georgia Douglas Johnson

Consider me a memory, a dream that passed away;
Or yet a flower that has blown and shattered in a day;
For passion sleeps alas and keeps no vigil with the years
And wakens to no conjuring of orisons or tears.

Consider me a melody that served its simple turn,
Or but the residue of fire that settles in the urn,
For love defies pure reasoning and undeterred flows
Within, without, the vassal heart—its reasoning who knows?

MY LITTLE DREAMS
by Georgia Douglas Johnson

I'm folding up my little dreams
Within my heart tonight,
And praying I may soon forget
The torture of their sight.

For time's deft fingers scroll my brow
With fell relentless art——
I'm folding up my little dreams
Tonight, within my heart.

RULERS
by Fenton Johnson

It is said that many a king in troubled Europe would sell his crown
for a day of happiness.
I have seen a monarch who held tightly the jewel of happiness.
On Lombard Street in Philadelphia, as evening dropped to earth, I
gazed upon a laborer duskier than a sky devoid of moon. He was
seated on a throne of flour bags, waving his hand imperiously as
two small boys played on their guitars the ragtime tunes of the day.
God's blessing on the monarch who rules on Lombard Street in Philadelphia.

THE BANJO PLAYER
by Fenton Johnson

There is music in me, the music of a peasant people.
I wander through the levee, picking my banjo and singing my songs of
the cabin and the field. At the Last Chance Saloon I am as welcome
as the violets in March;
there is always food and drink for me there, and the dimes of those
who love honest music. Behind the railroad tracks the little children clap their hands and love me as they love Kris Kringle.
But I fear that I am a failure.
Last night a woman called me a troubadour.
What is a troubadour?

THE SCARLET WOMAN
by Fenton Johnson

Once I was good like the Virgin Mary and the Minister's wife.
My father worked for Mr. Pullman and white people's tips; but he died
two days after his insurance expired.

I had nothing, so I had to go to work.

All the stock I had was a white girl's education and a face that enchanted the men of both races.

Starvation danced with me.

So when Big Lizzie, who kept a house for white men, came to me with tales of fortune that I could reap from the sale of my virtue I bowed my head to Vice.

Now I can drink more gin than any man for miles around.

Gin is better than all the water in Lethe.

TIRED
by Fenton Johnson

I am tired of work; I am tired of building up somebody else's civilization.

Let us take a rest, M'Lissy Jane.

I will go down to the Last Chance Saloon, drink a gallon or two of gin, shoot a game or two of dice and sleep the rest of the night on one of Mike's barrels.

You will let the old shanty go to rot, the white people's clothes turn to dust, and the Calvary Baptist Church sink to the bottomless pit.

You will spend your days forgetting you married me and your nights hunting the warm gin Mike serves the ladies in the rear of the Last Chance Saloon.

Throw the children into the river; civilization has given us too many. It is better to die than to grow up and find that you are colored.

Pluck the stars out of the heavens. The stars mark our destiny. The stars marked my destiny.

I am tired of civilization.

AUNT JANE ALLEN
by Fenton Johnson

State Street is lonely today. Aunt Jane Allen has driven her chariot to Heaven.

I remember how she hobbled along, a little woman, parched of skin, brown as the leather of a satchel and with eyes that had scanned eighty years of life.

Have those who bore her dust to the last resting place buried with her the basket of aprons she went up and down State Street trying to sell?

Have those who bore her dust to the last resting place buried with her the gentle worn *Son* that she gave to each of the seed of Ethiopia?

WHEN I DIE
by Fenton Johnson

When I die my song shall be
Crooning of the summer breeze;
When I die my shroud shall be
Leaves plucked from the maple trees;
On a couch as green as moss
And a bed as soft as down,
I shall sleep and dream my dream
Of a poet's laurel crown.

When I die my star shall drop
Singing like a nightingale;
When I die my soul shall rise
Where the lyre-strings never fail;
In the rose my blood shall lie,
In the violet the smile,
And the moonbeams thousand strong
Past my grave each night shall file.

THE LONELY MOTHER
by Fenton Johnson

Oh, my mother's moaning by the river,
My poor mother's moaning by the river,
For her son who walks the earth in sorrow.

Long my mother's moaned beside the river,
And her tears have filled an angel's pitcher:
"Lord of Heaven, bring to me my honey,
Bring to me the darling of my bosom,
For a lonely mother by the river."

Cease, O mother, moaning by the river;
Cease, good mother, moaning by the river.
I have seen the star of Michael shining,
Michael shining at the Gates of Morning.
Row, O mighty angel, down the twilight,
Row until I find a lonely woman,
Swaying long beneath a tree of cypress,
Swaying for her son who walks in sorrow.

WHO IS THAT A-WALKING IN THE CORN?
by Fenton Johnson

Who is that a-walking in the corn?
I have looked to East and looked to West
But nowhere could I find Him who walks
    Master's cornfield in the morning.

Who is that a-walking in the corn?
Is it Joshua, the son of Nun?—
Or King David come to fight the giant
    Near the cornfield in the morning?

Who is that a-walking in the corn?
Is it Peter jangling Heaven's keys?—
Or old Gabriel come to blow his horn
    Near the cornfield in the morning?

Who is that a-walking in the corn?
I have looked to East and looked to West
But nowhere could I find Him who walks
    Master's cornfield in the morning.

ENIGMA
by Jessie Redmond Fauset

There is no peace with you,
Nor any rest!
Your presence is a torture to the brain.
Your words are barbed arrows to the breast,
And one but greets
To wish you sped again.
Frustrate you make desire
And action vain.
There is no peace with you . . .
No peace . . .
Nor any rest.

Yet in your absence
Longing springs anew,
And hopefulness besets the baffled brain.
"If only you were you and yet not you!"
If you such joy could give as you give pain!
Then what an unguent for the burning breast!
And for the harassed heart
What rapture true!
"If only you were you and yet not you!"
There is no peace with you
Nor ever any rest!

LA VIE C'EST LA VIE
by Jessie Redmond Fauset

On summer afternoons I sit
Quiescent by you in the park,
And idly watch the sunbeams gild
And tint the ash-trees' bark.

Or else I watch the squirrels frisk
And chaffer in the grassy lane;
And all the while I mark your voice
Breaking with love and pain.

I know a woman who would give
Her chance of heaven to take my place;
To see the love-light in your eyes,
The love-glow on your face!

And there's a man whose lightest word
Can set my chilly blood afire;
Fulfillment of his least behest
Defines my life's desire.

But he will none of me, nor I
Of you. Nor you of her. 'Tis said
The world is full of jests like these—
I wish that I were dead.

DEAD FIRES
by Jessie Redmond Fauset

If this is peace, this dead and leaden thing,
    Then better far the hateful fret, the sting.
Better the wound forever seeking balm
    Than this gray calm!

Is this pain's surcease? Better far the ache,
    The long-drawn dreary day, the night's white wake,
Better the choking sigh, the sobbing breath
    Than passion's death!

OBLIVION
by Jessie Redmond Fauset

From the French of
Massillon Coicou (Haiti)

I hope when I am dead that I shall lie
    In some deserted grave—I cannot tell you why,
But I should like to sleep in some neglected spot,
    Unknown to every one, by every one forgot.

There lying I should taste with my dead breath
    The utter lack of life, the fullest sense of death;
And I should never hear the note of jealousy or hate,
    The tribute paid by passers-by to tombs of state.

To me would never penetrate the prayers and tears
    That futilely bring torture to dead and dying ears;
There I should lie annihilate and my dead heart would bless
    Oblivion—the shroud and envelope of happiness.

STATUS QUO
by Binga Dismond

                Let Bourbons fight for status quo
                And battle to maintain jim crow
                A mere short span——they can decide
                With whom we eat; with whom we ride;
                With whom we pass the hours by;
                With whom we march; with whom we die.
                But they stay not time's endless rust
                When they and we will end in dust,
                And all in final chemistry
                Become as one immutably
                And shall remain a status quo——
                Without a vestige of jim crow.

AT EARLY MORN
by Binga Dismond

From the French
of Catulle Mendes

At early morn—the telephone;
She asked that I should come alone.

I obeyed.

An hour came and passed along;
She asked if I would play a song?

I played.

When shadows slowly came at eve,
She trembling, asked that I should leave.

I stayed.

SONG OF THE SON[25]
by Jean Toomer

Pour O pour that parting soul in song,
O pour it in the sawdust glow of night,
Into the velvet pine-smoke air to-night,
And let the valley carry it along.
And let the valley carry it along.

O land and soil, red soil and sweet-gum tree,
So scant of grass, so profligate of pines,
Now just before an epoch's sun declines
Thy son, in time, I have returned to thee,
Thy son, I have in time returned to thee.

[25]From *Cane*, by Jean Toomer. Reprinted by permission of Liveright Publishing Corp.

In time, for though the sun is setting on
A song-lit race of slaves, it has not set;
Though late, O soil, it is not too late yet
To catch thy plaintive soul, leaving, soon gone,
Leaving, to catch thy plaintive soul soon gone.

O Negro slaves, dark purple ripened plums,
Squeezed, and bursting in the pine-wood air,
Passing, before they stripped the old tree bare
One plum was saved for me, one seed becomes
An everlasting song, a singing tree,
Caroling softly souls of slavery,
What they were, and what they are to me,
Caroling softly souls of slavery.

BEEHIVE[26]
by Jean Toomer

Within this black hive to-night
There swarm a million bees;
Bees passing in and out the moon,
Bees escaping out the moon,
Bees returning through the moon,
Silver bees intently buzzing,
Silver honey dripping from the swarm of bees
Earth is a waxen cell of the world comb,
And I, a drone,
Lying on my back,
Lipping honey,
Getting drunk with silver honey,
Wish that I might fly out past the moon
And curl forever in some far-off farmyard flower.

[26]From *Cane*, by Jean Toomer. Reprinted by permission of Liveright Publishing Corp.

EVENING SONG[27]
by Jean Toomer

Full moon rising on the waters of my heart,
Lakes and moon and fires,
Cloine tires,
Holding her lips apart.

Promises of slumber leaving shore to charm the moon,
Miracle made vesper-keeps,
Cloine sleeps,
And I'll be sleeping soon.

Cloine, curled like the sleepy waters where the moon-waves start,
Radiant, resplendently she gleams,
Cloine dreams,
Lips pressed against my heart.

GEORGIA DUSK[28]
by Jean Toomer

The sky, lazily disdaining to pursue
    The setting sun, too indolent to hold
    A lengthened tournament for flashing gold,
Passively darkens for night's barbecue,

A feast of moon and men and barking hounds,
    An orgy for some genius of the South
    With blood-shot eyes and cane-lipped scented mouth,
Surprised in making folk-songs from soul sounds.

The sawmill blows its whistle, buzz-saws stop,
    And silence breaks the bud of knoll and hill,

[27,28]From *Cane*, by Jean Toomer. Reprinted by permission of Liveright Publishing Corp.

Soft settling pollen where plowed lands fulfill
Their early promise of a bumper crop.

Smoke from the pyramidal sawdust pile
   Curls up, blue ghosts of trees, tarrying low
   Where only chips and stumps are left to show
The solid proof of former domicile.

Meanwhile, the men, with vestiges of pomp,
   Race memories of king and caravan,
   High-priests, an ostrich, and a juju-man,
Go singing through the footpaths of the swamp.

Their voices rise . . . the pine trees are guitars,
   Strumming, pine-needles fall like sheets of rain . . .
   Their voices rise . . . the chorus of the cane
Is caroling a vesper to the stars . . .

O singers, resinous and soft your songs
   Above the sacred whisper of the pines,
   Give virgin lips to cornfield concubines,
Bring dreams of Christ to dusky cane-lipped throngs.

SUPPLICATION
by Joseph S. Cotter, Jr.

I am so tired and weary,
   So tired of the endless fight,
So weary of waiting the dawn
   And finding endless night.

That I ask but rest and quiet—
   Rest for the days that are gone,
And quiet for the little space
   That I must journey on.

AND WHAT SHALL YOU SAY?
by Joseph S. Cotter, Jr.

> Brother, come!
> And let us go unto our God.
> And when we stand before Him
> I shall say—
> "Lord, I do not hate,
> I am hated.
> I scourge no one,
> I am scourged.
> I covet no lands,
> My lands are coveted.
> I mock no peoples,
> My people are mocked."
> And, brother, what shall you say?

DARK SYMPHONY
by Melvin B. Tolson

I Allegro Moderato

> Black Crispus Attucks taught
>   Us how to die
> Before white Patrick Henry's bugle breath
> Uttered the vertical
>   Transmitting cry:
> "Yea, give me liberty or give me death."
>
> Waifs of the auction block,
>   Men black and strong
> The juggernauts of despotism withstood,
> Loin-girt with faith that worms
>   Equate the wrong
> And dust is purged to create brotherhood.

No Banquo's ghost can rise
  Against us now,
Aver we hobnailed Man beneath the brute,
Squeezed down the thorns of greed
  On Labor's brow,
Garroted lands and carted off the loot.

II Lento Grave

The centuries-old pathos in our voices
Saddens the great white world,
And the wizardry of our dusky rhythms
Conjures up shadow-shapes of ante-bellum years:

Black slaves singing *One More River to Cross*
In the torture tombs of slave-ships,
Black slaves singing *Steal Away to Jesus*
In jungle swamps,
Black slaves singing *The Crucifixion*
In slave-pens at midnight,
Black slaves singing *Swing Low, Sweet Chariot*
In cabins of death,
Black slaves singing *Go Down, Moses*
In the canebrakes of the Southern Pharaohs.

III Andante Sostenuto

They tell us to forget
The Golgotha we tread . . .
We who are scourged with hate,
A price upon our head.
They who have shackled us
Require of us a song,
They who have wasted us
Bid us condone the wrong.

They tell us to forget
Democracy is spurned.

They tell us to forget
The Bill of Rights is burned.
Three hundred years we slaved,
We slave and suffer yet:
Though flesh and bone rebel,
They tell us to forget!

Oh, how can we forget
Our human rights denied?
Oh, how can we forget
Our manhood crucified?
When Justice is profaned
And plea with curse is met,
When Freedom's gates are barred,
Oh, how can we forget?

IV Tempo Primo

The New Negro strides upon the continent
In seven-league boots . . .
The New Negro
Who sprang from the vigor-stout loins
Of Nat Turner, gallows-martyr for Freedom,
Of Joseph Cinquez, Black Moses of the Amistad Mutiny,
Of Frederick Douglass, oracle of the Catholic Man,
Of Sojourner Truth, eye and ear of Lincoln's legions,
Of Harriet Tubman, Saint Bernard of the Underground Railroad.

The New Negro
Breaks the icons of his detractors,
Wipes out the conspiracy of silence,
Speaks to *his* America:
"My history-moulding ancestors
Planted the first crops of wheat on these shores,
Built ships to conquer the seven seas,
Erected the Cotton Empire,
Flung railroads across a hemisphere,
Disemboweled the earth's iron and coal,
Tunneled the mountains and bridged rivers,

Harvested the grain and hewed forests,
Sentineled the Thirteen Colonies,
Unfurled Old Glory at the North Pole,
Fought a hundred battles for the Republic."

The New Negro:
His giant hands fling murals upon high chambers,
His drama teaches a world to laugh and weep,
His voice thunders the Brotherhood of Labor,
His science creates seven wonders,
His Republic of Letters challenges the Negro-baiters.

The New Negro,
Hard-muscled, Fascist-hating, Democracy-ensouled,
Strides in seven-league boots
Along the Highway of Today
Toward the Promised Land of Tomorrow!

V Larghetto

None in the Land can say
To us black men Today:
You send the tractors on their bloody path,
And create Okies for *The Grapes of Wrath*.
You breed the slum that breeds a *Native Son*
To damn the good earth Pilgrim Fathers won.

None in the Land can say
To us black men Today:
You dupe the poor with rags-to-riches tales,
And leave the workers empty dinner pails.
You stuff the ballot box, and honest men
Are muzzled by your demagogic din.

None in the Land can say
To us black men Today:
You smash stock markets with your coined blitzkriegs,
And make a hundred million guinea pigs.
You counterfeit our Christianity,
And bring contempt upon Democracy.

None in the Land can say
To us black men Today:
You prowl when citizens are fast asleep,
And hatch Fifth Column plots to blast the deep
Foundations of the State and leave the Land
A vast Sahara with a Fascist brand.

VI *Tempo di Marcia*

Out of abysses of Illiteracy,
Through labyrinths of Lies,
Across waste lands of Disease . . .
We advance!

Out of dead-ends of Poverty,
Through wildernesses of Superstition,
Across barricades of Jim Crowism . . .
We advance!

With the Peoples of the World . . .
We advance!

ON SEEING TWO BROWN BOYS IN A CATHOLIC CHURCH
by Frank Horne

It is fitting that you be here,
Little brown boys
With Christ-like eyes
And curling hair.

Look you on yonder crucifix
Where He hangs nailed and pierced
With head hung low
And eyes all blind with blood that drips
From a thorny crown . . .
Look you well,
You shall know this thing.

Judas' kiss shall burn your cheek
And you will be denied
By your Peter——

And Gethsemane . . .
You shall know full well. . . .
Gethsemane . . .

You, too, will suffer under Pontius Pilate
And feel the rugged cut of rough-hewn cross
Upon your surging shoulder—

They will spit in your face
And laugh . . .
They will nail you up twixt thieves
And gamble for your garments.

And in this you will exceed God
For on this earth
You shall know Hell—

O little brown boys
With Christ-like eyes
And curling hair,
It is fitting that you be here.

KID STUFF
by Frank Horne

December, 1942

The wise guys
tell me
that Christmas
is Kid Stuff . . .
Maybe they've got
something there——

Two thousand years ago
three wise guys
chased a star
across a continent
to bring
frankincense and myrrh
to a Kid
born in a manger
with an idea in his head . . .

And as the bombs
crash
all over the world
today
the real wise guys
know
that we've all
got to go chasing stars
again
in the hope
that we can get back
some of that
Kid Stuff
born two thousand years ago——

TOAST
by Frank Horne

Here's to your eyes
for the things I see
drowned in them.
Here's to your lips
Two livid streaks of flame. . . .
Here's to your heart
May it ever be full
of the love of loving. . . .

Here's to your body
a lithesome hill-top tree
swaying
to a spring's morning breath. . . .
Here's to your soul
as yet
unborn. . . .

LETTERS FOUND NEAR A SUICIDE
by Frank Horne

To all of you

My little stone
Sinks quickly
Into the bosom of this deep, dark pool
Of oblivion . . .
I have troubled its breast but little
Yet those far shores
That knew me not
Will feel the fleeting, furtive kiss
Of my tiny concentric ripples . . .

To Mother

I came
In the blinding sweep
Of ecstatic pain,
I go
In the throbbing pulse
Of aching space——
In the eons between
I piled upon you
Pain on pain
Ache on ache
And yet as I go
I shall know

That you will grieve
And want me back . . .

To Catalina

Love thy piano, Oh girl,
It will give you back
Note for note
The harmonies of your soul.
It will sing back to you
The high songs of your heart.
It will give
As well as take . . .

To Telie

You have made my voice
A rippling laugh
But my heart
A crying thing . . .
'Tis better thus:
A fleeting kiss
And then,
The dark . . .

To "Chick"

Oh Achilles of the moleskins
And the gridiron
Do not wonder
Nor doubt that this is I
That lies so calmly here——
This is the same exultant beast
That so joyously
Ran the ball with you
In those far-flung days of abandon.
You remember how recklessly

We revelled in the heat and the dust
And the swirl of conflict?
You remember they called us
The Terrible Two?
And you remember
After we had battered our heads
And our bodies
Against the stonewall of their defense,——
You remember the signal I would call
And how you would look at me
In faith and admiration
And say "Let's go," . . .
How the lines would clash
And strain,
And how I would slip through
Fighting and squirming
Over the line
To victory.
You remember, Chick? . . .
When you gaze at me here
Let that same light
Of faith and admiration
Shine in your eyes
For I have battered the stark stonewall
Before me . . .
I have kept faith with you
And now
I have called my signal,
Found my opening
And slipped through
Fighting and squirming
Over the line
To victory. . . .

To Wanda

To you, so far away
So cold and aloof,

To you, who knew me so well,
This is my last Grand Gesture
This is my last Great Effect
And as I go winging
Through the black doors of eternity
Is that thin sound I hear
Your applause? . . .

To James

Do you remember
How you won
That last race . . . ?
How you flung your body
At the start . . .
How your spikes
Ripped the cinders
In the stretch . . .
How you catapulted
Through the tape . . .
Do you remember . . . ?
Don't you think
I lurched with you
Out of those starting holes . . . ?
Don't you think
My sinews tightened
At those first
Few strides . . .
And when you flew into the stretch
Was not all my thrill
Of a thousand races
In your blood . . . ?
At your final drive
Through the finish line
Did not my shout
Tell of the
Triumphant ecstasy
Of victory . . . ?

Live
As I have taught you
To run, Boy—
It's a short dash
Dig your starting holes
Deep and firm
Lurch out of them
Into the straightaway
With all the power
That is in you
Look straight ahead
To the finish line
Think only of the goal
Run straight
Run high
Run hard
Save nothing
And finish
With an ecstatic burst
That carries you
Hurtling
Through the tape
To victory. . . .

THE CRAFTSMAN
by Marcus B. Christian

I ply with all the cunning of my art
This little thing, and with consummate care
I fashion it—so that when I depart,
Those who come after me shall find it fair
And beautiful. It must be free of flaws—
Pointing no laborings of weary hands;
And there must be no flouting of the laws
Of beauty—as the artist understands.

Through passion, yearnings infinite—yet dumb—
I lift you from the depths of my own mind
And gild you with my soul's white heat to plumb
The souls of future men. I leave behind
This thing that in return this solace gives:
"He who creates true beauty ever lives."

McDONOGH DAY IN NEW ORLEANS
by Marcus B. Christian

The cotton blouse you wear, your mother said,
After a day of toil, "I guess I'll buy it";
For ribbons on your head and blouse she paid
Two-bits a yard—as if you would deny it!

And nights, after a day of kitchen toil,
She stitched your re-made skirt of serge—once blue—
Weary of eye, beneath a lamp of oil:
McDonogh would be proud of her and you.

Next, came white "creepers" and white stockings, too—
They almost asked her blood when they were sold;
Like some dark princess, to the school go you,
With blue larkspur and yellow marigold;
But few would know—or even guess this fact:
How dear comes beauty when a skin is black.

NOCTURNE VARIAL
by Lewis Alexander

I came as a shadow,
I stand now a light;
The depth of my darkness
Transfigures your night.

My soul is a nocturne
Each note is a star;
The light will not blind you
So look where you are.

The radiance is soothing.
There's warmth in the light.
I came as a shadow,
To dazzle your night!

DREAM SONG
by Lewis Alexander

Walk with the sun,
Dance at high noon;
And dream when night falls black;
But when the stars
Vie with the moon,
Then call the lost dream back.

TRANSFORMATION
by Lewis Alexander

I return the bitterness,
Which you gave to me;
When I wanted loveliness
Tantalant and free.

I return the bitterness
It is washed by tears;
Now it is a loveliness
Garnished through the years.

I return it loveliness,
Having made it so;
For I wore the bitterness
From it long ago.

AFTER WINTER[29]
by Sterling A. Brown

He snuggles his fingers
In the blacker loam
The lean months are done with,
The fat to come.

His eyes are set
On a brushwood-fire
But his heart is soaring
Higher and higher.

Though he stands ragged
An old scarecrow,
This is the way
His swift thoughts go,

"Butter beans fo' Clara
Sugar corn fo' Grace
An' fo' de little feller
Runnin' space.

"Radishes and lettuce
Eggplants and beets
Turnips fo' de winter
An' candied sweets.

"Homespun tobacco
Apples in de bin
Fo' smokin' an' fo' cider
When de folks draps in."

He thinks with the winter
His troubles are gone;
Ten acres unplanted
To raise dreams on.

[29]From *Southern Road*, by Sterling A. Brown, copyright, 1932, by Harcourt, Brace
and Company, Inc.

The lean months are done with,
The fat to come.
His hopes, winter wanderers,
Hasten home.

"Butterbeans fo' Clara
Sugar corn fo' Grace
An' fo' de little feller
Runnin' space. . . ."

OLD LEM[30]
by Sterling A. Brown

I talked to old Lem
And old Lem said:
   "They weigh the cotton
   They store the corn
      We only good enough
      To work the rows;
   They run the commissary
   They keep the books
      We gotta be grateful
      For being cheated;
   Whippersnapper clerks
   Call us out of our name
      We got to say mister
      To spindling boys
   They make our figgers
   Turn somersets
   We buck in the middle
      Say, 'Thankyuh, sah.'
         They don't come by ones
         They don't come by twos
         But they come by tens.

[30]By permission of author.

"They got the judges
They got the lawyers
They got the jury-rolls
They got the law
     They don't come by ones
They got the sheriffs
They got the deputies
         They don't come by twos
They got the shotguns
They got the rope
     We git the justice
     In the end
         And they come by tens.

"Their fists stay closed
Their eyes look straight
     Our hands stay open
     Our eyes must fall
         They don't come by ones
They got the manhood
They got the courage
         They don't come by twos
     We got to slink around,
     Hangtailed hounds.
They burn us when we dogs
They burn us when we men
         They come by tens. . . .

"I had a buddy
Six foot of man
Muscled up perfect
Game to the heart
         They don't come by ones
Outworked and outfought
Any man or two men
         They don't come by twos
He spoke out of turn
At the commissary
They gave him a day

To git out the county.
He didn't take it.
He said 'Come and get me.'
They came and got him.
   And they came by tens.
He stayed in the county—
He lays there dead.

   They don't come by ones
   They don't come by twos
   But they come by tens."

FORECLOSURE[31]
by Sterling A. Brown

Father Missouri takes his own.
These are the fields he loaned them,
Out of hearts' fullness; gratuitously;
Here are the banks he built up for his children—
Here are the fields; rich, fertile silt.

Father Missouri, in his dotage
Whimsical and drunkenly turbulent,
Cuts away the banks; steals away the loam;
Washes the ground from under wire fences,
Leaves fenceposts grotesquely dangling in the air;
And with doddering steps approaches the shanties.

Father Missouri; far too old to be so evil.

Uncle Dan, seeing his garden lopped away,
Seeing his manured earth topple slowly in the stream,
Seeing his cows knee-deep in yellow water,
His pig-sties flooded, his flower beds drowned,
Seeing his white leghorns swept down the stream—

Curses Father Missouri, impotently shakes
His fist at the forecloser, the treacherous skinflint;
Who takes what was loaned so very long ago,
And leaves puddles in his parlor, and useless lakes
In his fine pasture land.
Sees years of work turned to nothing—
Curses, and shouts in his hoarse old voice,
"Ain't got no right to act dat way at all"
And the old river rolls on, slowly to the gulf.

REMEMBERING NAT TURNER[32]
by Sterling A. Brown

We saw a bloody sunset over Courtland, once Jerusalem,
As we followed the trail that old Nat took
When he came out of Cross Keys down upon Jerusalem,
In his angry stab for freedom a hundred years ago.
The land was quiet, and the mist was rising,
Out of the woods and the Nottaway swamp,
Over Southampton the still night fell,
As we rode down to Cross Keys where the march began.

When we got to Cross Keys, they could tell us little of him,
The Negroes had only the faintest recollections:
"I ain't been here so long, I come from up roun' Newsome;
Yassah, a town a few miles up de road,
The old folks who coulda told you is all dead an' gone.
I heard something, sometime; I doan jis remember what.
'Pears lak I heard that name somewheres or other.
So he fought to be free. Well. You doan say."

An old white woman recalled exactly
How Nat crept down the steps, axe in his hand,
After murdering a woman and child in bed,
"Right in this house at the head of these stairs."
(In a house built long after Nat was dead.)

[32]By permission of author.

She pointed to a brick store where Nat was captured,
(Nat was taken in a swamp, three miles away)
With his men around him, shooting from the windows
(She was thinking of Harper's Ferry and old John Brown.)
She cackled as she told how they riddled Nat with bullets
(Nat was tried and hanged at Courtland, ten miles away)
She wanted to know why folks would come miles
Just to ask about an old nigger fool.

    "Ain't no slavery no more, things is going all right,
    Pervided thar's a good goober market this year.
    We had a sign post here with printing on it,
    But it rotted in the hole and thar it lays;
    And the nigger tenants split the marker for kindling.
    Things is all right, naow, ain't no trouble with the niggers.
    Why they make this big to-do over Nat?"

As we drove from Cross Keys back to Courtland,
Along the way that Nat came down from Jerusalem,
A watery moon was high in the cloud-filled heavens,
The same moon he dreaded a hundred years ago.
The tree they hanged Nat on is long gone to ashes,
The trees he dodged behind have rotted in the swamps.

The bus for Miami and the trucks boomed by,
And touring cars, their heavy tires snarling on the pavement.
Frogs piped in the marshes, and a hound bayed long,
And yellow lights glowed from the cabin windows.

As we came back the way that Nat led his army,
Down from Cross Keys, down to Jerusalem,
We wondered if his troubled spirit still roamed the Nottaway,
Or if it fled with the cock-crow at daylight,
Or lay at peace with the bones in Jerusalem,
Its restlessness stifled by Southampton clay.

We remembered the poster rotted through and falling,
The marker split for kindling a kitchen fire.

SISTER LOU[33]
by Sterling A. Brown

Honey
When de man
Calls out de las' train
You're gonna ride,
Tell him howdy.

Gather up yo' basket
An' yo' knittin' an' yo' things,
An' go on up an' visit
Wid frien' Jesus fo' a spell.

Show Marfa
How to make yo' greengrape jellies,
An' give po' Lazarus
A passel of them Golden Biscuits.

Scald some meal
Fo' some rightdown good spoonbread
Fo' li'l box-plunkin' David.

An' sit aroun'
An' tell them Hebrew Chillen
All yo' stories. . . .

Honey
Don't be feared of them pearly gates,
Don't go 'round to de back,
No mo' dataway
Not evah no mo'.

Let Michael tote yo' burden
An' yo' pocketbook an' evah thing
'Cept yo' Bible,
While Gabriel blows somp'n
Solemn but loudsome
On dat horn of his'n.

Honey
Go Straight on to de Big House,
An' speak to yo' God
Widout no fear an' tremblin'.

Then sit down
An' pass de time of day awhile.

Give a good talkin' to
To yo' favorite 'postle Peter,
An' rub the po' head
Of mixed-up Judas,
An' joke awhile wid Jonah.

Then, when you gits de chance,
Always rememberin' yo' raisin',
Let 'em know youse tired
Jest a mite tired.

Jesus will find yo' bed fo' you
Won't no servant evah bother wid yo' room.
Jesus will lead you
To a room wid windows
Openin' on cherry trees an' plum trees
Bloomin' everlastin'.

An' dat will be yours
Fo' keeps.

Den take yo' time. . . .
Honey, take yo' bressed time.

THE MASK[34]
by Clarissa Scott Delany

So detached and cool she is
No motion e'er betrays
The secret life within her soul,
The anguish of her days.

She seems to look upon the world
With cold ironic eyes,
To spurn emotion's fevered sway,
To scoff at tears and sighs.

But once a woman with a child
Passed by her on the street,
And once she heard from casual lips
A man's name, bitter-sweet.

Such baffled yearning in her eyes,
Such pain upon her face!
I turned aside until the mask
Was slipped once more in place.

SOLACE[35]
by Clarissa Scott Delany

My window opens out into the trees
And in that small space
Of branches and of sky
I see the seasons pass
Behold the tender green
Give way to darker heavier leaves.
The glory of the autumn comes

[34,35]By permission of Justice H. T. Delany.

When steeped in mellow sunlight
The fragile, golden leaves
Against a clear blue sky
Linger in the magic of the afternoon
And then reluctantly break off
And filter down to pave
A street with gold.
Then bare, gray branches
Lift themselves against the
Cold December sky
Sometimes weaving a web
Across the rose and dusk of late sunset
Sometimes against a frail new moon
And one bright star riding
A sky of that dark, living blue
Which comes before the heaviness
Of night descends, or the stars
Have powdered the heavens.
Winds beat against these trees;
The cold, but gentle rain of spring
Touches them lightly
The summer torrents strive
To lash them into a fury
And seek to break them—
But they stand.
My life is fevered
And a restlessness at times
An agony—again a vague
And baffling discontent
Possesses me.
I am thankful for my bit of sky
And trees, and for the shifting
Pageant of the seasons.
Such beauty lays upon the heart
A quiet.
Such eternal change and permanence
Take meaning from all turmoil
And leave serenity
Which knows no pain.

JOY[36]
by Clarissa Scott Delany

Joy shakes me like the wind that lifts a sail,
Like the roistering wind
That laughs through stalwart pines.
It floods me like the sun
On rain-drenched trees
That flash with silver and green.

I abandon myself to joy—
I laugh—I sing.
Too long have I walked a desolate way,
Too long stumbled down a maze
Bewildered.

INTERIM[37]
by Clarissa Scott Delany

The night was made for rest and sleep,
For winds that softly sigh;
It was not made for grief and tears;
So then why do I cry?

The wind that blows through leafy trees
Is soft and warm and sweet;
For me the night is a gracious cloak
To hide my soul's defeat.

Just one dark hour of shaken depths,
Of bitter black despair—
Another day will find me brave,
And not afraid to dare.

[36],[37]By permission of Justice H. T. Delany.

I, TOO, SING AMERICA[38]
by Langston Hughes

I, too, sing America.

I am the darker brother.
They send me to eat in the kitchen
When company comes,
But I laugh,
And eat well,
And grow strong.

Tomorrow,
I'll sit at the table
When company comes.
Nobody'll dare
Say to me,
"Eat in the kitchen,"
Then.

Besides,
They'll see how beautiful I am
And be ashamed—

I, too, am America.

DREAM VARIATION[39]
by Langston Hughes

To fling my arms wide
In some place of the sun,
To whirl and to dance
Till the white day is done.

[38,39]From *The Weary Blues,* by Langston Hughes, copyright, 1926, by Alfred A. Knopf, Inc. Reprinted by permission of Alfred A. Knopf, Inc.

Then rest at cool evening
Beneath a tall tree
While night comes on gently,
            Dark like me——
That is my dream!

To fling my arms wide
In the face of the sun,
Dance! whirl! whirl!
Till the quick day is done.
Rest at pale evening. . . .
A tall, slim tree. . . .
Night coming tenderly
            Black like me.

THE WEARY BLUES[40]
by Langston Hughes

Droning a drowsy syncopated tune,
Rocking back and forth to a mellow croon,
        I heard a Negro play.
Down on Lenox Avenue the other night
By the pale dull pallor of an old gas light
        He did a lazy sway. . . .
        He did a lazy sway. . . .
To the tune o' those Weary Blues.
With his ebony hands on each ivory key
He made that poor piano moan with melody.
        O Blues!
Swaying to and fro on his rickety stool
He played that sad raggy tune like a musical fool.
        Sweet Blues!
Coming from a black man's soul.
        O Blues!

[40]From The Weary Blues, by Langston Hughes, copyright, 1926, by Alfred A. Knopf, Inc. Reprinted by permission of Alfred A. Knopf, Inc.

In a deep song voice with a melancholy tone
I heard that Negro sing, that old piano moan—
  "Ain't got nobody in all this world,
  Ain't got nobody but ma self.
  I's gwine to quit ma frownin'
  And put ma troubles on the shelf."
Thump, thump, thump, went his foot on the floor.
He played a few chords then he sang some more—
  "I got the Weary Blues
  And I can't be satisfied.
  Got the Weary Blues
  And can't be satisfied—
  I ain't happy no mo'
  And I wish that I had died."
And far into the night he crooned that tune.
The stars went out and so did the moon.
The singer stopped playing and went to bed
While the Weary Blues echoed through his head.
He slept like a rock or a man that's dead.

LITTLE GREEN TREE BLUES[41]
by Langston Hughes

  Looks like to me
  My good-time days done past.
  Yes, it looks like
  My good-time days done past.
  There's nothin' in this world
  I reckon's due to last.

  I used to play
  And I played so hard.
  I used to play,
  I played so dog-gone hard.
  Now old age is got me,
  Dealt me my bad-luck card.

I looked down the road
And I see a little tree.
Little piece down the road
I see a little tree.
Them cool green leaves
Is waitin' to shelter me.

Oh, little tree!

PERSONAL[42]
by Langston Hughes

In an envelope marked:
    Personal
God addressed me a letter.
In an envelope marked:
    Personal
I have given my answer.

HAVANA DREAMS[43]
by Langston Hughes

The dream is a cocktail at Sloppy Joe's—
(Maybe—nobody knows.)

The dream is the road to Batabano.
(But nobody knows if that is so.)

Perhaps the dream is only her face—
Perhaps it's a fan of silver lace—
Or maybe the dream's a Vedado rose—
(*Quien sabe?* Who really knows?)

HARLEM SWEETIES[44]
by Langston Hughes

Have you dug the spill
Of Sugar Hill?
Cast your gims
On this sepia thrill:
Brown sugar lassie,
Caramel treat,
Honey-gold baby
Sweet enough to eat.
Peach-skinned girlie,
Coffee and cream,
Chocolate darling
Out of a dream.
Walnut tinted
Or cocoa brown,
Pomegranate-lipped
Pride of the town.
Rich cream-colored
To plum-tinted black,
Feminine sweetness
In Harlem's no lack.
Glow of the quince
To blush of the rose.
Persimmon bronze
To cinnamon toes.
Blackberry cordial,
Virginia Dare wine—
All those sweet colors
Flavor Harlem of mine!
Walnut or cocoa,
Let me repeat:
Caramel, brown sugar,
A chocolate treat.

Molasses taffy,
Coffee and cream,
Licorice, clove, cinnamon
To a honey-brown dream.
Ginger, wine-gold,
Persimmon, blackberry,
All through the spectrum
Harlem girls vary—
So if you want to know beauty's
Rainbow-sweet thrill,
Stroll down luscious,
Delicious, *fine* Sugar Hill.

AFRO-AMERICAN FRAGMENT[45]
by Langston Hughes

So long,
So far away
Is Africa.
Not even memories alive
Save those that history books create,
Save those that songs
Beat back into the blood—
Beat out of blood with words sad-sung
In strange un-Negro tongue—
So long,
So far away
Is Africa.

Subdued and time-lost
Are the drums—and yet
Through some vast mist of race
There comes this song
I do not understand,
This song of atavistic land,

[45]Originally published in *The Crisis*, Vol. 37, No. 7, July 1930. Reprinted by permission of author.

Of bitter yearnings lost
Without a place—
So long,
So far away
Is Africa's
Dark face.

CROSS[46]
by Langston Hughes

My old man's a white old man
And my old mother's black.
If ever I cursed my white old man
I take my curses back.

If ever I cursed my black old mother
And wished she were in hell,
I'm sorry for that evil wish
And now I wish her well.

My old man died in a fine big house,
My ma died in a shack.
I wonder where I'm gonna die,
Being neither white nor black?

SONG FOR A DARK GIRL[47]
by Langston Hughes

Way Down South in Dixie
(Break the heart of me)
They hung my dark young lover
To a cross roads tree.

Way Down South in Dixie
　(Bruised body high in air)
I asked the white Lord Jesus
　What was the use of prayer.

Way Down South in Dixie
　(Break the heart of me)
Love is a naked shadow
　On a gnarled and naked tree.

MERRY-GO-ROUND[48]
Colored Child at Carnival
by Langston Hughes

Where is the Jim Crow section
On this merry-go-round,
Mister, cause I want to ride?
Down South where I come from
White and colored
Can't sit side by side.
Down South on the train
There's a Jim Crow car.
On the bus we're put in the back——
But there ain't no back
To a merry-go-round!
Where's the horse
For a kid that's black?

MOTHER TO SON[49]
by Langston Hughes

Well, son, I'll tell you:
Life for me ain't been no crystal stair.

[48]From *Shakespeare in Harlem,* by Langston Hughes, copyright, 1942, by Alfred A. Knopf, Inc. Reprinted by permission of Alfred A. Knopf, Inc.

[49]From *The Weary Blues,* by Langston Hughes, copyright, 1926, by Alfred A. Knopf, Inc. Reprinted by permission of Alfred A. Knopf, Inc.

It's had tacks in it,
And splinters,
And boards torn up,
And places with no carpet on the floor—
Bare.
But all the time
I'se been a-climbin' on,
And reachin' landin's,
And turnin' corners,
And sometimes goin' in the dark
Where there ain't been no light.
So, boy, don't you turn back.
Don't you set down on the steps
'Cause you finds it's kinder hard.
Don't you fall now—
For I'se still goin', honey,
I'se still climbin',
And life for me ain't been no crystal stair.

THE NEGRO SPEAKS OF RIVERS[50]
by Langston Hughes

I've known rivers:
I've known rivers ancient as the world and older than the flow of human
    blood in human veins.

My soul has grown deep like the rivers.

I bathed in the Euphrates when dawns were young.
I built my hut near the Congo and it lulled me to sleep.
I looked upon the Nile and raised the pyramids above it.
I heard the singing of the Mississippi when Abe Lincoln went down to
    New Orleans, and I've seen its muddy bosom turn all golden in the
    sunset.

I've known rivers:
Ancient, dusky rivers.

My soul has grown deep like the rivers.

LET AMERICA BE AMERICA AGAIN[51]
by Langston Hughes

Let America be America again.
Let it be the dream it used to be.
Let it be the pioneer on the plain
Seeking a home where he himself is free.

(America never was America to me.)

Let America be the dream the dreamers dreamed—
Let it be that great strong land of love
Where never kings connive nor tyrants scheme
That any man be crushed by one above.

(It never was America to me.)

O, let my land be a land where Liberty
Is crowned with no false patriotic wreath,
But opportunity is real, and life is free,
Equality is in the air we breathe.

(There's never been equality for me,
Nor freedom in this "homeland of the free.")

Say who are you that mumbles in the dark?
And who are you that draws your veil across the stars?

[51]Originally published in part in *Esquire*, July 1936. Reprinted by permission of author.

I am the poor white, fooled and pushed apart,
I am the Negro bearing slavery's scars.
I am the red man driven from the land,
I am the immigrant clutching the hope I seek—
And finding only the same old stupid plan
Of dog eat dog, of mighty crush the weak.

I am the young man, full of strength and hope,
Tangled in that ancient endless chain
Of profit, power, gain, of grab the land!
Of grab the gold! Of grab the ways of satisfying need!
Of work the men! Of take the pay!
Of owning everything for one's own greed!

I am the farmer, bondsman to the soil.
I am the worker sold to the machine.
I am the Negro, servant to you all.
I am the people, worried, hungry, mean—
Hungry yet today despite the dream.
Beaten yet today—O, Pioneers!
I am the man who never got ahead,
The poorest worker bartered through the years.

Yet I'm the one who dreamt our basic dream
In that Old World while still a serf of kings,
Who dreamt a dream so strong, so brave, so true,
That even yet its mighty daring sings
In every brick and stone, in every furrow turned
That's made America the land it has become.
O, I'm the man who sailed those early seas
In search of what I meant to be my home—
For I'm the one who left dark Ireland's shore,
And Poland's plain, and England's grassy lea,
And torn from Black Africa's strand I came
To build a "homeland of the free."

The free?

A dream—
Still beckoning to me!

O, let America be America again—
The land that never has been yet—
And yet must be—
The land where *every* man is free.
The land that's mine—
The poor man's, Indian's, Negro's, ME—
Who made America,
Whose sweat and blood, whose faith and pain,
Whose hand at the foundry, whose plow in the rain,
Must bring back our mighty dream again.

Sure, call me any ugly name you choose—
The steel of freedom does not stain.
From those who live like leeches on the people's lives,
We must take back our land again,
America!

O, yes,
I say it plain,
America never was America to me,
And yet I swear this oath—
America will be!
An ever-living seed,
Its dream
Lies deep in the heart of me.

We, the people, must redeem
Our land, the mines, the plants, the rivers,
The mountains and the endless plain—
All, all the stretch of these great green states—
And make America again!

SONNETS
by Gwendolyn B. Bennett

1

He came in silvern armour, trimmed with black—
A lover come from legends long ago—
With silver spurs and silken plumes a-blow,
And flashing sword caught fast and buckled back
In a carven sheath of Tamarack.
He came with footsteps beautifully slow,
And spoke in voice meticulously low.
He came and Romance followed in his track. . . .

I did not ask his name—I thought him Love;
I did not care to see his hidden face.
All life seemed born in my intaken breath;
All thought seemed flown like some forgotten dove.
He bent to kiss and raised his visor's lace . . .
All eager-lipped I kissed the mouth of Death.

2

Some things are very dear to me—
Such things as flowers bathed by rain
Or patterns traced upon the sea
Or crocuses where snow has lain . . .
The iridescence of a gem,
The moon's cool opalescent light,
Azaleas and the scent of them,
And honeysuckles in the night.
And many sounds are also dear—
Like winds that sing among the trees
Or crickets calling from the weir
Or Negroes humming melodies.
But dearer far than all surmise
Are sudden tear-drops in your eyes.

LINES WRITTEN AT THE GRAVE OF ALEXANDRE DUMAS
by Gwendolyn B. Bennett

Cemeteries are places for departed souls
And bones interred,
Or hearts with shattered loves.
A woman with lips made warm for laughter
Would find grey stones and roving spirits
Too chill for living, moving pulses . . .
And thou, great spirit, wouldst shiver in thy granite shroud
Should idle mirth or empty talk
Disturb thy tranquil sleeping.

A cemetery is a place for shattered loves
And broken hearts. . . .
Bowed before the crystal chalice of thy soul,
I find the multi-colored fragrance of thy mind
Has lost itself in Death's transparency.

Oh, stir the lucid waters of thy sleep
And coin for me a tale
Of happy loves and gems and joyous limbs
And hearts where love is sweet!

A cemetery is a place for broken hearts
And silent thought . . .
And silence never moves,
Nor speaks nor sings.

A BLACK MAN TALKS OF REAPING
by Arna Bontemps

I have sown beside all waters in my day.
I planted deep, within my heart the fear
That wind or fowl would take the grain away.
I planted safe against this stark, lean year.

I scattered seed enough to plant the land
In rows from Canada to Mexico
But for my reaping only what the hand
Can hold at once is all that I can show.

Yet what I sowed and what the orchard yields
My brother's sons are gathering stalk and root,
Small wonder then my children glean in fields
They have not sown, and feed on bitter fruit.

MIRACLES
by Arna Bontemps

> Doubt no longer miracles,
> This spring day makes it plain
> A man may crumble into dust
> And straightway live again
>
> A jug of water in the sun
> Will easy turn to wine
> If love is stopping at the well
> And love's brown arms entwine.
>
> And you who think him only man,
> I tell you faithfully
> That I have seen Christ clothed in rain
> Walking on the sea.

NOCTURNE AT BETHESDA
by Arna Bontemps

> I thought I saw an angel flying low,
> I thought I saw the flicker of a wing
> Above the mulberry trees; but not again.
> Bethesda sleeps. This ancient pool that healed
> A host of bearded Jews does not awake.

This pool that once the angels troubled does not move
No angel stirs it now, no Saviour comes
With healing in His hands to raise the sick
And bid the lame man leap upon the ground.

The golden days are gone. Why do we wait
So long upon the marble steps, blood
Falling from our open wounds? and why
Do our black faces search the empty sky?
Is there something we have forgotten? some precious **thing**
We have lost, wandering in strange lands?

There was a day, I remember now,
I beat my breast and cried, "Wash me God,
Wash me with a wave of wind upon
The barley; O quiet One, draw near, draw near!
Walk upon the hills with lovely feet
And in the waterfall stand and speak.

"Dip white hands in the lily pool and mourn
Upon the harps still hanging in the trees
Near Babylon along the river's edge,
But oh, remember me, I pray, before
The summer goes and rose leaves lose their red."

The old terror takes my heart, the fear
Of quiet waters and of faint twilights.
There will be better days when I am gone
And healing pools where I cannot be healed.
Fragrant stars will gleam forever and ever
Above the place where I lie desolate.

Yet I hope, still I long to live.
And if there can be returning after death
I shall come back. But it will not be here;
If you want me you must search for me
Beneath the palms of Africa. Or if
I am not there then you may call to me
Across the shining dunes, perhaps I shall
Be following a desert caravan.

I may pass through centuries of death
With quiet eyes, but I'll remember still
A jungle tree with burning scarlet birds.
There is something I have forgotten, some precious thing.
I shall be seeking ornaments of ivory,
I shall be dying for a jungle fruit.

You do not hear, Bethesda.
O still green water in a stagnant pool!
Love abandoned you and me alike.
There was a day you held a rich full moon
Upon your heart and listened to the words
Of men now dead and saw the angels fly.
There is a simple story on your face;
Years have wrinkled you. I know, Bethesda!
You are sad. It is the same with me.

SOUTHERN MANSION
by Arna Bontemps

Poplars are standing there still as death
And ghosts of dead men
Meet their ladies walking
Two by two beneath the shade
And standing on the marble steps.

There is a sound of music echoing
Through the open door
And in the field there is
Another sound tinkling in the cotton:
Chains of bondmen dragging on the ground.

The years go back with an iron clank,
A hand is on the gate,
A dry leaf trembles on the wall.
Ghosts are walking.
They have broken roses down
And poplars stand there still as death.

LENGTH OF MOON
by Arna Bontemps

Then the golden hour
Will tick its last
And the flame will go down in the flower.

A briefer length of moon
Will mark the sea-line and the yellow dune.

Then we may think of this, yet
There will be something forgotten
And something we should forget.

It will be like all things we know:
The stone will fail; a rose is sure to go.

It will be quiet then and we may stay
As long at the picket gate
But there will be less to say.

THE RETURN
by Arna Bontemps

Once more, listening to the wind and rain,
Once more, you and I, and above the hurting sound
Of these comes back the throbbing of remembered rain,
Treasured rain falling on dark ground.
Once more, huddling birds upon the leaves
And summer trembling on a withered vine.
And once more, returning out of pain,
The friendly ghost that was your love and mine.

II

Darkness brings the jungle to our room:
The throb of rain is the throb of muffled drums.
Darkness hangs our room with pendulums
Of vine and in the gathering gloom
Our walls recede into a denseness of
Surrounding trees. This is a night of love
Retained from those lost nights our fathers slept
In huts; this is a night that must not die.
Let us keep the dance of rain our fathers kept
And tread our dreams beneath the jungle sky.

III

And now the downpour ceases.
Let us go back once more upon the glimmering leaves
And as the throbbing of the drums increases
Shake the grass and dripping boughs of trees.
A dry wind stirs the palm; the old tree grieves.

Time has charged the years: the old days have returned.

Let us dance by metal waters burned
With gold of moon, let us dance
With naked feet beneath the young spice trees.
What was that light, that radiance
On your face?—something I saw when first
You passed beneath the jungle tapestries?

A moment we pause to quench our thirst
Kneeling at the water's edge, the gleam
Upon your face is plain: you have wanted this.
Let us go back and search the tangled dream
And as the muffled drum-beats throb and miss
Remember again how early darkness comes
To dreams and silence to the drums.

IV

Let us go back into the dusk again,
Slow and sad-like following the track
Of blowing leaves and cool white rain
Into the old gray dream, let us go back.
Our walls close about us we lie and listen
To the noise of the street, the storm and the driven birds.
A question shapes your lips, your eyes glisten
Retaining tears, but there are no more words.

IDOLATRY
by Arna Bontemps

You have been good to me, I give you this:
The arms of lovers empty as our own,
Marble lips sustaining one long kiss
And the hard sound of hammers breaking stone.

For I will build a chapel in the place
Where our love died and I will journey there
To make a sign and kneel before your face
And set an old bell tolling on the air.

CLOSE YOUR EYES!
by Arna Bontemps

Go through the gates with closed eyes.
Stand erect and let your black face front the west.
Drop the axe and leave the timber where it lies;
A woodman on the hill must have his rest.

Go where leaves are lying brown and wet.
Forget her warm arms and her breast who mothered you,
And every face you ever loved forget.
Close your eyes; walk bravely through.

GOLGOTHA IS A MOUNTAIN
by Arna Bontemps

Golgotha is a mountain, a purple mound
Almost out of sight.
One night they hanged two thieves there,
And another man.
Some women wept heavily that night;
Their tears are flowing still. They have made a river;
Once it covered me.
Then the people went away and left Golgotha
Deserted.
Oh, I've seen many mountains:
Pale purple mountains melting in the evening mists and blurring on the
    borders of the sky.

I climbed old Shasta and chilled my hands in its summer snows.
I rested in the shadow of Popocatepetl and it whispered to me of daring
    prowess.
I looked upon the Pyrenees and felt the zest of warm exotic nights.
I slept at the foot of Fujiyama and dreamed of legend and of death.
And I've seen other mountains rising from the wistful moors like the
    breasts of a slender maiden.
Who knows the mystery of mountains!
Some of them are awful, others are just lonely.

. . .

Italy has its Rome and California has San Francisco,
All covered with mountains.
Some think these mountains grew
Like ant hills
Or sand dunes.

That might be so—
I wonder what started them all!
Babylon is a mountain
And so is Nineveh,
With grass growing on them;
Palaces and hanging gardens started them.
I wonder what is under the hills
In Mexico
And Japan!
There are mountains in Africa too.
Treasure is buried there:
Gold and precious stones
And moulded glory.
Lush grass is growing there
Sinking before the wind.
Black men are bowing.
Naked in that grass
Digging with their fingers.
I am one of them:
Those mountains should be ours.
It would be great
To touch the pieces of glory with our hands.
These mute unhappy hills,
Bowed down with broken backs,
Speak often one to another:
"A day is as a year," they cry,
"And a thousand years as one day."
We watched the caravan
That bore our queen to the courts of Solomon;
And when the first slave traders came
We bowed our heads.
"Oh, Brothers, it is not long!
Dust shall yet devour the stones
But we shall be here when they are gone."
Mountains are rising all around me.
Some are so small they are not seen;
Others are large.
All of them get big in time and people forget
What started them at first.

Oh the world is covered with mountains!
Beneath each one there is something buried:
Some pile of wreckage that started it there.
Mountains are lonely and some are awful.

. . .

One day I will crumble.
They'll cover my heap with dirt and that will make a mountain.
I think it will be Golgotha.

A NOTE OF HUMILITY
by Arna Bontemps

When all our hopes are sown on stony ground,
And we have yielded up the thought of gain,
Long after our last songs have lost their sound,
We may come back, we may come back again.

When thorns have choked the last green thing we loved,
And we have said all that there is to say,
When love that moved us once leaves us unmoved,
Then men like us may come to have a day.

For it will be with us as with the bee,
The meager ant, the sea-gull and the loon;
We may come back to triumph mournfully
An hour or two, but it will not be soon.

THE DAYBREAKERS
by Arna Bontemps

We are not come to wage a strife
With swords upon this hill;

It is not wise to waste the life
  Against a stubborn will.
Yet would we die as some have done:
Beating a way for the rising sun.

EPITAPH FOR A BIGOT
by Dorothy Vena Johnson

Life to the bigot is a whip
That lashes creed and laity;
Here lies the one who lost his grip
And cringed to Death—a refugee.

GREEN VALLEY
by Dorothy Vena Johnson

I stood in a meadow,
  And all I could see
Was the green valley
  Surrounding me

Then the setting sun
  Burned a ghastly red:
Blood of young men
  Too soon dead.

A tawny lizard
  Crawled near my feet:
I visioned women
  Alone, deplete.

And now and then
  A fledgling cried,
Like destitute folk
  On the wayside.

When I beheld
　　The tallest tree,
My soul expanded
　　Inside of me.

I wished, as I viewed
　　The greenest pit,
To bury ugliness
　　In it.

The hills were rich
　　With buds impearled.
The valley seemed
　　To engulf the world.

I stood in the meadow,
　　And all I could see
Was that green valley
　　Surrounding me.

HERITAGE[52]
For Harold Jackman
by Countee Cullen

What is Africa to me:
Copper sun or scarlet sea,
Jungle star or jungle track,
Strong bronzed men, or regal black
Women from whose loins I sprang
When the birds of Eden sang?
One three centuries removed
From the scenes his fathers loved,
Spicy grove, cinnamon tree,
What is Africa to me?

So I lie, who all day long
Want no sound except the song

[52]From *Color*, by Countee Cullen, copyright, 1925, by Harper & Brothers.

Sung by wild barbaric birds
Goading massive jungle herds,
Juggernauts of flesh that pass
Trampling tall defiant grass
Where young forest lovers lie,
Plighting troth beneath the sky.
So I lie, who always hear,
Though I cram against my ear
Both my thumbs, and keep them there,
Great drums throbbing through the air.
So I lie, whose fount of pride,
Dear distress, and joy allied,
Is my somber flesh and skin,
With the dark blood dammed within
Like great pulsing tides of wine
That, I fear, must burst the fine
Channels of the chafing net
Where they surge and foam and fret.

Africa? A book one thumbs
Listlessly, till slumber comes.
Unremembered are her bats
Circling through the night, her cats
Crouching in the river reeds,
Stalking gentle flesh that feeds
By the river brink; no more
Does the bugle-throated roar
Cry that monarch claws have leapt
From the scabbards where they slept.
Silver snakes that once a year
Doff the lovely coats you wear,
Seek no covert in your fear
Lest a mortal eye should see;
What's your nakedness to me?
Here no leprous flowers rear
Fierce corollas in the air;
Here no bodies sleek and wet,
Dripping mingled rain and sweat,
Tread the savage measures of

Jungle boys and girls in love.
What is last year's snow to me,
Last year's anything? The tree
Budding yearly must forget
How its past arose or set—
Bough and blossom, flower, fruit,
Even what shy bird with mute
Wonder at her travail there,
Meekly labored in its hair.
One three centuries removed
From the scenes his fathers loved,
Spicy grove, cinnamon tree,
What is Africa to me?

So I lie, who find no peace
Night or day, no slight release
From the unremittent beat
Made by cruel padded feet
Walking through my body's street.
Up and down they go, and back,
Treading out a jungle track.
So I lie, who never quite
Safely sleep from rain at night—
I can never rest at all
When the rain begins to fall;
Like a soul gone mad with pain
I must match its weird refrain;
Ever must I twist and squirm,
Writhing like a baited worm,
While its primal measures drip
Through my body, crying, "Strip!
Doff this new exuberance.
Come and dance the Lover's Dance!"
In an old remembered way
Rain works on me night and day.

Quaint, outlandish heathen gods
Black men fashion out of rods,
Clay, and brittle bits of stone,

In a likeness like their own,
My conversion came high-priced;
I belong to Jesus Christ,
Preacher of Humility;
Heathen gods are naught to me.

Father, Son, and Holy Ghost,
So I make an idle boast;
Jesus of the twice-turned cheek,
Lamb of God, although I speak
With my mouth thus, in my heart
Do I play a double part.
Ever at Thy glowing altar
Must my heart grow sick and falter,
Wishing He I served were black,
Thinking then it would not lack
Precedent of pain to guide it,
Let who would or might deride it;
Surely then this flesh would know
Yours had borne a kindred woe.
Lord, I fashion dark gods, too,
Daring even to give You
Dark despairing features where,
Crowned with dark rebellious hair,
Patience wavers just so much as
Mortal grief compels, while touches
Quick and hot, of anger, rise
To smitten cheek and weary eyes.
Lord, forgive me if my need
Sometimes shapes a human creed.
All day long and all night through,
One thing only must I do:
Quench my pride and cool my blood,
Lest I perish in the flood,
Lest a hidden ember set
Timber that I thought was wet
Burning like the dryest flax,
Melting like the merest wax,
Lest the grave restore its dead.

Not yet has my heart or head
In the least way realized
They and I are civilized.

FOR A POET[53]
by Countee Cullen

I have wrapped my dreams in a silken cloth,
And laid them away in a box of gold;
Where long will cling the lips of the moth,
I have wrapped my dreams in a silken cloth;
I hide no hate; I am not even wroth
Who found earth's breath so keen and cold;
I have wrapped my dreams in a silken cloth,
And laid them away in a box of gold.

SIMON THE CYRENIAN SPEAKS[54]
by Countee Cullen

He never spoke a word to me,
And yet He called my name;
He never gave a sign to me,
And yet I knew and came.

At first I said, "I will not bear
His cross upon my back;
He only seeks to place it there
Because my skin is black."

But He was dying for a dream,
And He was very meek,
And in His eyes there shone a gleam
Men journey far to seek.

[53,54]From *Color*, by Countee Cullen, copyright, 1925, by Harper & Brothers.

It was Himself my pity bought;
I did for Christ alone
What all of Rome could not have wrought
With bruise of lash or stone.

THE WISE[55]
by Countee Cullen

Dead men are wisest, for they know
How far the roots of flowers go,
How long a seed must rot to grow.

Dead men alone bear frost and rain
On throbless heart and heatless brain,
And feel no stir of joy or pain.

Dead men alone are satiate;
They sleep and dream and have no weight,
To curb their rest, of love or hate.

Strange, men should flee their company,
Or think me strange who long to be
Wrapped in their cool immunity.

THAT BRIGHT CHIMERIC BEAST[56]
by Countee Cullen

That bright chimeric beast
Conceived yet never born,
Save in the poet's breast,
The white-flanked unicorn,

[55]From *Color*, by Countee Cullen, copyright, 1925, by Harper & Brothers.

[56]From *The Black Christ*, by Countee Cullen, copyright, 1929, by Harper & Brothers.

Never may be shaken
From his solitude;
Never may be taken
In any earthly wood.

That bird forever feathered,
Of its new self the sire,
After aeons weathered,
Reincarnate by fire,
Falcon may not nor eagle
Swerve from his eyrie,
Nor any crumb inveigle
Down to an earthly tree.

That fish of the dread regime
Invented to become
The fable and the dream
Of the Lord's aquarium,
Leviathan, the jointed
Harpoon was never wrought
By which the Lord's anointed
Will suffer to be caught.

Bird of the deathless breast,
Fish of the frantic fin,
That bright chimeric beast
Flashing the argent skin,—
If beasts like these you'd harry,
Plumb then the poet's dream;
Make it your aviary,
Make it your wood and stream.

There only shall the swish
Be heard of the regal fish;
There like a golden knife
Dart the feet of the unicorn,
And there, death brought to life,
The dead bird be reborn.

FOR A LADY I KNOW[57]
by Countee Cullen

> She even thinks that up in heaven
> Her class lies late and snores,
> While poor black cherubs rise at seven
> To do celestial chores.

INCIDENT[58]
by Countee Cullen

> Once riding in old Baltimore,
> Heart-filled, head-filled with glee,
> I saw a Baltimorean
> Keep looking straight at me.
>
> Now I was eight and very small,
> And he was no whit bigger,
> And so I smiled, but he poked out
> His tongue, and called me, "Nigger."
>
> I saw the whole of Baltimore
> From May until December;
> Of all the things that happened there
> That's all that I remember.

SATURDAY'S CHILD[59]
by Countee Cullen

> Some are teethed on a silver spoon,
> With the stars strung for a rattle;
> I cut my teeth as the black racoon——
> For implements of battle.

[57,58,59]From *Color*, by Countee Cullen, copyright, 1925, by Harper & Brothers.

Some are swaddled in silk and down,
And heralded by a star;
They swathed my limbs in a sackcloth gown
On a night that was black as tar.

For some, godfather and goddame
The opulent fairies be;
Dame Poverty gave me my name,
And Pain godfathered me.

For I was born on Saturday——
"Bad time for planting a seed,"
Was all my father had to say,
And, "One mouth more to feed."

Death cut the strings that gave me life,
And handed me to Sorrow,
The only kind of middle wife
My folks could beg or borrow.

FRUIT OF THE FLOWER[60]
by Countee Cullen

My father is a quiet man
With sober, steady ways;
For simile, a folded fan;
His nights are like his days.

My mother's life is puritan,
No hint of cavalier,
A pool so calm you're sure it can
Have little depth to fear.

And yet my father's eyes can boast
How full his life has been;
There haunts them yet the languid ghost
Of some still sacred sin.

[60]From *Color*, by Countee Cullen, copyright, 1925, by Harper & Brothers.

And though my mother chants of God,
And of the mystic river,
I've seen a bit of checkered sod
Set all her flesh aquiver.

Why should he deem it pure mischance
A son of his is fain
To do a naked tribal dance
Each time he hears the rain?

Why should she think it devil's art
That all my songs should be
Of love and lovers, broken heart,
And wild sweet agony?

Who plants a seed begets a bud,
Extract of that same root;
Why marvel at the hectic blood
That flushes this wild fruit?

YOUTH SINGS A SONG OF ROSEBUDS[61]
by Countee Cullen

Since men grow diffident at last,
And care no whit at all,
If spring be come, or the fall be past,
Or how the cool rains fall,

I come to no flower but I pluck,
I raise no cup but I sip,
For a mouth is the best of sweets to suck;
The oldest wine's on the lip.

If I grow old in a year or two,
And come to the querulous song
Of "Alack and aday" and "This was true,
And that, when I was young,"

[61]From *Copper Sun*, by Countee Cullen, copyright, 1927, by Harper & Brothers.

I must have sweets to remember by,
Some blossom saved from the mire,
Some death-rebellious ember I
Can fan into a fire.

THE LOSS OF LOVE[62]
by Countee Cullen

All through an empty place I go,
And find her not in any room;
The candles and the lamps I light
Go down before a wind of gloom.

Thick-spraddled lies the dust about,
A fit, sad place to write her name
Or draw her face the way she looked
That legendary night she came.

The old house crumbles bit by bit;
Each day I hear the ominous thud
That says another rent is there
For winds to pierce and storms to flood.

My orchards groan and sag with fruit;
Where, Indian-wise, the bees go round;
I let it rot upon the bough;
I eat what falls upon the ground.

The heavy cows go laboring
In agony with clotted teats;
My hands are slack; my blood is cold;
I marvel that my heart still beats.

I have no will to weep or sing,
No least desire to pray or curse;
The loss of love is a terrible thing;
They lie who say that death is worse.

[62]By permission of Mrs. Ida M. Cullen.

YET DO I MARVEL[63]
by Countee Cullen

I doubt not God is good, well-meaning, kind,
And did He stoop to quibble could tell why
The little buried mole continues blind,
Why flesh that mirrors Him must some day die,
Make plain the reason tortured Tantalus
Is baited by the fickle fruit, declare
If merely brute caprice dooms Sisyphus
To struggle up a never-ending stair.
Inscrutable His ways are, and immune
To catechism by a mind too strewn
With petty cares to slightly understand
What awful brain compels His awful hand.
Yet do I marvel at this curious thing:
To make a poet black, and bid him sing!

FROM THE DARK TOWER[64]
by Countee Cullen

We shall not always plant while others reap
The golden increment of bursting fruit,
Not always countenance, abject and mute,
That lesser men should hold their brothers cheap;
Not everlastingly while others sleep
Shall we beguile their limbs with mellow flute,
Not always bend to some more subtle brute;
We were not made eternally to weep.

The night whose sable breast relieves the stark,
White stars is no less lovely being dark,

And there are buds that cannot bloom at all
In light, but crumple, piteous, and fall;
So in the dark we hide the heart that bleeds,
And wait, and tend our agonizing seeds.

THE RESURRECTION
by Jonathan Henderson Brooks

His friends went off and left Him dead
In Joseph's subterranean bed,
Embalmed with myrrh and sweet aloes,
And wrapped in snow-white burial clothes.

Then shrewd men came and set a seal
Upon His grave, lest thieves should steal
His lifeless form away, and claim
For Him an undeserving fame.

"There is no use," the soldiers said,
"Of standing sentries by the dead."
Wherefore, they drew their cloaks around
Themselves, and fell upon the ground,
And slept like dead men, all night through,
In the pale moonlight and chilling dew.

A muffled whiff of sudden breath
Ruffled the passive air of death.

He woke, and raised Himself in bed;
      Recalled how He was crucified;
Touched both hands' fingers to His head,
      And lightly felt His fresh-healed side.

Then with a deep, triumphant sigh,
He coolly put His grave-clothes by—
Folded the sweet, white winding sheet,
      The toweling, the linen bands,
      The napkin, all with careful hands—
And left the borrowed chamber neat.

His steps were like the breaking day:
    So soft across the watch He stole,
    He did not wake a single soul,
Nor spill one dewdrop by the way.

Now Calvary was loveliness:
    Lilies that flowered thereupon
Pulled off the white moon's pallid dress,
    And put the morning's vesture on.

"Why seek the living among the dead?
He is not here," the angel said.

The early winds took up the words,
And bore them to the lilting birds,
The leafing trees, and everything
That breathed the living breath of spring.

MY ANGEL
by Jonathan Henderson Brooks

That night my angel stooped and strained
To lift me from the mud.
He could not lift my heaviness.
My angel sweated blood.
He said: You are the heaviest grief
In heaven since the flood.

All night my angel stooped and strained,
Loath to abandon me:
The heaviest load since Lucifer
Shook heaven's regency.
All night he interceded for
My black necessity.

He rose. And two wings hid his feet.
And two wings veiled his face,

And two wings took him, weary wings,
To angels' resting place.
He flew away. He left with me
Despair and my disgrace.

AND ONE SHALL LIVE IN TWO
by Jonathan Henderson Brooks

Though he hung dumb upon her wall
And was so very still and small—
A miniature, a counterpart,
Yet did she press him to her heart
On countless, little loving trips,
And six times pressed him to her lips!
As surely as she kissed him six,
As sure as sand and water mix,
Sure as canaries sweetly sing,
And lilies come when comes the spring,
The two have hopes for days of bliss
When four warm lips shall meet in kiss;
Four eyes shall blend to see as one,
Four hands shall do what two have done,
Two sorrow-drops will be one tear—
And one shall live in two each year.

MUSE IN LATE NOVEMBER
by Jonathan Henderson Brooks

I greet you, son, with joy and winter rue:
For you the fatted calf, the while I bind
Sackcloth against my heart for siring you
At sundown and the twilight. Child, you find
A sire sore tired of striving with the winds;
Climbing Mount Nebo with laborious breath
To view the land of promise through blurred lens,
Knowing he can not enter, feeling death.

And, as old Israel called his dozen sons
And placed his withered hands upon each head
Ere he was silent with the skeletons
In Mamre of the cold, cave-chambered dead,
So would I bless you with a dreamer's will:
The dream that baffles me, may you fulfill.

SHE SAID . . .
by Jonathan Henderson Brooks

*Remembering Corporal Arthur Long, Negro,
the first soldier from Alcorn County, Mississippi,
reported killed in action in the invasion of Normandy.*

She said, "Not only music; brave men marching
Under the stripes and stars and sun's shining:
War is sudden news. *Your son was killed
The tenth of June in France. Letter follows.*

"Oh, he was bold to hasten peace," she said.
"And he was brave. And he desired tomorrow.
He was too young to be compelled from sunlight,
And moonlight; from the light of stars forever."

She would ask questions, morbid on her mind:
*The fatal bullet found him; did he scream?
Lie on the beach and call unhurrying Death?
Lord, was he waiting long? How long he fought
In France, four days or one? Who saw him fall?
Cared that he fell in sunshine, lay in rain,
Or perished in the night? And what star cared
Above his battleground in Normandy?*

"Now I know why Mary of Galilee,
One morning, rose and went into the Garden.
And I know why she tarried and was sad.
Mary, it is the same with me," she said.

POET
by Donald Jeffrey Hayes

No rock along the road but knows
The inquisition of his toes;
No journey's end but what can say:
He paused and rested here a day!
No joy is there that you may meet
But what will say: His kiss was sweet!
No sorrow but will sob to you:
He knew me intimately too. . . . !

PRESCIENCE
by Donald Jeffrey Hayes

I grieve to think of you alone
That first night watch when I am gone:

How darkness will assault your breath
And mind with frightening thoughts of death;

How inescapable the stress
Of that strange new emptiness;

How dawn such as you've never seen
Will streak its gray and yellow-green;

How shadows in a drifting pall
Will shift across this friendly wall!

I grieve that I shall not be there
To talk with you in your despair—

To reassure you in a glance
Mastery of the circumstance,

Speaking a language coded to
The key that I have given you;

Whispering low some silly word
That but our rooms and we have heard—

Nomenclature which should confound
The horror of the underground!

I'd sit a little while and speak
With my lips moving on your cheek

To help you face the awful dread
Of watching by your newly dead . . . !

Oh, that somehow I might contrive
My first night dead to be alive . . . !

HAVEN
by Donald Jeffrey Hayes

I'll build a house of arrogance
A most peculiar inn
With only room for vanquished folk
With proud and tilted chin! . . .

APPOGGIATURA
by Donald Jeffrey Hayes

It was water I was trying to think of all the time
Seeing the way you moved about the house. . . .
It was water, still and grey—or dusty blue
Where late at night the wind and a half-grown moon
Could make a crazy quilt of silver ripples

And it little mattered what you were about;
Whether painting in your rainbow-soiled smock
Or sitting by the window with the sunlight in your hair
That boiled like a golden cloud about your head
Or whether you sat in the shadows
Absorbed in the serious business
Of making strange white patterns with your fingers—
Whether it was any of these things
The emotion was always the same with me
And all the time it was water I was trying to recall,
Water, silent, breathless, restless,
Slowly rising, slowly falling, imperceptibly. . . .
It was the memory of water and the scent of air
Blown from the sea
That bothered me!

When you laughed, and that was so rare a festival,
I wanted to think of gulls dipping—
Grey wings, white-faced, into a rising wind
Dipping. . . .
Do you remember the day
You held a pale white flower to the sun
That I might see how the yellow rays
Played through the petals?
As I remember now
The flower was beautiful—
And the sunrays playing through—
And your slim fingers
And your tilting chin
But then:
There was only the indistinguishable sound of water silence;
The inaudible swish of one wave breaking. . . .

And now that you have moved on into the past;
You and your slim fingers
And your boiling hair,
Now that you have moved on into the past,
And I have time to stroll back through the corridors of memory,

It is like meeting an old friend at dawn
To find carved here deep in my mellowing mind
These words:
        "Sea-Woman—slim-fingered-water-thing . . ."

BENEDICTION
by Donald Jeffrey Hayes

Not with my hands
But with my heart I bless you:
May peace forever dwell
Within your breast!

May Truth's white light
Move with you and possess you—
And may your thoughts and words
Wear her bright crest!

May Time move down
Its endless path of beauty
Conscious of you
And better for your being!

Spring after Spring
Array itself in splendor
Seeking the favor
Of your sentient seeing!

May hills lean toward you
Hills and windswept mountains
And trees be happy
That have seen you pass—

Your eyes dark kinsmen
To the stars above you—
Your feet remembered
By the blades of grass. . . . !

FOUR GLIMPSES OF NIGHT
by Frank Marshall Davis

I

Eagerly
Like a woman hurrying to her lover
Night comes to the room of the world
And lies, yielding and content
Against the cool round face
Of the moon.

II

Night is a curious child, wandering
Between earth and sky, creeping
In windows and doors, daubing
The entire neighborhood
With purple paint.
Day
Is an apologetic mother
Cloth in hand
Following after.

III

Peddling
From door to door
Night sells
Black bags of peppermint stars
Heaping cones of vanilla moon
Until
His wares are gone
Then shuffles homeward
Jingling the gray coins
Of daybreak.

IV

> Night's brittle song, silver-thin
> Shatters into a billion fragments
> Of quiet shadows
> At the blaring jazz
> Of a morning sun.

I SING NO NEW SONGS
by Frank Marshall Davis

Once I cried for new songs to sing . . . a black rose . . . a brown sky
. . . the moon for my buttonhole . . . pink dreams for the table

Later I learned life is a servant girl . . . dusting the same pieces yesterday, today, tomorrow . . . a never ending one two three one
two three one two three

The dreams of Milton were the dreams of Lindsay . . . drinking corn
liquor, wearing a derby, dancing a foxtrot . . . a saxophone for a
harp

Ideas rise with new mornings but never die . . . only names, places,
people change . . . you are born, love, fight, tire and stop being
. . . Caesar died with a knife in his guts . . . Jim Colosimo from
revolver bullets

So I shall take aged things . . . bearded dreams . . . a silver dollar
moon worn thin from the spending . . . model a new dress for this
one . . . get that one a new hat . . . teach the other to forget the
minuet . . . then I shall send them into the street

And if passersby stop and say "Who is that? I never saw this pretty girl
before" or if they say . . . "Is that old woman still alive? I thought
she died years ago" . . . if they speak these words, I shall neither
smile nor swear . . . those who walked before me, those who
come after me, may make better clothes, teach a more graceful
step . . . but the dreams of Homer neither grow nor wilt. . . .

ROBERT WHITMORE
by Frank Marshall Davis

Having attained success in business
possessing three cars
one wife and two mistresses
a home and furniture
talked of by the town
and thrice ruler of the local Elks
Robert Whitmore
died of apoplexy
when a stranger from Georgia
mistook him
for a former Macon waiter.

FLOWERS OF DARKNESS
by Frank Marshall Davis

Slowly the night blooms, unfurling
Flowers of darkness, covering
The trellised sky, becoming
A bouquet of blackness
Unending
Touched with sprigs
Of pale and budding stars

Soft the night smell
Among April trees
Soft and richly rare
Yet commonplace
Perfume on a cosmic scale

I turn to you Mandy Lou
I see the flowering night
Cameo condensed
Into the lone black rose
Of your face

The young woman-smell
Of your poppy body
Rises to my brain as opium
Yet silently motionless
I sit with twitching fingers
Yea, even reverently
Sit I
With you and the blossoming night
For what flower, plucked,
Lingers long?

NORTHBOUN'
by Ariel Williams Holloway

O' de wurl' ain't flat,
An' de wurl' ain't roun',
H'it's one long strip
Hangin' up an' down—
Jes' Souf an' Norf;
Jes' Norf an' Souf.

Talkin' 'bout sailin' 'round de wurl'—
Huh! I'd be so dizzy my head 'ud twurl.
If dis heah earf wuz jes' a ball
You no the people all 'ud fall.

O' de wurl' ain't flat,
An' de wurl' ain't roun',
H'it's one long strip
Hangin' up an' down—
Jes' Souf an' Norf;
Jes' Norf an' Souf.

Talkin' 'bout the City whut Saint John saw—
Chile you oughta go to Saginaw;
A nigger's chance is "finest kind,"
An' pretty gals ain't hard to find.

Huh! de wurl' ain't flat,
An' de wurl' ain't roun',
Jes' one long strip
Hangin' up an' down.
Since Norf is up,
An' Souf is down,
An' Hebben is up,
I'm upward boun'.

CONCEPTION
by Waring Cuney

Jesus' mother never had no man.
God came to her one day an' said,
"Mary, chile, kiss ma han'."

NO IMAGES
by Waring Cuney

She does not know
Her beauty,
She thinks her brown body
Has no glory.

If she could dance
Naked,
Under palm trees
And see her image in the river
She would know.

But there are no palm trees
On the street,
And dish water gives back no images.

FINIS
by Waring Cuney

Now that our love has drifted
To a quiet close,
Leaving the empty ache
That always follows when beauty goes;
Now that you and I,
Who stood tip-toe on earth
To touch our fingers to the sky,
Have turned away
To allow our little love to die—
Go, dear, seek again the magic touch.
But if you are wise,
As I shall be wise,
You will not again
Love over much.

BURIAL OF THE YOUNG LOVE
by Waring Cuney

Weep not,
You who love her.

Place your flowers
Above her
And go your way
Only I shall stay.

After you have gone
With grief in your hearts,
I will remove the flowers
You laid above her.
Yes, I who love her.

Do not weep,
Friends and lovers.

(Oh, the scent of flowers in the air!
Oh, the beauty of her body there!)

Gently now lay your flowers down.
When the last mourner has gone
And I have torn
Each flower;
When the last mourner has gone
And I have tossed
Broken stems and flower heads
To the winds . . . ah! . . .
I will gather withered leaves . . .
I will scatter withered leaves there.

Friends and lovers,
Do not weep.

Gently lay your flowers down . . .
Gently, now, lay your flowers down.

THE DEATH BED
by Waring Cuney

All the time they were praying
He watched the shadow of a tree
Flicker on the wall.

There is no need of prayer
He said,
No need at all.

The kin-folk thought it strange
That he should ask them from a dying bed.
But they left all in a row

And it seemed to ease him
To see them go.

There were some who kept on praying
In a room across the hall,
And some who listened to the breeze
That made the shadows waver
On the wall.

He tried his nerve
On a song he knew
And made an empty note
That might have come,
From a bird's harsh throat.

And all the time it worried him
That they were in there praying,
And all the time he wondered
What it was they could be saying.

GRAVE
by Waring Cuney

When I am in my grave
And none are there
Save those who like myself
Must sleep,
I shall wake at times
To weep.

I shall wake at times
To weep,
For I need have no fears
There
That someone see
My tears

I need have no fears.

LAME MAN AND THE BLIND MAN
by Waring Cuney

Lame man said to the blind man,
"Hope you're doing well."
Blind man said to the lame man,
"Can't you see me catching hell?"

Blind man said to the lame man,
"How's things with you?"
Lame man leading the blind man,
"I'm catching hell, too."

Blind man playing his old guitar.
"Somebody gimme a dime—
Tired o' singing the blues
For nothing all the time!"

Lame man said to the blind man,
"Can't I sing some bass?"
Blind man said to the lame man,
"Open up your face!"

Lame man and the blind man
Sang a too-sad song:
"Tain't right to be so far down!
It's wrong! Sure is wrong!"

Blind man said to the lame man,
"Do I feel rain or snow?"
Lame man said to the blind man,
"Rain! Let's go!"

FORGOTTEN DREAMS
by Edward Silvera

The soft gray hands of sleep
Toiled all night long
To spin a beautiful garment
Of dreams;
At dawn
The little task was done.
Awakening,
The garb so deftly spun
Was only a heap
Of ravelled thread—
A vague remembrance
In my head.

ON THE DEATH OF A CHILD
by Edward Silvera

You came like the dawn
With no voice
To proclaim your calm birth
Save the song of the lark;
And when shadows foretold
That the quick day was done,
Your little white shroud
Had already been spun,
So you stole away in the dark.

SUMMER MATURES
by Helene Johnson

Summer matures. Brilliant Scorpion
Appears. The Pelican's thick pouch
Hangs heavily with perch and slugs.

The brilliant-bellied newt flashes
Its crimson crest in the white water.
In the lush meadow, by the river,
The yellow-freckled toad laughs
With a toothless gurgle at the white-necked stork
Standing asleep on one red reedy leg.
And here Pan dreams of slim stalks clean for piping,
And of a nightingale gone mad with freedom.
Come. I shall weave a bed of reeds
And willow limbs and pale nightflowers.
I shall strip the roses of their petals,
And the white down from the swan's neck.
Come. Night is here. The air is drunk
With wild grape and sweet clover.
And by the sacred fount of Aganippe
Euterpe sings of love. Ah, the woodland creatures,
The doves in pairs, the wild sow and her shoats,
The stag searching the forest for a mate,
Know more of love than you, my callous Phaon.
The young moon is a curved white scimitar
Pierced thru the swooning night.
Sweet Phaon. With Sappho sleep like the stars at dawn.
This night was born for love, my Phaon.
Come

FULFILLMENT
by Helene Johnson

To climb a hill that hungers for the sky,
    To dig my hands wrist-deep in pregnant earth,
To watch a young bird, veering, learn to fly,
    To give a still, stark poem shining birth.

To hear the rain drool, dimpling, down the drain
    And splash with a wet giggle in the street,
To ramble in the twilight after supper,
    And to count the pretty faces that you meet.

To ride to town on trolleys, crowded, teeming
　　With joy and hurry and laughter and push and sweat—
Squeezed next a patent-leathered Negro dreaming
　　Of a wrinkled river and a minnow net.

To buy a paper from a breathless boy,
　　And read of kings and queens in foreign lands,
Hyperbole of romance and adventure,
　　All for a penny the color of my hand.

To lean against a strong tree's bosom, sentient
　　And hushed before the silent prayer it breathes
To melt the still snow with my seething body
　　And kiss the warm earth tremulous underneath.

Ah, life, to let your stabbing beauty pierce me
　　And wound me like we did the studded Christ,
To grapple with you, loving you too fiercely,
　　And to die bleeding—consummate with Life.

MAGALU
by Helene Johnson

Summer comes.
The ziczac hovers
'Round the greedy-mouthed crocodile.
A vulture bears away a foolish jackal.
The flamingo is a dash of pink
Against dark green mangroves,
Her slender legs rivalling her slim neck.
The laughing lake gurgles delicious music in its throat
And lulls to sleep the lazy lizard,
A nebulous being on a sun-scorched rock.
In such a place,
In this pulsing, riotous gasp of color,
I met Magalu, dark as a tree at night,
Eager-lipped, listening to a man with a white collar
And a small black book with a cross on it.

Oh Magalu, come! Take my hand and I will read you poetry,
Chromatic words,
Seraphic symphonies,
Fill up your throat with laughter and your heart with song.
Do not let him lure you from your laughing waters,
Lulling lakes, lissome winds.
Would you sell the colors of your sunset and the fragrance
Of your flowers, and the passionate wonder of your forest
For a creed that will not let you dance?

REMEMBER NOT
by Helene Johnson

Remember not the promises we made
In this same garden many moons ago.
You must forget them. I would have it so.
Old vows are like old flowers as they fade
And vaguely vanish in a feeble death.
There is no reason why your hands should clutch
At pretty yesterdays. There is not much
Of beauty in me now. And though my breath
Is quick, my body sentient, my heart
Attuned to romance as before, you must
Not, through mistaken chivalry, pretend
To love me still. There is no mortal art
Can overcome Time's deep, corroding rust.
Let Love's beginning expiate Love's end.

INVOCATION
by Helene Johnson

Let me be buried in the rain
In a deep, dripping wood,
Under the warm wet breast of Earth
Where once a gnarled tree stood.

And paint a picture on my tomb
With dirt and a piece of bough
Of a girl and a boy beneath a round, ripe moon
Eating of love with an eager spoon
And vowing an eager vow.
And do not keep my plot mowed smooth
And clean as a spinster's bed,
But let the weed, the flower, the tree,
Riotous, rampant, wild and free,
Grow high above my head.

THE ROAD
by Helene Johnson

Ah, little road all whirry in the breeze,
A leaping clay hill lost among the trees,
The bleeding note of rapture-streaming thrush
And stretched out in a single singing line of dusky song.
Ah, little road, brown as my race is brown,
Your trodden beauty like our trodden pride,
Dust of the dust, they must not bruise you down.
Rise to one brimming golden, spilling cry!

I HAVE SEEN BLACK HANDS[66]
by Richard Wright

I am black and I have seen black hands, millions and millions of them—
Out of millions of bundles of wool and flannel tiny black fingers have
    reached restlessly and hungrily for life.
Reached out for the black nipples at the black breasts of black mothers,
And they've held red, green, blue, yellow, orange, white, and purple
    toys in the childish grips of possession,
And chocolate drops, peppermint sticks, lollypops, wineballs, ice cream
    cones, and sugared cookies in fingers sticky and gummy,
And they've held balls and bats and gloves and marbles and jack-knives
    and sling-shots and spinning tops in the thrill of sport and play.

[66]Reprinted by permission of Paul R. Reynolds & Son.

And pennies and nickels and dimes and quarters and sometimes on
    New Year's, Easter, Lincoln's Birthday, May Day, a brand new
    green dollar bill,
They've held pens and rulers and maps and tablets and books in palms
    spotted and smeared with ink,
And they've held dice and cards and half-pint flasks and cue sticks and
    cigars and cigarettes in the pride of new maturity . . .

II

I am black and I have seen black hands, millions and millions of them—
They were tired and awkward and calloused and grimy and covered
    with hangnails,
And they were caught in the fast-moving belts of machines and snagged
    and smashed and crushed,
And they jerked up and down at the throbbing machines massing
    taller and taller the heaps of gold in the banks of bosses,
And they piled higher and higher the steel, iron, the lumber, wheat,
    rye, the oats, corn, the cotton, the wool, the oil, the coal, the meat,
    the fruit, the glass, and the stone until there was too much to be
    used,
And they grabbed guns and slung them on their shoulders and marched
    and groped in trenches and fought and killed and conquered
    nations who were customers for the goods black hands had made.
And again black hands stacked goods higher and higher until there was
    too much to be used,
And then the black hands held trembling at the factory gates the
    dreaded lay-off slip,
And the black hands hung idle and swung empty and grew soft and
    got weak and bony from unemployment and starvation,
And they grew nervous and sweaty, and opened and shut in anguish
    and doubt and hesitation and irresolution . . .

III

I am black and I have seen black hands, millions and millions of them—
Reaching hesitantly out of days of slow death for the goods they had
    made, but the bosses warned that the goods were private and did
    not belong to them,

And the black hands struck desperately out in defence of life and there was blood, but the enraged bosses decreed that this too was wrong,

And the black hands felt the cold steel bars of the prison they had made, in despair tested their strength and found that they could neither bend nor break them,

And the black hands fought and scratched and held back but a thousand white hands took them and tied them,

And the black hands lifted palms in mute and futile supplication to the sodden faces of mobs wild in the revelries of sadism,

And the black hands strained and clawed and struggled in vain at the noose that tightened about the black throat,

And the black hands waved and beat fearfully at the tall flames that cooked and charred the black flesh . . .

IV

I am black and I have seen black hands
Raised in fists of revolt, side by side with the white fists of white workers,
And some day—and it is only this which sustains me—
Some day there shall be millions and millions of them,
On some red day in a burst of fists on a new horizon!

BETWEEN THE WORLD AND ME[66]
by Richard Wright

And one morning while in the woods I stumbled suddenly upon the thing,
Stumbled upon it in a grassy clearing guarded by scaly oaks and elms.
And the sooty details of the scene rose, thrusting themselves between the world and me. . . .

There was a design of white bones slumbering forgottenly upon a cushion of ashes.
There was a charred stump of a sapling pointing a blunt finger accusingly at the sky.

There were torn tree limbs, tiny veins of burnt leaves, and a scorched
    coil of greasy hemp;

A vacant shoe, an empty tie, a ripped shirt, a lonely hat, and a pair of
    trousers stiff with black blood.

And upon the trampled grass were buttons, dead matches, butt-ends
    of cigars and cigarettes, peanut shells, a drained gin-flask, and a
    whore's lipstick;

Scattered traces of tar, restless arrays of feathers, and the lingering
    smell of gasoline.

And through the morning air the sun poured yellow surprise into the
    eye sockets of a stony skull. . . .

And while I stood my mind was frozen with a cold pity for the life that
    was gone.

The ground gripped my feet and my heart was circled by icy walls
    of fear—

The sun died in the sky; a night wind muttered in the grass and fum-
    bled the leaves in the trees; the woods poured forth the hungry
    yelping of hounds; the darkness screamed with thirsty voices; and
    the witnesses rose and lived:

The dry bones stirred, rattled, lifted, melting themselves into my bones.

The grey ashes formed flesh firm and black, entering into my flesh.

The gin-flask passed from mouth to mouth; cigars and cigarettes
    glowed, the whore smeared the lipstick red upon her lips,

And a thousand faces swirled around me, clamoring that my life be
    burned. . . .

And then they had me, stripped me, battering my teeth into my throat
    till I swallowed my own blood.

My voice was drowned in the roar of their voices, and my black wet
    body slipped and rolled in their hands as they bound me to the
    sapling.

And my skin clung to the bubbling hot tar, falling from me in limp
    patches.

And the down and quills of the white feathers sank into my raw flesh,
    and I moaned in my agony.

Then my blood was cooled mercifully, cooled by a baptism of gasoline.

And in a blaze of red I leaped to the sky as pain rose like water, boiling
    my limbs.

Panting, begging I clutched childlike, clutched to the hot sides of
    death.
Now I am dry bones and my face a stony skull staring in yellow sur-
    prise at the sun. . . .

ADJURATION
by Charles Enoch Wheeler

> Let the knowing speak
> Let the oppressed tell of their sorrows,
> Of their salt and boundless grief.
> Since even the wise and the brave
> Must wonder, and the creeping mists
> Of doubt, creep along the trough
> Of pursuing woe . . .
> To curl among the crevices
> Of the most cannily armored brain.
> Let those who can endure their doubts
> Speak for the comfort of the weary
> Who weep to know.

TUMULT
by Charles Enoch Wheeler

> Until your laughter
> Dusk was good, and quiet.
> Until your laughter went up
> A rocket against the dark,
> That broke in spatter of flame.
> There will never be peace again.
> The heart remembers too well,
> A rocket sang upward and broke
> Against the dark, dripping fire
> . . . And the heart is in tumult.

WITHOUT NAME[67]
by Pauli Murray

Call it neither love nor spring madness,
Nor chance encounter nor quest ended.
Observe it casually as pussy-willows
Or push-cart pansies on a city street.
Let this seed growing in us
Granite-strong with persistent root
Be without name, or call it the first
Warm wind that caressed your cheek
And traded unshared kisses between us.
Call it the elemental earth
Bursting the clasp of too-long winter
And trembling for the plough-blade.

Let our blood chant it
And our flesh sing anthems to its arrival,
But our lips shall be silent, uncommitted.

HEART OF THE WOODS
by Wesley Curtright

Deep in the woods we'll go,
Hand in hand
Let the woods close about us,
Let the world outside be lost—
And let us find that Secret City
Lost so long ago—
In the Heart of the Woods.

[67]By permission of *The Saturday Review of Literature* and the author.

FREEDOM IN MAH SOUL
by David Wadsworth Cannon, Jr.

I

Fo'ty acres jes' fo' me!
And freedom in mah soul!
Great pines lickin' up de sky,
Hickories too and oaks so high,
And freedom in mah soul!

I can see it jes' as plain
As if it all was done now.
Fo'ty acres, mule an' plow—
Cabin big enuf fo' foah,
Garden 'fo' mah own front do',
And freedom in mah soul!

Den we gotta dig a well
Deep, so she'll be plenty cool,
Next we're goin' to raise a church,
And den, we'll build a school.
Lawd, if dis ain't jes' too grand,
Led us straight to de promised land,
Freedom in mah soul.

WESTERN TOWN
by David Wadsworth Cannon, Jr.

Dry Gap—a dingy general store.
A sign said, "Population Seven."
I found a universe for two:
One sun, one moon, and called it heaven.

A BOY'S NEED[68]
by Herbert Clark Johnson

A boy should have an open fireplace
To sit beside, a place to warm his feet
And have the peace of firelight on his face.

A boy should know the songs that wood worms sing
In burning logs in winter time, as well
As those of robins on the boughs in spring.

Aside from these, a hearth, like a meadow's stream,
Has a strange old way of making boys sit down
And dream of being men—and boys should dream.

CROSSING A CREEK
by Herbert Clark Johnson

He who has rolled his pants up to his knee
And walked a lowland creek from bank to bank
Has mixed his pulse with that of land and sea.
And though, in after days, he cross his streams
By bridge or log, he'll always feel its beat
Against his body, even in his dreams.

WILLOW BEND AND WEEP[69]
by Herbert Clark Johnson

Bend willow, willow bend down deep
And dip your branches into cold
Brown river water and then weep,
Weep, willow, for my land-sick soul.

[68]From *Poems from Flat Creek*, by Herbert Clark Johnson; originally published in *Yankee*, April 1941.

[69]From *Poems from Flat Creek*, by Herbert Clark Johnson; originally published in *Opportunity: A Journal of Negro Life*, November 1940.

Let river tears wash out land grief,
Let river water wash wounds made
By too much toil without relief
While you, willow, stood in the shade.

Willow, you owe this much to me,
I spared the ax for many years,
Your roots are in my land, now, tree
Bend down and weep. I have not tears.

ON CALVARY'S LONELY HILL
by Herbert Clark Johnson

Let's not be slow in knowing
That these cold drops of rain
Have not the power to cleanse
The sinner's crimson stain.

For each sweet stolen hour
There'll be a bitter one
On some high lonely hill
Before the cleansing's done.

THE LETTER[70]
by Beatrice M. Murphy

Please excuse this letter;
I know we said we're through
But there's something very precious
Of mine you took with you
And I must have it back.

[70]From *Love Is a Terrible Thing,* by Beatrice M. Murphy. Reprinted by permission.

I'm sure that you will find it
If you search among your pack
Way down in the innermost part.

Please wrap it carefully
Before you mail——
You see, it is my heart.

O DAEDALUS FLY AWAY HOME
by Robert E. Hayden

Drifting scent of the Georgia pines,
coonskin drum and jubilee banjo:
   pretty Malinda, dance with me.

Night is juba, night is conjo,
   pretty Malinda, dance with me. . . .

Night is an African juju man
weaving a wish and a weariness together
to make two wings.

   O fly away home, fly away

Do you remember Africa?

   O cleave the air, fly away home

I knew all the stars of Africa.

   Spread my wings and cleave the air

My gran, he flew back to Africa,
just spread his arms and flew away home. . . .

Drifting night in the windy pines,
night is a laughing, night is a longing:
   duskrose Malinda, come to me. . . .

Night is a mourning juju man
weaving a wish and a weariness together
to make two wings.

O fly away home, fly away

HOMAGE TO THE EMPRESS OF THE BLUES
by Robert E. Hayden

Because somewhere there was a man in a candystripe silk shirt
gracile and dangerous as a jaguar and because some woman moaned
for him in sixty watt gloom and mourned him Faithless Love
Twotiming Love Oh Love Oh Careless Aggravating Love,
     She came out on the stage in yards of pearls, emerging like
     a favorite scenic view, flashed her golden teeth, and sang.

Because somewhere the lathes began to show from underneath
torn hurdygurdy lithographs of dollfaced heaven,
because there were those who feared alaruming fists of snow upon
the door and those who feared the riotsquad of statistics,
     She came out on the stage in ostrich feathers, beaded satin,
     and shone that smile on us and didn't need the lights and sang.

LETTER FROM THE SOUTH
by Robert E. Hayden

This is no dreamworld, no nightmare country, no landscape
                    by Tanguy, Ernst, or Fini.
No. But as charged with the presence of a sleeping,
                    an easily-aroused terror,
as specialized, as selective, as trademarked in its neurosis,
                    as beaked, as hideous-feathered, as gothic.

If you have seen a battered jukebox light up in the primitive
                    colors that mean sex, joy, abandon,

if you have watched it wake into garishness and, lo, heard it
                          begin a waxen funeral music,
you will understand how the heart is harried here, is never
                          at home here, continues a stranger.

No terrain of delirium tremens. No. But wherever I turn, wherever,
                          there are divisions and amputations
and masks that leer and lour and grin and evade and dissemble
                          and try to be human faces.
Wherever I turn, wherever I turn, I see the deformed and the injured,
                          distortions of double-exposure,
pathetic processions hobbling, faltering on stumps of feet, on
                          burnt-matchstick legs, getting nowhere.

If you have read, and shuddered upon the reading, of England's
                          plague-year, when the infected,
made vicious by their fear, breathed upon the untainted,
                          hoping to avenge themselves, then surely
you will understand this pity, this revulsion, this angry compassion
                          the heart here experiences.

This is no feverchart territory, no shifting cinematic acre
                          of the mad, certainly,
but as tentacular, as non sequitur, as phosphorescent
                          with imageries of guilt;
as savage in its threats of death by claustrophobia, death by
                          castration, death by division. Death.

A BALLAD OF REMEMBRANCE
by Robert E. Hayden

> Quadroon mermaids, Afro angels, saints
> blackgilt balanced upon the switchblades of that air
> and sang. Tight streets unfolding to the eye
> like fans of corrosion and elegiac lace
> crackled with their singing: Shadow of time. Shadow of blood.

Shadow, echoed the zulu king, dangling
from a cluster of balloons. Blood,
whined the gunmetal priestess, floating
out from the courtyard where dead men sat at dice.

What will you have? she inquired, the sallow vendeuse
of prepared tarnishes and jokes of nacre and ormolu.
What but those gleamings, oldrose graces,
manners like scented gloves? Contrived ghosts
rapped to metronome clack of lavalieres.

Contrived illuminations riding a threat
of river, masked Negroes wearing chameleon
satins gaudy now as an undertaker's dream
of disaster, lighted the crazy flopping dance
of my heart, dance of love and hate among joys, rejections.

Accommodate, muttered the zulu king, throned
like a copper toad in a glaucous poison jewel.
Love, chimed the saints and the angels and the mermaids.
Hate, shrieked the gunmetal priestess
from her spiked bellcollar curved like a fleur-de-lys:

As well have a talon as a finger, a muzzle
as a mouth. As well have a hollow as a heart.
And she pinwheeled away in coruscations
of laughter, scattering those others before her.

But my heart continued its dance—now among
metaphorical doors, decors of illusion,
coffeecups floating poised hysterias;
now among mazurka dolls offering
deaths-heads of peppermint roses and real violets.

Then you arrived, meditative, ironic,
richly human. And your presence was shore where my heart
rested, released, from the hoodoo of that dance,
where I spoke with my human voice again and saw
the minotaurs of edict dwindle feckless, foolish.

And this is not only, therefore, a ballad
of remembrance for the down-South arcane city
with death in its jaws like gold teeth and archaic
cusswords; not only a token
for Bernice and Grady, for Mentor, for George and Oscar,
held in the schizoid fists of that city like flowers,
but also, Mark Van Doren,
a poem of remembrance, a gift, a souvenir for you.

A PHOTOGRAPH OF ISADORA DUNCAN
by Robert E. Hayden

How like the consummation and despair
of a medium's gifts she seems,
how like a revenant, receding yet
approaching, whose message is the holiness
of art, whose valedictory word is: Live.

Uncouth skull and crossbones rattle wrangle
but cannot clamor down
what weeps and sings in these translucid fixed
and fluent gestures: fusion of the soul's
the body's splendor into most godly fire.

EINE KLEINE NACHTMUSIK
by Robert E. Hayden

I

The siren cries that ran like mad and naked screaming women
with hair ablaze all over Europe, that like ventriloquists
made steel and stone speak out in the wild idiom of the damned,
oh now they have ceased but have created a groaning aftersilence.

And the mended ferris wheel turns to a tune again
in nevermore Alt Wien and poltergeists in imperials

and eau de cologne go up and up on the ferris wheel la la
in contagious dark where only the dead are relaxed and warm.

II

Anton the student hunches in a frigid room and reads and hears
the clawfoot sarabande, the knucklebone passacaglia coming close:
he has put on the requisite ancestral blue,
and his hair would glister festive as opals if the girandole

Had its way. A single prism is left to exclaim
at the dear iota of warmth and light a burntdown candle
salvages. Anton aching reads re-reads the dimming lines,
warms thumb and finger at the candleshine and turns the page.

III

Now as the ferris wheel revolves to extrovert neomusic
and soldiers pay with cigarettes and candybars
for rides for rides with the famished girls whose colloquies
with death have taught them how to play at being whores:

Now as skin-and-bones Europe hurts all over from the swastika's
hexentanz: oh think of Anton, Anton brittle, Anton crystalline;
think what the winter moon, the leper beauty of a Gothic tale, must see:
the ice-azure likeness of a young man reading, carved most craftily.

RUNAGATE RUNAGATE
by Robert E. Hayden

I

And it's fare you well, fare you well,
I'm on my way to Canaan, fare you well.

O freedom   mythic North

like some rock-crystal far-off Bible city

Runs falls rises stumbles on
from darkness into darkness and the darkness
thicketed with shapes of fear and the hounds behind
and the hunters behind and the night cold and the night long
and the river to cross and blackness ahead keep on
and doubt ahead   when shall I reach that somewhere
that tomorrow and if they find me if they overtake me
die fighting   keep on   never turn back

            Runagate nigger   Runagate

Many thousands rise and go,
many thousands done crossed over.

        Some go weeping and some rejoicing,
        some in coffins and some in carriages,
        some in silk, most in shackles.
           Rise and go or fare you well
        Blind and halt and tired and lonely,
        hunched and straight and proud and humble.

          Come along, brother, or fare you well

No more auction-block for me,
no more driver's lash for me.

        Rise and go

          Runagate   Runagate

        If you catch a Sambo disguised as a dandy,
        if you catch a Mandy mincing like a lady,
        notify subscriber and claim reward;
           but it's only fair to warn you:

        They will run underground when you try to catch them,
        plunge into quicksands, whirlpools, mazes,

they will turn to scorpions when you try to catch them,
salamanders, nettles; they will turn to fire.

And before I'll be a slave
I'll be buried in my grave.

North Star and bonanza gold
I'm bound for the freedom, freedom-bound
and oh Susanna don't you cry for me
                                        Runagate

II

And it is now she comes,
            summoned by their need:

                                    Harriet Tubman,
            whipscarred woman of earth, risen out of bondage,
            risen from their anguish and their power
            for to be a calling, for to be a shining.

                                    Mean to be free.
Emerges from unnatural shadow,
accomplice of that host whose crime
is the opening of a door, the lighting of a lamp,
the whispering of a name;

Is strategist of stars and ghostly silences.

Walks that panthergloom of trauma and decay
with pistol and disguises,
equal to all the gothic role requires:

            Hairbreadth escape by iceblock, hidden stair,
            hand-to-hand encounters with the hooded stalkers,
            despair and panic and betrayal.

                                    Mean to be free.

Wanted: the negress Harriet Tubman,
alias The General, alias Conductor, alias Moses:
stealer of slaves, in league
with the bigots Alcott and Emerson, Hussey and Haviland,
with the traitors Garrison, Still, Thoreau,
the troublemakers Loguen, Douglass, Coffin, old John Brown:

Reward

Godgazing Ezekiel, oh tell me do you see
mailed Jehovah coming to deliver me?

Dead or Alive

Come ride this train. Mean to be free.

FREDERICK DOUGLASS
by Robert E. Hayden

When it is finally ours, this freedom, this liberty,
        this beautiful
and terrible thing, needful to man as air,
usable as the earth; when it belongs at last to our children,
when it is truly instinct, brainmatter, diastole, systole,
reflex action; when it is finally won; when it is more
than the gaudy mumbo jumbo of politicians:
this man, this Douglass, this former slave, this Negro
beaten to his knees, exiled, visioning a world
where none is lonely, none hunted, alien,
this man, superb in love and logic, this man
shall be remembered——oh, not with statues' rhetoric,
not with legends and poems and wreaths of bronze alone,
but with the lives grown out of his life, the lives
fleshing his dream of the needful beautiful thing.

CREOLE GIRL
by Leslie M. Collins

When you dance,
Do you think of Spain,—
Purple skirts and clipping castanets,
Creole Girl?

When you laugh,
Do you think of France,—
Golden wine and mincing minuets,
Creole Girl?

When you sing,
Do you think of young America,—
Grey guns and battling bayonets,
Creole Girl?

When you cry,
Do you think of Africa,—
Blue nights and casual canzonets,
Creole Girl?

SIX O'CLOCK
by Owen Dodson

I have a river in my mind
Where I have drowned myself
So many times I feel sharp flesh
Of water underneath
My eyelids; and between my toes
The minnows smuggle time
And heard it where all shells begin
To grow what children on the shore
Will beg to listen to.

Horizon, water, land
For me at six o'clock:
A scarlet time of sky
That drinks your rim, horizon;
Turns your blue to blood,
Oh sea; absorbs your green,
Oh land: in scarlet time
I'll see the wave,
The quicksand arm ascend
To master and control
All teeth, death-growing hair,
(Goodbye) Each cell that loves.
(Goodbye my dear goodbye)

RAG DOLL AND SUMMER BIRDS
For Frank Harriott
by Owen Dodson

II

The snow cannot melt too soon for the birds left behind.
The crumbs fall in the crevices of snow
And the birds taste winter in their throats,
Wonder where the warm seasons went.
Their wings do not know the directions
The other flocks are gone, the signs are covered with winter.
There are no signals . . . Directionless . . . Lost . . . Alone . . .

Why are the flowers on the trees so white?
Why are these flowers so cold?

Smoke is in the chimneys where warmth is,
The sky is low and dark and level in the barns,
The intricate cobwebs are thinner than branches:
They are not singing places, not resting places,
Hay has not the smell of their nests,
Their songs turn to ice in the air.

The dark stiff little compact spots you see on these white fields are not
   shadows.

COUNTERPOINT
by Owen Dodson

> *Terror does not belong to open day*

> Picnics on the beach, all along
> The unmined water children play,
> A merry-go-round begins a jingle song,
> Horses churn up and down the peppermint poles,
> Children reach for the brassy ring,
> Children laugh while the platform rolls
> Faster and faster while the horses sing:

> merry-ro, merry-o,
> this is the way your lives should go:
> up and down and all around
> listening to this merry sound.

> *Terror does not belong to open day*

> merry-ro, merry-ha,
> snatch this ring and plant a star;
> grow a field of magic light,
> reap it on a winter night.

> *Terror does not belong to open day*

EPITAPH FOR A NEGRO WOMAN
by Owen Dodson

> How cool beneath this stone the soft moss lies,
> How smooth and long the silken threads have kept
> Without the taste of slender rain or stars,
> How tranquilly the outer coats have slept.

Alone with only wind, with only ice,
The moss is growing, clinging to the stone;
And seeing only what the darkness shows,
It thrives without the moon, it thrives alone.

THE DECISION
by Owen Dodson

Who are these among you
Homesick for home, longing for peace—
The summer going and the war going
And all the sharp promises of peace?

Watch from your foxholes
For fire on distant mountains,
Fire flags lit with peace
Waving on the mountains.

There are other journeys
You must make after your journey home,
Other journeys you must make alone
Into the countries of the heart
To sit with silence and decide alone

If your final home will be
Where brother knows brother,
Chews meat, breaks bread
Together with his brother;

Or where a man will trample again
His neighbor, shake no hands,
Scorn fellowship, light fires
Of dark bones and flesh to warm his hands.

Who are these among you
Longing for peace among all men,
Longing for each homesick heart
To make a pilgrimage among all men?

POEMS FOR MY BROTHER KENNETH
by Owen Dodson

VII

Sleep late with your dream.
The morning has a scar
To mark on the horizon
With death of the morning star.

The color of blood will appear
And wash the morning sky,
Aluminum birds flying with fear
Will scream to your waking,
Will send you to die;

Sleep late with your dream.
Pretend that the morning is far,
Deep in the horizon country,
Unconcerned with the morning star.

OCTOBER JOURNEY[71]
by Margaret Walker

Traveller take heed for journeys undertaken in the dark of the year.
Go in the bright blaze of Autumn's equinox.
Carry protection against ravages of a sun-robber, a vandal, and a thief.
Cross no bright expanse of water in the full of the moon.
Choose no dangerous summer nights;
no heady tempting hours of spring;
October journeys are safest, brightest, and best.

I want to tell you what hills are like in October
when colors gush down mountainsides
and little streams are freighted with a caravan of leaves.

[71]From *For My People*, by Margaret Walker. Reprinted by permission of Yale University Press.

I want to tell you how they blush and turn in fiery shame and joy,
how their love burns with flames consuming and terrible
until we wake one morning and woods are like a smoldering plain—
a glowing caldron full of jewelled fire:
the emerald earth a dragon's eye
the poplars drenched with yellow light
and dogwoods blazing bloody red.

Travelling southward earth changes from gray rock to green velvet.
Earth changes to red clay
with green grass growing brightly
with saffron skies of evening setting dully
with muddy rivers moving sluggishly.

In the early spring when the peach tree blooms
wearing a veil like a lavender haze
and the pear and plum in their bridal hair
gently snow their petals on earth's grassy bosom below
then the soughing breeze is soothing
and the world seems bathed in tenderness,
but in October
blossoms have long since fallen.
A few red apples hang on leafless boughs;
wind whips bushes briskly.
And where a blue stream sings cautiously
a barren land feeds hungrily.

An evil moon bleeds drops of death.
The earth burns brown.
Grass shrivels and dries to a yellowish mass.
Earth wears a dun-colored dress
like an old woman wooing the sun to be her lover,
be her sweetheart and her husband bound in one.
Farmers heap hay in stacks and bind corn in shocks
against the biting breath of frost.

The train wheels hum, "I am going home, I am going home,
I am moving toward the South."

Soon cypress swamps and muskrat marshes
and black fields touched with cotton will appear.
I dream again of my childhood land
of a neighbor's yard with a redbud tree
the smell of pine for turpentine
an Easter dress, a Christmas eve
and winding roads from the top of a hill.
A music sings within my flesh
I feel the pulse within my throat
my heart fills up with hungry fear
while hills and flatlands stark and staring
before my dark eyes sad and haunting
appear and disappear.

Then when I touch this land again
the promise of a sun-lit hour dies.
The greenness of an apple seems
to dry and rot before my eyes.
The sullen winter rains
are tears of grief I cannot shed.
The windless days are static lives.
The clock runs down
timeless and still.
The days and nights turn hours to years
and water in a gutter marks the circle of another world
hating, resentful, and afraid
stagnant, and green, and full of slimy things.

MOLLY MEANS[72]
by Margaret Walker

Old Molly Means was a hag and a witch;
Chile of the devil, the dark, and sitch.
Her heavy hair hung thick in ropes
And her blazing eyes was black as pitch.

[72]From *For My People*, by Margaret Walker. Reprinted by permission of Yale University Press.

Imp at three and wench at 'leben
She counted her husbands to the number seben.
    O Molly, Molly, Molly Means
    There goes the ghost of Molly Means.

Some say she was born with a veil on her face
So she could look through unnatchal space
Through the future and through the past
And charm a body or an evil place
And every man could well despise
The evil look in her coal black eyes.
    Old Molly, Molly, Molly Means
    Dark is the ghost of Molly Means.

And when the tale begun to spread
Of evil and of holy dread:
Her black-hand arts and her evil powers
How she cast her spells and called the dead,
The younguns was afraid at night
And the farmers feared their crops would blight.
    Old Molly, Molly, Molly Means
    Cold is the ghost of Molly Means.

Then one dark day she put a spell
On a young gal-bride just come to dwell
In the lane just down from Molly's shack
And when her husband come riding back
His wife was barking like a dog
And on all fours like a common hog.
    O Molly, Molly, Molly Means
    Where is the ghost of Molly Means?

The neighbors come and they went away
And said she'd die before break of day
But her husband held her in his arms
And swore he'd break the wicked charms;
He'd search all up and down the land
And turn the spell on Molly's hand.
    O Molly, Molly, Molly Means
    Sharp is the ghost of Molly Means.

So he rode all day and he rode all night
And at the dawn he come in sight
Of a man who said he could move the spell
And cause the awful thing to dwell
On Molly Means, to bark and bleed
Till she died at the hands of her evil deed.
　　Old Molly, Molly, Molly Means
　　This is the ghost of Molly Means.

Sometimes at night through the shadowy trees
She rides along on a winter breeze.
You can hear her holler and whine and cry.
Her voice is thin and her moan is high,
And her cackling laugh or her barking cold
Bring terror to the young and old.
　　O Molly, Molly, Molly Means
　　Lean is the ghost of Molly Means.

WE HAVE BEEN BELIEVERS[73]
by Margaret Walker

We have been believers believing in the black gods of an old land,
　　believing in the secrets of the seeress and the magic of the charmers
　　and the power of the devil's evil ones.

And in the white gods of a new land we have been believers believing
　　in the mercy of our masters and the beauty of our brothers, be-
　　lieving in the conjure of the humble and the faithful and the pure.

Neither the slavers' whip nor the lynchers' rope nor the bayonet could
　　kill our black belief. In our hunger we beheld the welcome table
　　and in our nakedness the glory of a long white robe. We have been
　　believers in the new Jerusalem.

[73]From For My People, by Margaret Walker. Reprinted by permission of Yale University Press.

We have been believers feeding greedy grinning gods, like a Moloch demanding our sons and our daughters, our strength and our wills and our spirits of pain. We have been believers, silent and stolid and stubborn and strong.

We have been believers yielding substance for the world. With our hands have we fed a people and out of our strength have they wrung the necessities of a nation. Our song has filled the twilight and our hope has heralded the dawn.

Now we stand ready for the touch of one fiery iron, for the cleansing breath of many molten truths, that the eyes of the blind may see and the ears of the deaf may hear and the tongues of the people be filled with living fire.

Where are our gods that they leave us asleep? Surely the priests and the preachers and the powers will hear. Surely now that our hands are empty and our hearts too full to pray they will understand. Surely the sires of the people will send us a sign.

We have been believers believing in our burdens and our demigods too long. Now the needy no longer weep and pray; the long-suffering arise, and our fists bleed against the bars with a strange insistency.

HARRIET TUBMAN[74]
by Margaret Walker

> Dark is the face of Harriet,
> Darker still her fate
> Deep in the dark of southern wilds
> Deep in the slavers' hate.
>
> Fiery the eye of Harriet,
> Fiery, dark, and wild;
> Bitter, bleak, and hopeless
> Is the bonded child.

[74]From *For My People,* by Margaret Walker. Reprinted by permission of Yale University Press.

Stand in the fields, Harriet,
Stand alone and still
Stand before the overseer
Mad enough to kill.

This is slavery, Harriet,
Bend beneath the lash;
This is Maryland, Harriet,
Bow to poor white trash.

You're a field hand, Harriet,
Working the corn;
You're a grubber with the hoe
And a slave child born.

You're just sixteen, Harriet,
And never had a beau;
Your mother's dead long time ago,
Your daddy you don't know.

This piece of iron's not hard enough
To kill you with a blow,
This piece of iron can't hurt you,
Just let you slaves all know.

I'm still the overseer,
Old marster'll believe my tale;
I know that he will keep me,
From going to the jail.

Get up, bleeding Harriet,
I didn't hit you hard;
Get up, bleeding Harriet,
And grease your head with lard.

Get up, sullen Harriet,
Get up and bind your head.
Remember this is Maryland
And I can beat you dead.

How far is the road to Canada?
How far do I have to go?
How far is the road from Maryland
And the hatred that I know?

I stabbed that overseer;
I took his rusty knife;
I killed that overseer;
I took his lowdown life.

For three long years I waited,
Three years I kept my hate,
Three years before I killed him,
Three years I had to wait.

Done shook the dust of Maryland
Clean off my weary feet;
I'm on my way to Canada
And Freedom's golden street.

I'm bound to git to Canada
Before another week;
I come through swamps and mountains,
I waded many a creek.

Now tell my brothers yonder
That Harriet is free;
Yes, tell my brothers yonder
No more auction block for me.

* * * *

Come down from the mountain, Harriet,
Come down to the valley at night,
Come down to your weeping people
And be their guiding light.

Sing Deep Dark River of Jordan,
Don't you want to cross over today?
Sing Deep Wide River of Jordan,
Don't you want to walk Freedom's way?

I stole down in the night time,
I come back in the day,
I stole back to my Maryland
To guide the slaves away.

I met old marster yonder
A-coming down the road,
And right past me in Maryland
My old marster strode.

I passed beside my marster
And covered up my head;
My marster didn't know me
I guess he heard I'm dead.

I wonder if he thought about
That overseer's dead;
I wonder if he figured out
He ought to know this head?

You better run, brave Harriet,
There's ransom on your head;
You better run, Miss Harriet,
They want you live or dead.

Been down in valleys yonder
And searching round the stills,
They got the posse after you,
A-riding through the hills.

They got the blood hounds smelling,
They got their guns cocked too;
You better run, bold Harriet,
The white man's after you.

They got ten thousand dollars
Put on your coal-black head;
They'll give ten thousand dollars;
They're mad because you fled.

I wager they'll be riding
A long, long time for you.
Yes, Lord, they'll look a long time
Till Judgment Day is due.

* * * *

I'm Harriet Tubman, people,
I'm Harriet the slave,
I'm Harriet, free woman,
And I'm free within my grave.

> *Come along, children, with Harriet*
> *Come along, children, come along*
> *Uncle Sam is rich enough*
> *To give you all a farm.*

I killed the overseer.
I fooled old marster's eyes,
I found my way to Canada
With hundreds more besides.

> *Come along to Harper's Ferry*
> *Come along to brave John Brown*
> *Come along with Harriet, children,*
> *Come along ten million strong.*

I met the mighty John Brown,
I know Fred Douglass too
Enlisted Abolitionists
Beneath the Union blue.

I heard the mighty trumpet
That sent the land to war;
I mourned for Mister Lincoln
And saw his funeral car.

> *Come along with Harriet, children,*
> *Come along to Canada.*
> *Come down to the river, children,*
> *And follow the northern star.*

I'm Harriet Tubman, people,
I'm Harriet, the slave,
I'm Harriet, free woman,
And I'm free beyond my grave.

Come along to freedom, children,
Come along ten million strong;
Come along with Harriet, children,
Come along ten million strong.

FOR MY PEOPLE[75]
by Margaret Walker

For my people everywhere singing their slave songs repeatedly: their dirges and their ditties and their blues and jubilees, praying their prayers nightly to an unknown god, bending their knees humbly to an unseen power;

For my people lending their strength to the years, to the gone years and the now years and the maybe years, washing ironing cooking scrubbing sewing mending hoeing plowing digging planting pruning patching dragging along never gaining never reaping never knowing and never understanding;

For my playmates in the clay and dust and sand of Alabama backyards playing baptizing and preaching and doctor and jail and soldier and school and mama and cooking and playhouse and concert and store and hair and Miss Choomby and company;

For the cramped bewildered years we went to school to learn to know the reasons why and the answers to and the people who and the places where and the days when, in memory of the bitter hours when we discovered we were black and poor and small and different and nobody cared and nobody wondered and nobody understood;

[75]From *For My People*, by Margaret Walker. Reprinted by permission of Yale University Press.

For the boys and girls who grew in spite of these things to be man and woman, to laugh and dance and sing and play and drink their wine and religion and success, to marry their playmates and bear children and then die of consumption and anemia and lynching;

For my people thronging 47th Street in Chicago and Lenox Avenue in New York and Rampart Street in New Orleans, lost disinherited dispossessed and happy people filling the cabarets and taverns and other people's pockets needing bread and shoes and milk and land and money and something—something all our own;

For my people walking blindly spreading joy, losing time being lazy, sleeping when hungry, shouting when burdened, drinking when hopeless, tied and shackled and tangled among ourselves by the unseen creatures who tower over us omnisciently and laugh;

For my people blundering and groping and floundering in the dark of churches and schools and clubs and societies, associations and councils and committees and conventions, distressed and disturbed and deceived and devoured by money-hungry glory-craving leeches, preyed on by facile force of state and fad and novelty, by false prophet and holy believer;

For my people standing staring trying to fashion a better way from confusion, from hypocrisy and misunderstanding, trying to fashion a world that will hold all the people, all the faces, all the adams and eves and their countless generations;

Let a new earth rise. Let another world be born. Let a bloody peace be written in the sky. Let a second generation full of courage issue forth; let a people loving freedom come to growth. Let a beauty full of healing and a strength of final clenching be the pulsing in our spirits and our blood. Let the martial songs be written, let the dirges disappear. Let a race of men now rise and take control.

FOR MARY McLEOD BETHUNE
by Margaret Walker

Great Amazon of God behold your bread
washed home again from many distant seas.
The cup of life you lift contains no less,
no bitterness to mock you. In its stead
this sparkling chalice many souls has fed,
and broken hearted people on their knees
lift up their eyes and suddenly they seize
on living faith, and they are comforted.

Believing in the people who are free,
who walk uplifted in an honest way,
you look at last upon another day
that you have fought with God and men to see.
Great Amazon of God behold your bread.
We walk with you and we are comforted.

KITCHENETTE BUILDING[76]
by Gwendolyn Brooks

We are things of dry hours and the involuntary plan,
Grayed in, and gray. "Dream" makes a giddy sound, not strong
Like "rent," "feeding a wife," "satisfying a man."

But could a dream send up through onion fumes
Its white and violet, fight with fried potatoes
And yesterday's garbage ripening in the hall,
Flutter, or sing an aria down these rooms

Even if we were willing to let it in,
Had time to warm it, keep it very clean,
Anticipate a message, let it begin?

[76]From A Street in Bronzeville, by Gwendolyn Brooks, copyright, 1945, by Gwendolyn Brooks Blakely. Reprinted by permission of Harper & Brothers.

We wonder. But not well! not for a minute!
Since Number Five is out of the bathroom now,
We think of lukewarm water, hope to get in it.

OF DE WITT WILLIAMS ON HIS WAY TO LINCOLN CEMETERY[77]
by Gwendolyn Brooks

He was born in Alabama.
He was bred in Illinois.
He was nothing but a
Plain black boy.

Swing low swing low sweet sweet chariot.
Nothing but a plain black boy.

Drive him past the Pool Hall.
Drive him past the Show.
Blind within his casket,
But maybe he will know.

Down through Forty-seventh Street:
Underneath the L,
And—Northwest Corner, Prairie,
That he loved so well.

Don't forget the Dance Halls—
Warwick and Savoy,
Where he picked his women, where
He drank his liquid joy.

Born in Alabama.
Bred in Illinois.
He was nothing but a
Plain black boy.

Swing low swing low sweet sweet chariot.
Nothing but a plain black boy.

THE OLD-MARRIEDS[78]
by Gwendolyn Brooks

But in the crowding darkness not a word did they say.
Though the pretty-coated birds had piped so lightly all the day.
And he had seen the lovers in the little side-streets.
And she had heard the morning stories clogged with sweets.
It was quite a time for loving. It was midnight. It was May.
But in the crowding darkness not a word did they say.

LOVE NOTE[79]
II: FLAGS
by Gwendolyn Brooks

Still, it is dear defiance now to carry
Fair flags of you above my indignation,
Top, with a pretty glory and a merry
Softness, the scattered pound of my cold passion.
I pull you down my foxhole. Do you mind?
You burn in bits of saucy color then.
I let you flutter out against the pained
Volleys. Against my power crumpled and wan.
You, and the yellow pert exuberance
Of dandelion days, unmocking sun;
The blowing of clear wind in your gay hair;
Love changeful in you (like a music, or
Like a sweet mournfulness, or like a dance,
Or like the tender struggle of a fan).

[78,79]From *A Street in Bronzeville*, by Gwendolyn Brooks, copyright, 1945, by Gwendolyn Brooks Blakely. Reprinted by permission of Harper & Brothers.

THE BIRTH IN A NARROW ROOM[80]
by Gwendolyn Brooks

Weeps out of Kansas country something new.
Blurred and stupendous. Wanted and unplanned.
    Winks. Twines, and weakly winks
Upon the milk-glass fruit bowl, iron pot,
The bashful china child tipping forever
Yellow apron and spilling pretty cherries.

Now, weeks and years will go before she thinks
"How pinchy is my room! how can I breathe!
I am not anything and I have got
Not anything, or anything to do!"——
But prances nevertheless with gods and fairies
Blithely about the pump and then beneath
The elms and grapevines, then in darling endeavor
By privy foyer, where the screenings stand
And where the bugs buzz by in private cars
Across old peach cans and old jelly jars.

MENTORS[81]
by Gwendolyn Brooks

For I am rightful fellow of their band.
My best allegiances are to the dead.
I swear to keep the dead upon my mind,
Disdain for all time to be overglad.
Among spring flowers, under summer trees,
By chilling autumn waters, in the frosts
Of supercilious winter—all my days
I'll have as mentors those reproving ghosts.

[80]Reprinted by special permission from the author.

[81]From *A Street in Bronzeville*, by Gwendolyn Brooks, copyright, 1945, by Gwendolyn Brooks Blakely. Reprinted by permission of Harper & Brothers.

And at that cry, at that remotest whisper,
I'll stop my casual business. Leave the banquet.
Or leave the ball—reluctant to unclasp her
Who may be fragrant as the flower she wears,
Make gallant bows and dim excuses, then quit
Light for the midnight that is mine and theirs.

PIANO AFTER WAR[82]
by Gwendolyn Brooks

On a snug evening I shall watch her fingers,
Cleverly ringed, declining to clever pink,
Beg glory from the willing keys. Old hungers
Will break their coffins, rise to eat and thank.
And music, warily, like the golden rose
That sometimes after sunset warms the west,
Will warm that room, persuasively suffuse
That room and me, rejuvenate a past.
But suddenly, across my climbing fever
Of proud delight—a multiplying cry.
A cry of bitter dead men who will never
Attend a gentle maker of musical joy.
Then my thawed eye will go again to ice.
And stone will shove the softness from my face.

HERE AND NOW[83]
by Catharine Cater

If here and now be but a timely span
Between today's unhappiness, tomorrow's
Joys, what if today's abundant sorrows
Never end, tomorrow never comes, what then?

[82]From *A Street in Bronzeville*, by Gwendolyn Brooks, copyright, 1945, by Gwendolyn Brooks Blakely. Reprinted by permission of Harper & Brothers.

[83]From *Phylon*, with special permission of the author.

If youth, impatient of the disrespect
Accorded it, yearns to be old,
Age chafes beneath the manifold
Losses of its prime and mourns neglect;

So let it be for here and now, my dear,
Not for the when of an eternity;
No gazer in the crystal ball can see
The future as we see the now and here.

TO AN AVENUE SPORT
by Helen Johnson Collins

Here lies the street of the three balls
the BUY, TRADE, SELL
your new suit that cost too much,
the loaded dice that overplayed their luck,
the cow-hide grip that should have left the town
with you that night when hell
played boogie-woogie at a card game.
Here lies . . . but what do you care now
for shining switchblades, roadsters,
and flashy women always tuning in
on some man's heart, picking his bankroll
to chicken bones and lashing him
with whips of harpy-laughter?

The stakes were high in your crazy race of life,
and you were in the lead . . . pompous, grand . . .
until a knife
pierced you out of jealousy
and you fell
scattering your winning hand!

BLUES FOR BESSIE[84]
by Myron O'Higgins

> *Bessie Smith, the greatest of the early blues singers,*
> *died violently after an auto accident*
> *while on a theatrical tour of the South in 1937.*
> *The newspapers reported that she bled to death*
> *when the only hospital in the vicinity*
> *refused her emergency medical attention*
> *because she was a Negro woman.*

Let de peoples know (unnh)
 what dey did in dat Southern Town
Let de peoples know
 what dey did in dat Southern Town
Well, dey lef' po' Bessie dyin'
 wid de blood (Lawd) a-streamin' down

Bessie lef' Chicago
 in a bran' new Cadillac;
 didn' take no suitcase
 but she wore her mournin' black (unnh)
Bessie, Bessie,
 she wore her mournin' black
She went ridin' down to Dixie (Lawd)
 an' dey shipped her body back

Lawd, wasn't it a turr'ble
 when dat rain come down
Yes, wasn't it a turr'ble
 when de rain come down
An' ol' Death caught po' Bessie
 down in 'at Jim Crow town

[84]From *Portfolio*, Paris, France.

Well, de thunder rolled
   an' de lightnin' broke de sky
Lawd, de thunder rolled
   an' de lightnin' broke de sky
An' you could hear po' Bessie moanin',
   "Gret Gawd, please doan lemme die!"

She holler, "Lawd, please hep me!",
   but He never heerd a word she say
Holler, "Please, *some*body hep me!",
   but dey never heerd a word she say
Frien', when yo' luck run out in Dixie,
   well, it doan do no good to pray

Well, dey give po' Bessie
   to de undertaker man;
   ol' Death an' Jim Crow (Lawd)
   done de job, hand in han'
Well, Bessie, Bessie,
   she won't sing de blues no mo'
Cause dey let her go down bloody (Lawd)
   trav'lin' from door to do'

Bessie lef' Chicago
   in a bran' new Cad'lac Eight
Yes, Bessie lef' Chicago
   in a gret big Cad'lac Eight
But dey shipped po' Bessie back (Lawd)
   on dat lonesome midnight freight

Lawd, let de peoples know
   what dey did in dat Southern Town
Yes, let de peoples know
   what dey did in dat Southern Town
Well, dey lef' po' Bessie dyin'
   wid de blood (Lawd) a-streamin' down

TWO LEAN CATS . . .[85]
by Myron O'Higgins

I remember Wednesday was the day
the rain came down in ragged jets
and made a grave along my street . . .

And Friday was the day that brought
impatient winds to swell the
blood-stained garments on my line

But that day in between
comes back with two lean cats
who run in checkered terror
through a poolroom door
and bolting from a scream
a keen knife marks with sudden red
the gaming green
. . . a purple billiard ball
explodes the color scheme.

YOUNG POET[86]
by Myron O'Higgins

Somebody,
Cut his hair
And send him out to play.

Someone,
While there is time,
Call him down from his high place.

[85],[86]From *The Lion and the Archer*. Counterpoise Series, No. 1. Special permission of the author.

Tell him,
Before terror marks his face,
He will belong to the hunted.

Say
He will be betrayed,
Or high on some fruited hill
Die naked with thieves.

Go to him
While fire is in his flesh:
Take him whole
And kiss his young mouth into wisdom
And healing.

SUNSET HORN[87]
by Myron O'Higgins

*"Enduring peace is the only monument civilization can raise
to the millions who have perished in its cause"*

I

Block the cannon; let no trumpets sound!
Our power is manifest in other glory;
Our flesh in this contested slope of ground.

In thin silences we lie, pale strangers to the corn-gold morning,
Repeating what the fathers told . . . the promised legacy of tall sons;
The hushed sibilants of peace; and the far tomorrow on the hills.

O we went quickly or a little longer
And for a space saw caste and categories, creeds and race
Evaporate into the flue of common circumstance.
We sought transcendent meaning for our struggle,

[87]From *Motive*. With special permission of the author.

And in that rocking hour, each minute, each narrow second
Fell upon us like a rain of knives.
We grappled here an instant, then singly, or in twos or tens, or by be-
    wildered hundreds,
Were pulverized . . . Reduced . . . Wiped out—
Made uniform and *equal!*
                              And let us tell you this:
Death is indiscriminate . . . and easier . . . than sorrow, fear, or
    fallen pride.
There is no road back. We rest in ultimates;
In calmness come abrupt by bomb, or bullet, or abbreviated dream;
With conflicts spent.
This stark convergent truth continues,
Linking us through slim unseen dimensions—we to you, we to you . . .

II

While you cry Victory! or Surrender!
Turn these figures in the head,
Clean impersonal round numbers,
Ordered inventory of the dead.

Regard these slender nines and ones;
These trailing threes and fives; these fours and sevens, bent and angular;
Delicately drawn, divided into ranks by commas,
Staggered down the page in regimented squads and columns:
These are our mute effigies, trim and shining,
Passing in review . . .
                              O, Drummer, obediently we come,
Down through the assassin's street,
The company of death in splendid array! . . .

But leave us to the terrible fields.
Yours is the pomp of brasses, the counterfeit peace, the dynasty of
    lies . . .
We are but dabs of flesh blown to the cliffs,
Or ragged stumps of legs that moved too slowly toward the brush.
And our song: we joined no swelling harmony of voices.

Those final incoherent sounds we made;
Those startled oaths that bubbled through the blood bogged in our
    throats;
That last falsetto cry of terror;
Were a jagged threnody, swallowed whole and drowned in cacophonic
    floods.
This was our sunset horn . . .

Let these be added with the spoils for quick division!
Set these down in sharp italics on the page
For scholars' documents!

III

Raise no vain monuments; bury us down!
Our power is manifest in other glory;
Our flesh in this contested slope of ground.
There is no more but these, a legacy, a grim prediction . . .
Let the scent and sounds of death go limp
And flounder in the valleys and the streets.
And for those crafty ones—those who speak our names in brief profes-
    sional remembrance
To garner votes and profits, or practice quick extortion—
Let other music find their ears.
And give them for a souvenir this clown's disguise
Of swastikas and Roman standards, of scythes and suns and dollar
    signs . . .
One day the rest of you will know the meaning of annihilation.
And the hills will rock with voltage;
And the forests burn like a flaming broom;
And the stars explode and drop like cinders on the land.
And these steel cities where no love is—
You shall see them fall and vanish in a thunder of erupting suns!

O you shall know; and in that day, traveler, O in that day
When the tongues confound, and breath is total in the horn,
Your judas eyes, seeking truth at last, will search for us
And borrow ransom from this bowel of violence!

JOURNEY TO A PARALLEL
Summer—1947
by Bruce McM. Wright

I remember distinctly the tired tumult of my urges
and the sun shining, and the dust, and the clouds,
and how I turned my rifle down;
I remember the cow stinking in the street
and a woman sweeping dung,
and Prague and Pilsen just forty kilometers:
I recall that songs were sung,
attention stood, allegiance re-asserted,
and I saw two colonels cry.
There was a first night of awkward peace
with pillows
trimmed in *böhmisch* lace, lettered *schlafe wohl,*
and hugged into humanity:
I trembled, and felt quite old.

How distant is any day,
How many hurts away?

And there were Prague and Pilsen,
and I,
having dug holes in history,
stretched out alive
on the Continent with Paris—
just some wars and worlds removed
from Miss Upjohn's geography and P.S. 89,
and all the things she never taught me.
I remember, though, that Sheffield made
fine cutlery,
and coal was made at Newcastle,
and dry-docks at Southampton:
I should have known that France had beaches,
that Normandy must be noted for this, or that,
plus D-Day, plus one, plus two, plus et cetera,
and divers things from Carentan to Mons.

I should have known of Omaha
And Utah—
American Indian hinterlands—
as French as Bar-le-Duc;
But Miss Upjohn was a virgin,
then a spinster;
she shied away from Flesh and French facts,
she disapproved of certain acts:
Between us there can be no bond,
Now that I can teach Upjohn.

THE AFRICAN AFFAIR
by Bruce McM. Wright

Black is what the prisons are,
The stagnant vortex of the hours
Swept into totality,
Creeping in the perjured heart,
Bitter in the vulgar rhyme,
Bitter on the walls;

Black is where the devils dance
With time within
The creviced wall. Time pirouettes
A crippled orbit in a trance,
And crawls below, beneath the flesh
Where darkness flows;

Black is where the deserts burn,
The Niger and Sasandra flow,
From where the Middle Passage went
Within the Continent of Night
From Cameroons to Carisbrooke
And places conscience cannot go;

Black is where thatched temples burn
Incense to carved ebon-wood;
Where traders shaped my father's pain,
His person and his place,
Among dead statues in a frieze,
In the spectrum of his race.

PORTRAIT PHILIPPINES
by Alfred A. Duckett

The Philippines were drenched in sun.
The maidens, gold and brown.
But children cried with hunger
When the angry sun went down.

Children laughed and sang and danced
all the livelong day.
At night they begged for garbage
the soldiers cast away.

SONNET
by Alfred A. Duckett

Where are we to go when this is done?
Will we slip into old, accustomed ways,
finding remembered notches, one by one?
Thrashing a hapless way through quickening haze?

Who is to know us when the end has come?
Old friends and families, but could we be
strange to the sight and stricken dumb
at visions of some pulsing memory?

Who will love us for what we used to be
who now are what we are, bitter or cold?

Who is to nurse us with swift subtlety
back to the warm and feeling human fold?

Where are we to go when this is through?
We are the war-born. What are we to do?

SONG
by M. Carl Holman

Dressed up in my melancholy
With no place to go,
Sick as sin of inwardness
And sick of being so

I walked out on the avenue,
Eager to give my hand
To any with the health to heal
Or heart to understand.

I had not walked a city block
And met with more than ten
Before I read the testament
Stark behind each grin:

Beneath the hat brims haunting me,
More faithful than a mirror,
The figuration of my grief,
The image of my error.

NOTES FOR A MOVIE SCRIPT
by M. Carl Holman

Fade in the sound of summer music,
Picture a hand plunging through her hair,
Next his socked feet and her scuffed dance slippers
Close, as they kiss on the rug-stripped stair.

Catch now the taxi from the station,
Capture her shoulders' sudden sag;
Switch to him silent in the barracks
While the room roars at the corporal's gag.

Let the drums dwindle in the distance,
Pile the green sea above the land;
While she prepares a single breakfast,
Reading the v-mail in her hand.

Ride a cold moonbeam to the pillbox,
Sidle the camera to his feet
Sprawled just outside in the gummy grasses,
Swollen like nightmare and not neat.

Now doorbell nudges the lazy morning:
She stills the sweeper for a while,
Twitches her dress, swings the screendoor open,
Cut—with no music—on her smile.

LETTER ACROSS DOUBT AND DISTANCE
by M. Carl Holman

I dreamed all my fortitude screamed
And fled down the strict corridor,
Entered in greedy and unashamed
At the seductive door;
Or your eyes winked from the tabloid,
Your silence raised a wraith
Which lured me nearer that void
Where fact prepares its ambuscade for faith.

Carved keen in the spring-green bark
Your long absence does not congeal,
No cement sutures the cruel crack
Where the hot sap weeps still

And will furrow and blister this sand
Though vanes claim weather is north
Until your gifted hand
Heals the shocked tissues and late buds flame forth:

O girl waking now where the swirl
Of gulls scatters across white hulls
And the wind hurtling the marshy field
Spurs the green bay into hills,
All my pain falls at your power,
Slacks and comes softly to rest.
Calmed, as that gray church tower
Checks the wild pigeons taking them to breast.

AND ON THIS SHORE
by M. Carl Holman

Alarm and time clock still intrude too early,
Sun on the lawns at morning is the same,
Across the cups we yawn at private murders,
Accustomed causes leave us gay or glum.

(I feel the streaming wind in my eyes,
the highway swimming under the floor,
music flung comically over the hills,
Remember your profile, your pilot's body at ease,
the absolute absence of boredom, the absence of fear)

The swingshift workers are snoring at noon,
The armywife's offspring dumb in his crib,
The private, patron of blackmarket still,
Sleeps long past reveille stark on his slab.

(The chimes were musing far beyond soft hills,
I brushed an ant from your arm,
The leaves lifted, shifted like breathing to pour
Light on your lids, seemed then no end of time)

The streets re-wind to spools of home,
Dials usher in the bland newscaster,
From the mail box's narrow room
Lunges the cobra of disaster.

(Kissed and were happy at the door,
showered, pretending this would last,
Stones down dead wells, the calendar
counts summers that are lost, are lost)

II

Is it yourself he loves
Or the way you arranged your hair?
The book which taught you to listen while he talked?
The cute dance steps and that night on the Navy pier?
Did he see yours or another's face when he waked?
On what does this shadow feed
And shall it not fade?

Is it yourself she loves
Or the easy-come money you breezily spend?
The 4-F, convertible, "A" coupons, dark market Scotch?
Would she stick if she found she could interest your friend:
When the man on her dresser returns will you prove his match?
On what does this shadow feed
And shall it not fade?

Is it yourself they love
Or the victories panted with vibrant voice?
(Mellow for brave boys sleeping their last long sleep)
Will sponsor and fan abide when bulletins burst in your face,
Raw stumps and barricades explode through the map?
On what does this shadow feed,
And shall it not fade?

Is it yourself they love,
You brief-cased and lens-familiar,

Invoking spring from the smoke of our heaviest winter?
Their mouths adore—but fangs may lurk for anger;
Watching night wither do you not sometimes wonder
On what does this shadow feed
And shall it not fade?

REFUGEE
by Naomi Long Witherspoon

Say, bud, ya got a cigarette?
Yeah, man, dat's ALL I got!
Go 'way! I ain't got even that.
A cigarette's a lot.

I had a home, a wife and kid,
And I was ridin' high.
Along came white Jim from the hill
And said I had to die.

He tol' da law his po' white wife
Had suffered by my gang.
When Manny came to tip me off,
He said: *Skip town or hang!*

I lef' my wife, my little kid,
And Nineteen Cherry Street,
And in da moonless Georgia night
I moved my weary feet.

When I remember Cherry Street
It hurts me to da bone.
But hell! I'm here up North—alive,
Although I am alone.

Ain't got no job, no fine blue suit,
No new ten-gallon hat.
I only got one cigarette—
You might as well take that.

POEM
by Russell Atkins

Upstood upstaffed passing sinuously away over an airy arch
    Streaming where all the lustres
    Streaming sinuously shone
    bright where more sky
Upstood upstaffed the sumptuously ready
    flags full
    (the shaded soothed and blowing softly
    the underlings smoothly
    with horses wavering with winds gently
    and smooth the men and manners soft
    tangling with manly manners thick
    gathering the steeds) that
    forthwith
    up up
    Christophe
    appearing in the imminent
    and the passion overjoying the hour
    unfolded flaming for
Highly the imperial sign
    shone in his huge glory!

FOR WILLIAM EDWARD BURGHARDT DUBOIS
ON HIS EIGHTIETH BIRTHDAY
by Bette Darcie Latimer

*He does not lounge with the old men
on their thrones in the sun. . . .*

I have awakened from the unknowing to the knowing
hoping to see the fathomless. . . .

But I saw the old men
on their thrones in the sun,
with aged eyes
and dust in their beards.

      Mixed with the shadows,
      veiled and unthroned,
      the brown one smiles.

I meet them at the turnpike,
but they point signward,
waving the crutches of empty years.

      The brown one, smiling, led me on
      with wisdom as a sturdy cane.
      "The masterpiece is there," he said—
      and the dread beauty of living
      crushed us into reverence.

2 TRIBUTARY POEMS BY NON-NEGROES

THE RUNAWAY SLAVE[1]
From *Song of Myself*
by Walt Whitman

The runaway slave came to my house and stopt outside,
I heard his motions crackling the twigs of the woodpile,
Through the swung half-door of the kitchen I saw him limpsy and weak,
And went where he sat on a log and led him in and assured him,
And brought water and fill'd a tub for his sweated body and bruis'd
    feet,
And gave him a room that enter'd from my own, and gave him some
    coarse clean clothes,
And remember perfectly well his revolving eyes and his awkwardness,
And remember putting plasters on the galls of his neck and ankles;
He staid with me a week before he was recuperated and pass'd North,
I had him sit next me at table. . . .

THE WOUNDED PERSON[2]
From *Song of Myself*
by Walt Whitman

The hounded slave that flags in the race, leans by the fence, blowing,
    cover'd with sweat,
The twinges that sting like needles his legs and neck, the murderous
    buckshot and the bullets,
All these I feel or am.

I am the hounded slave, I wince at the bite of the dogs,
Hell and despair are upon me, crack and again crack the marksmen,
I clutch the rails of the fence, my gore dribs, thinn'd with the ooze of
    my skin,
I fall on the weeds and stones,
The riders spur their unwilling horses, haul close,
Taunt my dizzy ears and beat me violently over the head with whip-
    stocks.

[1,2]From *Leaves of Grass*, by Walt Whitman. Reprinted by permission of Double-day & Company, Inc.

Agonies are one of my changes of garments.
I do not ask the wounded person how he feels, I myself become the
　　wounded person.

THE DRAYMAN[3]
From *Song of Myself*
by Walt Whitman

The Negro holds firmly the reins of his four horses, the block swags
　　underneath on its tied-over chain,
The Negro that drives the long dray of the stone-yard, steady and tall
　　he stands pois'd on one leg on the stringpiece,
His blue shirt exposes his ample neck and breast and loosens over his
　　hip-band,
His glance is calm and commanding, he tosses the slouch of his hat
　　away from his forehead,
The sun falls on his crispy hair and mustache, falls on the black of his
　　polish'd and perfect limbs.
I behold the picturesque giant and love him, and I do not stop there,
I go with the team also.
In me the caresser of life wherever moving, backward as well as for-
　　ward sluing,
To niches aside and junior bending, not a person or object missing,
Absorbing all to myself and for this song.

ETHIOPIA SALUTING THE COLORS[4]
From *Drum-Taps*
by Walt Whitman

　　Who are you dusky woman, so ancient hardly human,
　　With your woolly-white and turban'd head, and bare bony feet?
　　Why rising by the roadside here, do you the colors greet?

[3,4] From *Leaves of Grass*, by Walt Whitman. Reprinted by permission of Double-
day & Company, Inc.

('Tis while our army lines Carolina's sands and pines,
Forth from thy hovel door thou Ethiopia com'st to me,
As under doughty Sherman I march toward the sea.)

Me master years a hundred since from my parents sunder'd,
A little child, they caught me as the savage beast is caught,
Then hither me across the sea the cruel slaver brought.

No further does she say, but lingering all the day,
Her high-borne turban'd head she wags, and rolls her darkling eye,
And courtesies to the regiments, the guidons moving by.

What is it fateful woman, so blear, hardly human?
Why wag your head with turban bound, yellow, red and green?
Are the things so strange and marvelous you see or have seen?

THE LITTLE BLACK BOY
by William Blake

My mother bore me in the southern wild,
And I am black, but O! my soul is white;
White as an angel is the English child,
But I am black, as if bereav'd of light.

My mother taught me underneath a tree,
And sitting down before the heat of day,
She took me on her lap and kissed me,
And, pointing to the east, began to say:

"Look on the rising sun,—there God does live,
And gives his light, and gives his heat away;
And flowers and trees and beasts and men receive
Comfort in morning, joy in the noonday.

"And we are put on earth a little space,
That we may learn to bear the beams of love;
And these black bodies and this sunburnt face
Is but a cloud, and like a shady grove.

"For when our souls have learn'd the heat to bear,
The cloud will vanish; we shall hear his voice,
Saying: 'Come out from the grove, my love and care,
And round my golden tent like lambs rejoice.' "

Thus did my mother say, and kissed me;
And thus I say to little English boy:
When I from black, and he from white cloud free,
And round the tent of God like lambs we joy,

I'll shade him from the heat, till he can bear
To lean in joy upon our Father's knee;
And then I'll stand and stroke his silver hair,
And be like him, and he will then love me.

(1789)

THE RUNAWAY SLAVE AT PILGRIM'S POINT
by Elizabeth Barrett Browning

I

I stand on the mark, beside the shore,
    Of the first white pilgrim's bended knee;
Where exile turned to ancestor,
    And God was thanked for liberty.
I have run through the night—my skin is as dark—
    I bend my knee down on this mark—
I look on the sky and the sea.

II

O, pilgrim-souls, I speak to you:
    I see you come out proud and slow
From the land of the spirits, pale as dew,
    And round me and round me ye go.
O, pilgrims, I have gasped and run
    All night long from the whips of one
Who in your names works sin and woe!

III

And thus I thought that I would come
  And kneel here where ye knelt before,
And feel your souls around me hum
  In undertone to the ocean's roar;
And lift my black face, my black hand,
  Here in your names, to curse this land
Ye blessed in Freedom's heretofore.

IV

I am black, I am black,
  And yet God made me, they say:
But if He did so—smiling back
  He must have cast his work away
Under the feet of His white creatures
  With a look of scorn, that the dusky features
Might be trodden again to clay.

V

And yet He has made dark things
  To be glad and merry as light;
There's a little dark bird sits and sings;
  There's a dark stream ripples out of sight;
And the dark frogs chant in the safe morass,
  And the sweetest stars are made to pass
O'er the face of the darkest night.

VI

But *we* who are dark, we are dark!
  Ah God, we have no stars!

About our souls, in care and cark,
   Our blackness shuts like prison-bars!
The poor souls crouch so far behind,
   That never a comfort can they find,
By reaching through the prison bars.

VII

And still God's sunshine and His frost
   They make us hot, they make us cold,
As if we were not black and lost;
   And the beasts and birds in wood and fold,
Do fear us and take us for very men;—
   Could the weep-poor-will or the cat of the glen
Look into my eyes and be bold?

VIII

I am black, I am black,
   And once I laughed in girlish glee;
For one of my colour stood in the track
   Where the drivers drove, and looked at me;
And tender and full was the look he gave!
   A Slave looked so at another Slave,—
I look at the sky and the sea.

IX

And from that hour our spirits grew
   As free as if unsold, unbought;
We were strong enough, since we were two,
   To conquer the world, we thought.
The drivers drove us day by day:
   We did not mind; we went one way,
And no better a freedom sought.

X

In the sunny ground between the canes,
   He said "I love you" as he passed
When the shingle-roof rang sharp with the rains,
   I heard how he vowed it fast,
While other trembled, he sat in the hut
   And carved me a bowl of the cocoa-nut
Through the roar of the hurricanes.

XI

I sang his name instead of a song;
   Over and over I sang his name.
Upward and downward I drew it along
   My notes,—the same, the same!
I sang it low, that the slave-girls near
   Might never guess, from aught they could hear,
It was only a name—a name.

XII

I look on the sky and the sea!
   We were two to love, and two to pray,—
Yes, two, O God, who cried to Thee,
   Though nothing didst Thou say,
Coldly Thou sat'st behind the sun,
   And now I cry, who am but one,—
Thou wilt not speak to-day!

XIII

We were black, we were black,
   We had no claim to love and bliss—

What marvel, if each went to wrack?
    They wrung my cold hands out of his—
They dragged him—where,—I crawled to touch
    His blood's mark in the dust—not much,
Ye pilgrim-souls,—though plain as THIS!

XIV

Wrong, followed by a deeper wrong!
    Mere grief's too good for such as I;
So the white men brought the shame ere long
    To strangle the sob of my agony.
They would not leave me for my dull
    Wet eyes!—it was too merciful
To let me weep pure tears, and die.

XV

I am black, I am black!
    I wore a child upon my breast,—
An amulet that hung too slack,
    And, in my unrest, could not rest!
Thus we went moaning, child and mother,
    One to another, one to another.
Until all ended for the best.

XVI

For hark! I will tell you low—low—
    I am black, you see;
And the babe, that lay on my bosom so,
    Was far too white—too white for me,
As white as the ladies who scorned to pray
    Beside me at the church but yesterday,
Though my tears had washed a place for my knee.

XVII

My own, own child—I could not bear
   To look in his face, it was so white;
I covered him up with a kerchief there;
   I covered his face in close and tight!
And he moaned and struggled as well as might be,
   For the white child wanted his liberty,—
Ha, ha! he wanted the master-right.

XVIII

He moaned and beat with his head and feet—
   His little feet that never grew!
He struck them out as it was meet
   Against my heart to break it through.
I might have sung and made him mild,
   But I dared not sing to the white faced child
The only song I knew.

XIX

I pulled the kerchief very close;
   He could not see the sun, I swear,
More then, alive, than now he does
   From between the roots of the mango—where?
I know where—close! a child and mother
   Do wrong to look at one another
When one is black and one is fair.

XX

Even in that single glance I had
   Of my child's face,—I tell you all,—

I saw a look that made me mad,—
   The *master's* look, that used to fall
On my soul like his lash,—or worse,—
   And so, to save it from my curse,
I twisted it round in my shawl.

XXI

And he moaned and trembled from foot to head,—
   He shivered from head to foot,—
Till after a time, he lay, instead,
   Too suddenly still and mute;
And I felt, beside, a creeping cold,—
   I dared to lift up just a fold,
As in lifting a leaf of the mango-fruit.

XXII

But *my* fruit! ha, ha!—there, had been
   (I laugh to think on't at this hour!)
Your fine white angels,—who have been
   Nearest the secret of God's power—
And plucked my fruit to make them wine,
   And sucked the soul of that child of mine,
As the humming-bird sucks the soul of the flower.

XXIII

Ha, ha! the trick of the angels white!
   They freed the white child's spirit so;
I said not a word but day and night
   I carried the body to and fro;
And it lay on my heart like a stone—as chill;
   The sun may shine out as much as he will,—
I am cold, though it happened a month ago.

XXIV

From the white man's house and the black man's hut,
    I carried the little body on;
The forest's arms did around us shut,
    And silence through the trees did run!
They asked no questions as I went,—
    They stood too high for astonishment,—
They could see God sit on his throne.

XXV

My little body, kerchief-fast,
    I bore it on through the forest—on—
And when I felt it was tired at last,
    I scooped a hole beneath the moon.
Through the forest-tops the angels far,
    With a white sharp finger in every star
Did point and mock at what was done.

XXVI

Yet when it all was done aright,
    Earth twixt me and my baby strewed,—
All, changed to black earth,—nothing white—
    A dark child in the dark—ensued
Some comfort, and my heart grew young;
    I sate down smiling there, and sung
The song I learnt in my maidenhood.

XXVII

And thus we two were reconciled,
    The white child and black mother, thus;

For, as I sang it,—soft and wild,
   The same song, more melodious,
Rose from the grave whereon I sat!
   It was the dead child singing that,
To join the souls of both of us.

XXVIII

I look on the sea and the sky!
   Where the pilgrims' ships first anchored lay,
The great sun rideth gloriously!
   But the pilgrim-ghosts have slid away
Through the first faint streaks of the morn!
   My face is black, but it glares with a scorn
Which they dare not meet by day.

XXIX

Ah! in their stead their hunter sons!
   Ah, ah! they are on me! they form in a ring!
Keep off—I brave you all at once,—
   I throw off your eyes like snakes that sting!
You have killed the black eagle at nest, I think;
   Did you ever stand still in your triumph, and shrink
From the stroke of her wounded wing?

XXX

(Man, drop that stone you dared to lift!)
   I wish you, who stand there, five abreast,
Each, for his own wife's joy and gift,
   A little corpse as safely at rest,
As mine in the mangoes! Yes, but *she*
   May keep live babies on her knee,
And sing the song she likes the best.

XXXI

I am not mad,—I am black!
  I see you staring in my face,—
I know you staring, shrinking back,—
  Ye are born of the Washington-race!
And this land is the Free America,—
  And this mark on my wrist,—(I prove what I say)
Ropes tied me up here to the flogging place.

XXXII

You think I shrieked then? not a sound!
  I hung as a gourd hangs in the sun;
I only cursed them all around
  As softly as I might have done
My very own child. From these sands
  Up to the mountains, lift your hands,
O slaves, and end what I begun.

XXXIII

Whips, curses! these must answer those!
  For in this Union, ye have set
Two kinds of men in adverse rows,
  Each loathing each! and all forget
The seven wounds in Christ's body fair;
  While he sees gaping everywhere
Our countless wounds that pay no debt.

XXXIV

Our wounds are different—your white men
  Are, after all, not gods indeed,

Nor able to make Christs again
Do good with bleeding. We who bleed,—
(Stand off!)—we help not in our loss—
We are too heavy for our cross,
And fall and crush you and your seed.

XXXV

I fall,—I swoon,—I look at the sky!
The clouds are breaking on my brain:
I am floated along, as if I should die
Of Liberty's exquisite pain!
In the name of the white child waiting for me
In the death-dark where we may kiss and agree—
White men, I leave you all curse-free,
In my broken heart's disdain!

TO TOUSSAINT L'OUVERTURE
by William Wordsworth

TOUSSAINT, the most unhappy man of men!
Whether the whistling Rustic tend his plough
Within thy hearing, or thy head be now
Pillowed in some deep dungeon's earless den;—
O miserable Chieftain! where and when
Wilt thou find patience? Yet die not; do thou
Wear rather in thy bonds a cheerful brow:
Though fallen thyself, never to rise again,
Live, and take comfort. Thou hast left behind
Powers that will work for thee; air, earth, and skies;
There's not a breathing of the common wind
That will forget thee; thou hast great allies;
Thy friends are exultations, agonies,
And love, and man's unconquerable mind.

TOUSSAINT L'OUVERTURE[5]
Chateau de Joux, 1803
by Edwin Arlington Robinson

Am I alone—or is it you, my friend?
I call you friend, but let it not be known
That such a word was uttered in this place.
You are the first that has forgotten duty
So far as to be sorry—and perilously,
For you—that I am not so frozen yet,
Or starved, or blasted, that I cannot feel.
Yes, I can feel, and hear. I can hear something
Behind me. Is it you? There is no light,
But there's a gray place where a window was
Before the sun went down. Was there a sun?
There must have been one; for there was a light,
Or sort of light—enough to make me see
That I was here alone. Was I forgotten?
I have been here alone now for three days,
Without you, and with nothing here to eat
Or drink; and for God knows how many months,
Or years, before you came, have I been here—
But never alone so long. You must be careful,
Or they will kill you if they hear you asking
Questions of me as if I were a man.
I did not know that there was anything left
Alive to see me, or to consider me,
As more than a transplanted shovelful
Of black earth, with a seed of danger in it—
A seed that's not there now, and never was.
When was I dangerous to Napoleon?
Does a perfidious victor fear the victim
That he has trapped and harassed? No, he hates him.
The only danger that was ever in me
Was food that his hate made to feed itself.

[5]From *Nicodemus*, copyright, 1932, by Edwin Arlington Robinson; used by permission of The Macmillan Company, New York, and Macmillan & Co., Ltd.. London.

There lives in hate a seed more dangerous
To man, I fear, than any in time's garden
That has not risen to full stalk and flower
In history yet. I am glad now for being
So like a child as to believe in him
As long as there was hope. And what was hope?
Hope was a pebble I brought here to play with,
And might as well have dropped into the ocean
Before there was a bitter league of it
Between me and my island. It was well
Not to do that. Not that it matters now.

My friend, I do not hear you any longer.
Are you still there? Are you afraid to speak?
You are the first thing fashioned as a man
That has acknowledged me since I came here—
To die, as I see now—with word or motion
Of one man in the same world with another;
And you may be afraid of saying to me
Some word that hurts your tongue. Have they invented
A last new misery fit for the last days
Of an old sick black man who says tonight
He does not think that he shall have to live
Much longer now? If there were left in me
A way to laugh, I might as well be laughing
To think of that. Say to Napoleon
That he has made an end of me so slowly,
And thoroughly, that only God Almighty
Shall say what is to say. And if God made him,
And made him as he is, and has to be,
Say who shall answer for a world where men
Are mostly blind, and they who are the blindest
Climb to cold heights that others cannot reach,
And there, with all there is for them to see,
See nothing but themselves. I am not one
To tell you about that, for I am only
A man destroyed, a sick man, soon to die;
A man betrayed, who sees his end a ruin,
Yet cannot see that he has lived in vain.

Though he was crushed and humbled at the last
As things are that are crawling in man's way,
He was a man. God knows he was a man,
And tells him so tonight. Another man
Mixed fear with power and hate and made of it
A poison that was death, and more than death,
And strangled me to make me swallow it—
And here I am. I shall not be here long
To trouble you; and I shall not forget
Your seeing in me a remnant of mankind,
And not a piece of God's peculiar clay
Shaped as a reptile, or as a black snake.
A black man, to be sure; and that's important.

I cannot tell you about God, my friend,
But in my life I have learned more of men
Than would be useful now, or necessary,
If a man's life were only a man's life.
Sometimes it is, or looks to be, no better
Than a weed growing to be crushed or cut,
Or at the most and best, or worst, to live
And shrivel and slowly die and be forgotten.
Others are not like that; and it appears
That mine was not. Mine was a million lives,
And millions after them. Why am I here!
What have I done to die in a cold hole
In a cold land that has no need of me?
Men have been mightier than in doing this thing
To me, I think. Yet who am I to say it?
An exile, buried alive in a cold grave
For serving man, as men may still remember.
There are diseased and senseless ways of hate
That puzzle me—partly because I'm black,
Perhaps, though more because of things that are,
And shall be, and for God may say how long.

Hear me, and I will tell you a strange thing—
Which may be new and of an interest

To many who may not know so much of me
As even my name until my name shall have
A meaning in this world's unhappy story.
Napoleon cannot starve my name to death,
Or blot it out with his. There is an island
Where men remember me; and from an island
Surprising freight of dreams and deeds may come,
To make men think. Is it not strange, my friend—
If you are there—that one dishonored slave,
One animal owned and valued at a price,
One black commodity, should have seen so early
All that I saw? When I filled sight with action,
I could see tyranny's blood-spattered eyes
That saw no farther, laughing at God and fate,
Than a day's end, or possibly one day more,—
Until I made them see. Was it not strange?
Drivers and governors of multitudes
Must be more than themselves, and have more eyes
Than one man's eyes, or scorn will bury them,
Or leave them worse uncovered; and time will pass them
Only to kick their bones. I could see that;
And my prophetic eyes, where God had fixed them
In this black face, could see in front of them
A flaming shambles of men's ignorance
Of all that men should know. I could see farther;
And in a world far larger than my island
Could see the foul indifferent poison wreaking
Sorrow and death and useless indignation
On millions who are waiting to be born;
And this because the few that have the word
Are mostly the wrong few in the wrong places.
On thrones or chairs of state too high for them,
Where they sit swollen or scared, or both, as may be,
They watch, unseen, a diligent see-saw
Played by their privileged and especial slaves
On slippery planks that shake and smell of blood
That flows from crushed and quivering backs and arms
Of slaves that hold them up. There are more slaves
Than have yet felt or are to feel, and know it,

An iron or a lash. This will go on
Until more slaves like me, and more, and more,
Throw off their shackles and make swords of them
For those to feel who have not felt before,
And will not see. It will go on as long
As men capitulate who feel and see,
And men who know say nothing. If this means
It must go on for always—well I have done
All that one man—one black man, I should say—
Could do against a madness and a system
And a malicious policy, all rotten
With craft and hate. It will be so again:
Humanity will hear the lash of scorn
And ignorance again falling on hope,
And hearing it will feel it. Ignorance,
Always a devil, is a father of devils
When it has power and fire and hate to play with,
And goes down with the noise of its own house
Falling, always too late to save itself,
Because it has no eyes. That's power, my friend.
If you are sorry to be born without it,
Be sorry for something else, and answer me:
Is power a breaking down of flesh and spirit?
Is foresight a word lost with a lost language?
Is honor incomprehensible? Is it strange,
That I should sit here and say this to you—
Here in the dark? . . . Nothing to eat or drink,
Nothing to do but die? This is not right. . . .
Hear me, and I will tell you what I saw.

Last night I saw Napoleon in hell.
He was not dead, but I knew where he was,
For there was fire and death surrounding him
Like red coals ringed around a scorpion
To make him sting himself rather than burn.
Napoleon burned. I saw his two hands flaming;
And while I saw him I could see that hate
For me was still alive in his blind eyes.
I was no happier for the sight of him,

For that would not help me; and I had seen
Too much already of crime and fire at work
Before I made an end of it—for him
To make of peace a useless waste and fury.
I have not yet gone mad, for I have known
That I was right. It seems a miracle,
Yet I am not so sure it is a mercy
That I have still my wits and memories
For company in this place. I saw him there,
And his hands that were flaming with a fire
They caught from the same fire that they had lighted.
So fire will act, sometimes, apparently.
Well, there he was, and if I'm not in error,
He will be there again before he dies;
And that will not be medicine here for this.
There is no cure for this, except to die,
And there is nothing left that is worth hating—
Not even the hate of him that kills with hate.
Is it that I am weak—or am I wise?
Can a black man be wise? He would say not.
Having his wisdom, he would have to say it
To keep his hate alive; and without that
He would soon hate the sound of his own name.
Prisons have tongues, and this will all be told;
And it will not sound well when men remember.

Where are you now? Is this another night?
Another day—and now another night?
I do not hear you any more, my friend.
Where are you? Were you ever here at all?
I have been here alone now for too long.
They will not let you come to me again
Until you come to carry a dead man—
I see it now—out of this cold and darkness
To a place where black and white are dark together.
Nothing to eat or drink—nothing to do
But wait, and die. No, it will not sound well.
Where are you now, my friend? I cannot hear you;
I cannot feel you. Are you dead, perhaps?

I said to you it would be perilous
Not to remember that I'm not a man,
But an imprudent piece of merchandise
To buy and sell—or this time rather to steal;
To catch and steal, and carry from my island
To France, and to this place. And in this place,
Is it not strange, my friend, for me to see
So clearly, and in the dark, more than he sees
Who put me here—as I saw long ago
More than a man could do, till it was done?
Yes, it is done, and cannot be undone.
I know, because I know; and only those
Whose creed and caution has been never to know
Will see in that no reason . . . Yes, I know,
My friend, but I do not know where you are.
If you are here, help me to rise and stand
Once more. I cannot sleep. I cannot see.
Nothing to eat or drink—nothing to see
But night. Good night, my friend—if you are here.

Nothing to see but night—and a long night,
My friend. I hear you now. I hear you moving,
And breathing. I can feel you in the dark,
Although I cannot see you. . . . Is this night?
Or is it morning! No, it is not night—
For now I see. You were a dream, my friend!
Glory to God, who made a dream of you,
And of a place that I believed a prison.
There were no prisons—no Napoleons.
I must have been asleep for a long time.
Now I remember. I was on a ship—
A ship they said was carrying me to France.
Why should I go to France? I must have slept,
And sailed away asleep, and sailed on sleeping.
I am not quite awake; yet I can see
White waves, and I can feel a warm wind coming—
And I can see the sun! . . . This is not France—
This is a ship; and France was never a ship.

France was a place where they were starving me
To death, because a black man had a brain.
I feel the sun! Now we going faster—
Now I see land—I see land and a mountain!
I see white foam along a sunny shore—
And there's a town. Now there are people in it,
Shouting and singing, waving wild arms at me,
And crowding down together to the water!
You know me—and you knew that I was coming!
O you lost faces! My lost friends! My island!
You knew that I was coming. . . .
                                        You are gone.
Where are you gone? Is this the night again?
I cannot see you now. But you are there—
You are still there. And I know who is here.

THE SLAVE'S DREAM
by Henry Wadsworth Longfellow

Beside the ungathered rice he lay,
    His sickle in his hand;
His breast was bare, his matted hair
    Was buried in the sand.
Again, in the mist and shadow of sleep,
    He saw his Native Land.

Wide through the landscape of his dreams
    The lordly Niger flowed;
Beneath the palm-trees on the plain
    Once more a king he strode;
And heard the tinkling caravans
    Descend the mountain road.

He saw once more his dark-eyed queen
    Among her children stand;
They clasped his neck, they kissed his cheeks,
    They held him by the hand!—

A tear burst from the sleeper's lids
  And fell into the sand.

And then at furious speed he rode
  Along the Niger's bank;
His bridle-reins were golden chains,
  And, with a martial clank,
At each leap he could feel his scabbard of steel
  Smiting his stallion's flank.

Before him, like a blood-red flag,
  The bright flamingoes flew;
From morn till night he followed their flight,
  O'er plains where the tamarind grew,
Till he saw the roofs of Caffre huts,
  And the ocean rose to view.

At night he heard the lion roar,
  And the hyena scream,
And the river-horse, as he crushed the reeds
  Beside some hidden stream;
And it passed, like a glorious roll of drums,
  Through the triumph of his dream.

The forests, with their myriad tongues,
  Shouted of liberty;
And the Blast of the Desert cried aloud,
  With a voice so wild and free,
That he started in his sleep and smiled
  At their tempestuous glee.

He did not feel the driver's whip,
  Nor the burning heat of day;
For Death had illumined the Land of Sleep,
  And his lifeless body lay
A worn-out fetter, that the soul
  Had broken and thrown away!

THE FAREWELL
by John Greenleaf Whittier

Of a Virginia Slave Mother to Her Daughters,
Sold into Southern Bondage

Gone, gone—sold and gone,
To the rice-swamp dank and lone.
Where the slave-whip ceaseless swings,
Where the noisome insect stings,
Where the fever demon strews
Poison with the falling dews,
Where the sickly sunbeams glare
Through the hot and misty air,—
Gone, gone—sold and gone,
To the rice-swamp dank and lone,
From Virginia's hills and waters,—
Woe is me, my stolen daughters!

Gone, gone—sold and gone,
To the rice-swamp dank and lone.
There no mother's eye is near them,
There no mother's ear can hear them;
Never, when the torturing lash
Seams their back with many a gash,
Shall a mother's kindness bless them,
Or a mother's arms caress them.
Gone, gone—sold and gone,
To the rice-swamp dank and lone,
From Virginia's hills and waters—
Woe is me, my stolen daughters!

Gone, gone—sold and gone,
To the rice-swamp dank and lone.
Oh, when weary, sad, and slow,
From the fields at night they go,

Faint with toil, and racked with pain,
To their cheerless homes again—
There no brother's voice shall greet them—
There no father's welcome meet them.
    Gone, gone—sold and gone,
    To the rice-swamp dank and lone,
    From Virginia's hills and waters—
    Woe is me, my stolen daughters!

    Gone, gone—sold and gone,
    To the rice-swamp dank and lone,
From the tree whose shadow lay
On their childhood's place of play—
From the cool spring where they drank—
Rock, and hill, and rivulet bank—
From the solemn house of prayer,
And the holy counsels there—
    Gone, gone—sold and gone,
    To the rice-swamp dank and lone,
    From Virginia's hills and waters,—
    Woe is me, my stolen daughters!

    Gone, gone—sold and gone,
    To the rice-swamp dank and lone—
Toiling through the weary day,
And at night the spoiler's prey.
Oh, that they had earlier died,
Sleeping calmly, side by side,
Where the tyrant's power is o'er
And the fetter galls no more!
    Gone, gone—sold and gone,
    To the rice-swamp dank and lone,
    From Virginia's hills and waters,—
    Woe is me, my stolen daughters!

    Gone, gone—sold and gone,
    To the rice-swamp dank and lone.
By the holy love He beareth—
By the bruised reed He spareth—

Oh, may He, to whom alone
All their cruel wrongs are known,
Still their hope and refuge prove,
With a more than mother's love.
　　Gone, gone—sold and gone,
　　To the rice-swamp dank and lone,
　　From Virginia's hills and waters,—
　　Woe is me, my stolen daughters!

STANZAS ON FREEDOM
by James Russell Lowell

Men! whose boast it is that ye
Come of fathers brave and free,
If there breathe on earth a slave,
Are ye truly free and brave?
If ye do not feel the chain,
When it works a brother's pain,
Are ye not base slaves, indeed,
Slaves unworthy to be freed?

Women! who shall one day bear
Sons to breathe New England air,
If ye hear without a blush
Deeds to make the roused blood rush
Like red lava through your veins,
For your sisters now in chains,—
Answer! are ye fit to be
Mothers of the brave and free?

Is true Freedom but to break
Fetters for our own dear sake,
And with leathern hearts forget
That we owe mankind a debt?
No! true Freedom is to share
All the chains our brothers wear,

And with heart and hands to be
Earnest to make others free!

They are slaves who fear to speak
For the fallen and the weak;
They are slaves who will not choose
Hatred, scoffing and abuse,
Rather than in silence shrink
From the truth they needs must think;
They are slaves who dare not be
In the right with two or three.

HOW OLD BROWN TOOK HARPERS FERRY[6]
by Edmund Clarence Stedman

John Brown in Kansas settled, like a steadfast Yankee farmer,
Brave and godly, with four sons, all stalwart men of might.
There he spoke aloud for freedom, and the Border-strife grew warmer,
Till the Rangers fired his dwelling, in his absence, in the night;
                    And Old Brown,
                    Osawatomie Brown,
Came homeward in the morning—to find his house burned down.

Then he grasped his trusty rifle and boldly fought for freedom;
    Smote from border unto border the fierce, invading band;
And he and his brave boys vowed—so might Heaven help and speed
    'em!—
    They would save those grand old prairies from the curse that blights
    the land;
                    And Old Brown,
                    Osawatomie Brown,
Said, "Boys, the Lord will aid us!" and he shoved his ramrod down.

And the Lord *did* aid these men, and they labored day and even,
    Saving Kansas from its peril; and their very lives seemed charmed,

[6]Reprinted by permission of Houghton Mifflin Company.

Till the ruffians killed one son, in the blessed light of Heaven,—
  In cold blood the fellows slew him, as he journeyed all unarmed;
Then Old Brown,
Osawatomie Brown,
Shed not a tear, but shut his teeth, and frowned a terrible frown!

Then they seized another brave boy,—not amid the heat of battle,
  But in peace, behind his ploughshare,—and they loaded him with chains,
And with pikes, before their horses, even as they goad their cattle,
  Drove him cruelly, for their sport, and at last blew out his brains;
Then Old Brown,
Osawatomie Brown,
Raised his right hand up to Heaven, calling Heaven's vengeance down.

And he swore a fearful oath, by the name of the Almighty,
  He would hunt this ravening evil that had scathed and torn him so;
He would seize it by the vitals; he would crush it day and night; he
  Would so pursue its footsteps, so return it blow for blow,
That Old Brown,
Osawatomie Brown,
Should be a name to swear by, in backwoods or in town!

Then his beard became more grizzled, and his wild blue eye grew wilder,
  And more sharply curved his hawk's-nose, snuffing battle from afar,
And he and the two boys left, though the Kansas strife waxed milder,
  Grew more sullen, till was over the bloody Border War,
And Old Brown,
Osawatomie Brown,
Had gone crazy, as they reckoned by his fearful glare and frown.

So he left the plains of Kansas and their bitter woes behind him,
  Slipt off into Virginia, where the statesmen all are born,
Hired a farm by Harpers Ferry, and no one knew where to find him,
  Or whether he'd turned parson, or was jacketed and shorn;
For Old Brown,
Osawatomie Brown,
Mad as he was, knew texts enough to wear a parson's gown.

He bought no ploughs and harrows, spades and shovels, and such trifles;
　　But quietly to his rancho there came, by every train,
Boxes full of pikes and pistols, and his well-beloved Sharp's rifles;
　　And eighteen other madmen joined their leader there again.
　　　　　　　　Says Old Brown,
　　　　　　　　Osawatomie Brown,
"Boys, we've got an army large enough to march and take the town!

"Take the town, and seize the muskets, free the Negroes and then arm
　　them;
　　Carry the County and the State, ay, and all the potent South.
On their own heads be the slaughter, if their victims rise to harm them—
　　These Virginians! who believed not, nor would heed the warning
　　mouth."
　　　　　　　　Says Old Brown,
　　　　　　　　Osawatomie Brown,
"The world shall see a Republic, or my name is not John Brown."

'Twas the sixteenth of October, on the evening of a Sunday:
　　"This good work," declared the captain, "shall be on a holy night!"
It was on a Sunday evening, and before the noon of Monday,
　　With two sons, and Captain Stephens, fifteen privates—black and
　　white,
　　　　　　　　Captain Brown,
　　　　　　　　Osawatomie Brown,
Marched across the bridged Potomac, and knocked the sentry down;

Took the guarded armory-building, and the muskets and the cannon;
　　Captured all the county majors and the colonels, one by one;
Scared to death each gallant scion of Virginia they ran on,
　　And before the noon of Monday, I say, the deed was done.
　　　　　　　　Mad Old Brown,
　　　　　　　　Osawatomie Brown,
With his eighteen other crazy men, went in and took the town.

Very little noise and bluster, little smell of powder made he;
　　It was all done in the midnight, like the Emperor's *coup d'état.*

"Cut the wires! Stop the rail-cars! Hold the streets and bridges!" said he,
  Then declared the new Republic, with himself for guiding star,—
                    This Old Brown,
                    Osawatomie Brown;
And the bold two thousand citizens ran off and left the town.

Then was riding and railroading and expressing here and thither;
  And the Martinsburg Sharpshooters and the Charlestown Volunteers,
And the Shepherdstown and Winchester Militia hastened whither
  Old Brown was said to muster his ten thousand grenadiers.
                    General Brown!
                    Osawatomie Brown! !
Behind whose rampant banner all the North was pouring down.

But at last, 'tis said, some prisoners escaped from Old Brown's durance,
  And the effervescent valor of the Chivalry broke out,
When they learned that nineteen madmen had the marvellous assur-
      ance—
    Only nineteen—thus to seize the place and drive them straight about;
                    And Old Brown,
                    Osawatomie Brown,
Found an army come to take him, encamped around the town.

But to storm, with all the forces I have mentioned, was too risky;
  So they hurried off to Richmond for the Government Marines,
Tore them from their weeping matrons, fired their souls with Bourbon
      whiskey,
    Till they battered down Brown's castle with their ladders and ma-
      chines;
                    And Old Brown,
                    Osawatomie Brown,
Received three bayonet stabs, and a cut on his brave old crown.

Tallyho! the old Virginia gentry gather to the baying!
  In they rushed and killed the game, shooting lustily away;
And when'er they slew a rebel, those who came too late for slaying,
  Not to lose a share of glory, fired their bullets in his clay;
                    And Old Brown,
                    Osawatomie Brown,
Saw his sons fall dead beside him and between them laid him down.

How the conquerors wore their laurels; how they hastened on the trial;
   How Old Brown was placed, half dying, on the Charlestown court-
      house floor;
How he spoke his grand oration, in the scorn of all denial;
   What the brave old madman told them,—these are known the coun-
      try o'er.

"Hang Old Brown,
Osawatomie Brown,"

Said the judge, "and all such rebels!" with his most judicial frown.

But, Virginians, don't do it! for I tell you that the flagon,
   Filled with blood of Old Brown's offspring, was first poured by
      Southern hands;
And each drop from Old Brown's life-veins, like the red gore of the
      dragon,
   May spring up a vengeful Fury, hissing through your slave-worn
      lands!

And Old Brown,
Osawatomie Brown,

May trouble you more than ever, when you've nailed his coffin down!

JOHN BROWN'S PRAYER[7]
From *John Brown's Body*
by Stephen Vincent Benét

Omnipotent and steadfast God,
Who, in Thy mercy, hath
Upheaved in me Jehovah's rod
And his chastising wrath,

For fifty-nine unsparing years
Thy Grace hath worked apart
To mould a man of iron tears
With a bullet for a heart.

[7]From "John Brown's Body," in *Selected Works of Stephen Vincent Benét,* copyright, 1927, 1928, by Stephen Vincent Benét. Published by Rinehart & Company,
Inc.

Yet, since this body may be weak
With all it has to bear,
Once more, before Thy thunders speak,
Almighty, hear my prayer.

I saw Thee when Thou did display
The black man and his lord
To bid me free the one, and slay
The other with the sword.

I heard Thee when Thou bade me spurn
Destruction from my hand
And, though all Kansas bleed and burn,
It was at Thy command.

I hear the rolling of the wheels,
The chariots of war!
I hear the breaking of the seals
And the opening of the door!

The glorious beasts with many eyes
Exult before the Crowned.
The buried saints arise, arise
Like incense from the ground!

Before them march the martyr-kings,
In bloody sunsets drest,
O, Kansas, bleeding Kansas,
You will not let me rest!

I hear your sighing corn again,
I smell your prairie-sky,
And I remember five dead men
By Pottawattomie.

Lord God it was a work of Thine,
And how might I refrain?
But Kansas, bleeding Kansas,
I hear her in her pain.

Her corn is rustling in the ground,
An arrow in my flesh.
And all night long I staunch a wound
That ever bleeds afresh.

Get up, get up, my hardy sons,
From this time forth we are
No longer men, but pikes and guns
In God's advancing war.

And if we live, we free the slave,
And if we die, we die.
But God has digged His saints a grave
Beyond the western sky.

Oh, fairer than the bugle-call
Its walls of jasper shine!
And Joshua's sword is on the wall
With space beside for mine.

And should the Philistine defend
His strength against our blows,
The God who doth not spare His friend,
Will not forget His foes.

HARPERS FERRY[8]
by Selden Rodman

Everything was wrong; the local slaves wore smiles,
At least on Sundays; freedom could be bought;
There was no cotton within fifty miles.
Brown and his eighteen roughnecks never thought
To stand, but the attack went un-rehearsed
And with the Shenandoah crossed, retreat
Was out of question; reckless, he dispersed
His men; no hour of withdrawal was set.

[8]From *The Amazing Year,* by Selden Rodman. Charles Scribner's Sons, publishers.

The first man to be shot was free, and black.
Liquor at Wager House began to flow.
Brown, while his time ran out, rode four miles back
To steal George Washington's pistols for a Negro.
Trapped in the engine-house, he burnt the brief
Stuart prepared, and when they beat him flat
Told gentlemanly Lee: "You . . . are the thief;
We came to free the slaves and only that . . ."

And like a thief America slept on,
Dreaming of where two angry rivers met,
And the trains howled in the mountain, and a town
Crouched like a black child, shivering and wet,
Until the voice that had aroused to murder
Before the circle of the noose had set
Screamed at the sleeping Giant, and so stirred her
She took a million lives to pay the debt.

"FORMERLY A SLAVE"
by Herman Melville

An idealized portrait by E. Vedder,
in the spring exhibition
of the National Academy, 1865

The sufferance of her race is shown,
    And retrospect of life,
Which now too late deliverance dawns upon;
    Yet is she not at strife.

Her children's children they shall know
    The good withheld from her;
And so her reverie takes prophetic cheer——
    In spirit she sees the stir.

Far down the depth of thousand years,
    And marks the revel shine;
Her dusky face is lit with sober light,
    Sibylline, yet benign.

ECHOES OF CHILDHOOD[9]
A Folk-Medley
From *Echoes of Childhood*
by Alice Corbin

UNCLE JIM

Old Uncle Jim was as blind as a mole,
But he could fiddle Virginia Reels,
Till you felt the sap run out of your heels,
Till you knew the devil had got your soul——

Down the middle and swing yo' partners,
Up agin and salute her low,
Shake yo' foot an' keep a-goin'
Down the middle an' do-se-do!

Mind yo' manners an' doan git keerless,
Swing yo' lady and bow full low,
S'lute yo' partner an' turn yo' neighbor,
Gran'-right-an'-left, and aroun' you go!

DELPHY

Delphy's breast was wide and deep,
A shelf to lay a child asleep,
   Swing low, sweet chariot, swing low;
Rocking like a lifted boat
On lazy tropic seas afloat,
   Swing low, sweet chariot, swing low.

Delphy, when my mother died,
Taught me wisdom, curbed my pride,
   Swing low, sweet chariot, swing low;

[9]By permission of author.

And when she laid her body down,
It shone, a jewel, in His crown,
    Swing low, sweet chariot, swing low.

.   .   .

(*Underneath the southern moon*
I was cradled to the tune
Of the banjo and the fiddle
And the plaintive Negro croon.)

MANDY'S RELIGION

I'se got religion an' I doan care
Who knows that God an' I are square,
I wuz carryin' home my mistis' wash
When God came an' spoke to me out'n de hush.

An' I th'ew de wash up inter de air,
An' I climbed a tree to de golden stair;
Ef it hadn't a been fur Mistah Wright
I'd had ter stayed dere all de night!

.   .   .

(*Underneath the southern moon*
I was cradled to the tune
Of the banjo and the fiddle
And the plaintive Negro croon.)

.   .   .

NEGRO SPIRITUAL
by Perient Trott

Sable is my throat
golden the cable
golden the column of its sound—
firm, my transplanted feet
upon this soil—
deep, my roots

I am the sounding board
the maker of songs—
mine, the folk song of America!
Sensitive, my transplanted feet
to the rhythm of the earth:
deep, my roots
in the somnambulant greatness
of the earth
in the nostalgia
of my race
in the drama
of my people
uprooted
dispossessed
transplanted—
the song of America
wells full-bodied
in my throat . . .

I am the maker of songs
the voice of colony
the folk song of empire

Oh, sable is my throat. . . .
golden, the rich cable. . . .
rich, the column of my song!
Sable, sable!
Golden, golden!

Oh, sable is my throat!

THE CONGO[10]
A Study of the Negro Race
by Vachel Lindsay

I—THEIR BASIC SAVAGERY

Fat black bucks in a wine-barrel room,
Barrel-house kings, with feet unstable,

A deep roll-
ing bass
Sagged and reeled and pounded on the table,
Pounded on the table,
Beat an empty barrel with the handle of a broom,
Hard as they were able,
Boom, boom, BOOM,
With a silk umbrella and the handle of a broom,
Boomlay, boomlay, boomlay, BOOM.
THEN I had religion, THEN I had a vision.
I could not turn from their revel in derision.

More deliber-
ate. Solemnly
chanted
THEN I SAW THE CONGO, CREEPING
    THROUGH THE BLACK,
CUTTING THROUGH THE JUNGLE WITH A
    GOLDEN TRACK.
Then along that river bank
A thousand miles
Tattooed cannibals danced in files;
Then I heard the boom of the blood-lust song
And a thigh-bone beating on a tin-pan gong.

A rapidly pil-
ing climax of
speed and
racket
And "BLOOD!" screamed the whistles and the fifes
    of the warriors,
"BLOOD!" screamed the skull-faced, lean witch-doc-
    tors;
"Whirl ye the deadly voo-doo rattle,
Harry the uplands,
Steal all the cattle,
Rattle-rattle, rattle-rattle,
Bing!
Boomlay, boomlay, boomlay, BOOM!"

[10]From *The Congo & Other Poems,* by Vachel Lindsay; copyright, 1914, by The Macmillan Company. Reprinted with their permission.

With a philo-sophic pause	A roaring, epic, rag-time tune From the mouth of the Congo To the Mountains of the Moon. Death is an Elephant,
Shrilly and with a heavily accented meter	Torch-eyed and horrible, Foam-flanked and terrible. BOOM, steal the pygmies, BOOM, kill the Arabs, BOOM, kill the white men, HOO, HOO, HOO.
Like the wind in the chimney	Listen to the yell of Leopold's ghost Burning in Hell for his hand-maimed host. Hear how the demons chuckle and yell Cutting his hands off down in Hell. Listen to the creepy proclamation,
All the O sounds very golden. *Heavy ac-cents very heavy. Light accents very light. Last line whis-pered*	Blown through the lairs of the forest-nation, Blown past the white-ants' hill of clay, Blown past the marsh where the butterflies play:— "Be careful what you do, Or Mumbo-Jumbo, god of the Congo, And all of the other Gods of the Congo, Mumbo-Jumbo will hoo-doo you, Mumbo-Jumbo will hoo-doo you, Mumbo-Jumbo will hoo-doo you."

II—THEIR IRREPRESSIBLE HIGH SPIRITS

Rather shrill and high	Wild crap-shooters with a whoop and a call Danced the juba in their gambling-hall, And laughed fit to kill, and shook the town, And guyed the policemen and laughed them down With a boomlay, boomlay, boomlay, BOOM. THEN I SAW THE CONGO CREEPING THROUGH THE BLACK,
Read exactly as in first sec-tion. Lay em-phasis on the delicate ideas.	CUTTING THROUGH THE JUNGLE WITH A GOLDEN TRACK. A Negro fairyland swung into view, A minstrel river Where dreams come true.

Keep as light-
footed as pos-
sible

The ebony palace soared on high
Through the blossoming trees to the evening sky.
The inlaid porches and casements shone
With gold and ivory and elephant-bone.
And the black crowd laughed till their sides were sore
At the baboon butler in the agate door,
And the well-known tunes of the parrot band
That trilled on the bushes of that magic land.

With pom-
posity

A troop of skull-faced witch-men came
Through the agate doorway in suits of flame—
Yea, long-tailed coats with a gold-leaf crust
And hats that were covered with diamond-dust.
And the crowd in the court gave a whoop and a call

With a great
deliberation
and ghostli-
ness

And danced the juba from wall to wall.
But the witch-men suddenly stilled the throng
With a stern cold glare, and a stern old song:
"Mumbo-Jumbo will hoo-doo you." . . .

With over-
whelming as-
surance, good
cheer, and
pomp

Just then from the doorway, as fat as shotes
Came the cake-walk princes in their long red coats,
Canes with a brilliant lacquer shine,
And tall silk hats that were red as wine.
And they pranced with their butterfly partners there,
Coal-black maidens with pearls in their hair,

With growing
speed and
sharply
marked
dance-
rhythm

Knee-skirts trimmed with the jassamine sweet,
And bells on their ankles and little black feet.
And the couples railed at the chant and the frown
Of the witch-men lean, and laughed them down.
(Oh, rare was the revel, and well worth while
That made those glowering witch-men smile.)
The cake-walk royalty then began
To walk for a cake that was tall as a man
To the tune of "Boomlay, boomlay, BOOM,"

With a touch
of Negro dia-
lect, and as
rapidly as
possible to-
ward the end

While the witch-men laughed, with a sinister air,
And sang with the scalawags prancing there:
"Walk with care, walk with care,
Or Mumbo-Jumbo, god of the Congo,
And all of the other
Gods of the Congo,

Mumbo-Jumbo will hoo-doo you.
Beware, beware, walk with care,
Boomlay, boomlay, boomlay, boom,
Boomlay, boomlay, boomlay, boom,
Boomlay, boomlay, boomlay, boom,
Boomlay, boomlay, boomlay,
BOOM."

Slow philo-
sophic calm

Oh, rare was the revel, and well worth while
That made those glowering witch-men smile.

III—THE HOPE OF THEIR RELIGION

Heavy bass.
With a literal
imitation of
camp-meet-
ing racket
and trance

A good old Negro in the slums of the town
Preached at a sister for her velvet gown.
Howled at a brother for his low-down ways,
His prowling, guzzling, sneak-thief days.
Beat on the Bible till he wore it out
Starting the jubilee revival shout.
And some had visions, as they stood on chairs,
And sang of Jacob, and the golden stairs.
And they all repented, a thousand strong,
From their stupor and savagery and sin and wrong,
And slammed with their hymn-books till they shook
    the room
With "Glory, glory, glory,"
And "Boom, boom, Boom."
THEN I SAW THE CONGO, CREEPING
    THROUGH THE BLACK,

Exactly as in
the first sec-
tion. Begin
with terror
and power,
end with joy.
Sung to the
tune of "Hark,
ten thousand
harps and
voices"

CUTTING THROUGH THE JUNGLE WITH A
    GOLDEN TRACK.
And the gray sky opened like a new-rent veil
And showed the apostles with their coats of mail.
In bright white steel they were seated round,
And their fire-eyes watched where the Congo wound.
And the twelve Apostles, from their thrones on high,
Thrilled all the forest with their heavenly cry:
"Mumbo-Jumbo will die in the jungle;
Never again will he hoo-doo you,
Never again will he hoo-doo you."

	Then along that river, a thousand miles,
With growing	The vine-snared trees fell down in files.
deliberation	Pioneer angels cleared the way
and joy	For a Congo paradise, for babes at play,
	For sacred capitals, for temples clean.
	Gone were the skull-faced witch-men lean;
In a rather	There, where the wild ghost-gods had wailed,
high key—as	A million boats of the angels sailed
delicately as	With oars of silver, and prows of blue,
possible	And silken pennants that the sun shone through.
	'Twas a land transfigured, 'twas a new creation.
To the tune	Oh, a singing wind swept the Negro nation,
of "Hark, ten	And on through the backwoods clearing flew:—
thousand	"Mumbo-Jumbo is dead in the jungle.
harps and	Never again will he hoo-doo you.
voices"	Never again will he hoo-doo you."

Redeemed were the forests, the beasts and the men,
And only the vulture dared again

Dying down   By the far lone mountains of the moon
into a pene-   To cry, in the silence, the Congo tune:
trating, ter-   "Mumbo-Jumbo will hoo-doo you,
rified whisper Mumbo-Jumbo will hoo-doo you.

Mumbo . . . Jumbo . . . will . . . hoo-doo . . . you."

BLACK TAMBOURINE[11]
by Hart Crane

The interests of a black man in a cellar
Mark tardy judgment on the world's closed door.
Gnats toss in the shadow of a bottle,
And a roach spans a crevice in the floor.

[11]From *The Collected Poems of Hart Crane*. Reprinted by permission of Liveright Publishing Corporation.

Aesop, driven to pondering, found
Heaven with the tortoise and the hare;
Fox brush and sow ear top his grave
And mingling incantations on the air.

The black man, forlorn in the cellar,
Wanders in some mid-kingdom, dark, that lies,
Between his tambourine, stuck on the wall,
And, in Africa, a carcass quick with flies.

ELEGY ON A NORDIC WHITE PROTESTANT[12]
by John Gould Fletcher

Lazy petals of magnolia-bloom float down the sluggish river,
Borne by the wind from deep bayous, where loose lithe boughs are
    trailing
Grey-green beards of Spanish moss; white flowers in the sluggish cur-
    rent;
But the black tide beneath them is rising.

Lofty and still, the trees
Stand like a columned ballroom for the dance
Of fireflies; green-white they spurt and flicker.
Down in the marsh the bullfrogs with bassoons
Hold a deep raucous bass above the chorus
Of katydid and cricket in the stillness:—
Remote and lone, the trees
Look down long clearings, grey-green in dense moonlight;
The hound-dogs bay, and glimmering lights peep out
From low dark cabin-doors.
But the white house keeps cold and high, aloof,
Its classic columns not yet given to decay:
It brings a day
To memory, when under its broad roof
Over unrotted and new-polished floors,
There flowed no grace

[12]From *XXIV Elegies*, copyright, 1935, by John Gould Fletcher. Published by
Writers' Editions, Santa Fe, New Mexico.

Like this, nor was there ever seen a face
So white, unearthly fair
As yours:—
But the moon in the woods knows better, for it has looked on despair.

Pale petals of magnolia-bloom thrust out white cups for coolness,
Magnolia-buds thrust up, hold themselves taut to the thunder
That beats across the ragged hills to southward
Its dull deep-muttering drum;
Between snake-fences staggering off over fields,
The strong green plumes of warrior-corn, the white dense clumps of
    cotton,
And miles away the strong and eddying current of the river
Fretting the green levees, night after night in the moonlight,
Where the strong black tide is rising, ever rising,
As it would rise forever.

Voices speak in the trees;
Voices shake in the leaves, as the leaves shake before thunder;
Ku-klux, the faint snick-snick of rifles,
Galloping horses, voices, crackle of twigs on the trail.
White figures flit past swiftly
Dissolving into moonbeams, that dapple the earth with shadows;
For tonight the eternal forest
Is filled with the hunt for blood.

(When a dry rain of mandolins, pulsing and fluttering, beats on the
    stiffened tuberoses
That hold up their chaste waxlike chalices, chill to the breeze of the
    night,
That runs out of red-gullied hills, and creaks through the pomegranate
    bushes
That flare out in startling scarlet all down the long avenue,
Under the sombre magnolias with the trail of the Milky Way going
    southwestward,
You whom I loved so of old—you whom I hold in my heart still—
I shall often think that I come back only to you).

Slowly, the moon, bronzed by the heat of the day,
Passes, a lithe brown fluteplayer;—

Slowly on streets where the dust hovers and settles,
From the mule-drays that rattled along
Bearing their bales in the morning;
Swinging the brown-bagged cotton,
Out of the fields to the town;—
Slowly the red earth cracks, and the white fronts of the houses
Stare into hopeless silence;
And slowly rises the river,
Seething, chocolate-brown;
Stealthily drifts on its current,
Sweeping, with many a shiver,
Over the cottonwoods, roosting on sandbanks, spectrally grey and
    surprising:
Writhing their branches to the sky;—
Slowly the black tide is rising.

Batter on your banjoes, roar you golden saxophones,
Beat your sullen bass-drums, jingle loud your tambourines,
Shout loud deep trombone voices, swell in amazing chorus;
White mobs of lynchers, vain is your work;
Vain is the web of your terror, you pass like mist in the morning:
Shifting and ebbing forever, leaving the land dark and naked;
Under the hail of your bullets, the river runs on still triumphant,
And the black tide in its banks is rising,
Rising, forever, rising!

THE BIRD AND THE TREE[13]
by Ridgely Torrence

> Blackbird, blackbird in the cage,
> There's something wrong tonight.
> Far off the sheriff's footfall dies,
> The minutes crawl like last year's flies
> Between the bars, and like an age
> The hours are long tonight.

[13]From Poems, by Ridgely Torrence, copyright, 1941, by The Macmillan Company. Used with their permission.

The sky is like a heavy lid
Out here beyond the door tonight.
What's that? A mutter down the street.
What's that? A sound of yells and feet.
For what you didn't do or did
You'll pay the score tonight.

No use to reek with reddened sweat,
No use to whimper and to sweat.
They've got the rope; they've got the guns,
They've got the courage and the guns;
And that's the reason why tonight;
No use to ask them any more.
They'll fire the answer through the door—
You're out to die tonight.

There where the lonely cross-road lies,
There is no place to make replies;
But silence, inch by inch, is there,
And the right limb for a lynch is there;
And a lean daw waits for both your eyes,
Blackbird.

Perhaps you'll meet again some place.
Look for the mask upon the face:
That's the way you'll know them there—
A white mask to hide the face:
And you can halt and show them there
The things that they are deaf to now,
And they can tell you what they meant—
To wash the blood with blood. But how
If you are innocent?

Blackbird singer, blackbird mute,
They choked the seed you might have found.
Out of a thorny field you go—
For you it may be better so—
And leave the sowers of the ground
To eat the harvest of the fruit,
Blackbird.

THE LYNCHING BEE[14]
by William Ellery Leonard

I

Here at the crossroads is the night so black
It swallows tree and thicket, barn and stack,
Even though the sickle of the new moon hang,
Keen as a knife, bent like a boomerang,
A witch's bangle in the Zodiac.

Black on the crossroads . . . but in skies off yonder
There broods a fiery gloom, a hectic glow,
Like the last twilight just before the thunder,
Or omens of doomed soothsayers, long ago . . .
To-day the veriest dog or mule would know
It only means a lighted town thereunder.

II

Honk, Honk!
On to the fork! Honk! Honk!
You hear?
From hand-squeezed bulb and belching conch!
Honk! Honk!
Down in the hollow now, but near.
How many there?—
Honk! Honk!
Topping the hill off there—
Behind the foremost cone of glare—
That, like the swift typhoon,
Sweeps on along each length of rut
And makes their ridges as clear cut
As in Uganda at high noon
Stand out the Mountains of the Moon.

[14]From *The Lynching Bee and Other Poems,* by William Ellery Leonard, copyright, 1920, by B. W. Huebsch, Inc., 1948, by Charlotte Charlton Leonard.

Honk,—for the brasses and cat-gut!
Honk, Honk,—for cymbals and bassoon!
New times, new music and new fun!
Though Bottom's gone and Oberon,
With Satyr, Dwarf, and pet Baboon,
Midsummer nights have still their rites.
Honk, Honk: "We've caught the coon!"
("Honk" means they've caught the coon.)

III

They stop—they jerk—they chug—they back.
And in a monstrous ring they park,
With ghostly cones converging from the dark
Upon a central tree all split and black,
Whose limbs and leaves are caverned out of sight
In the eternity of night.
It's like a magic circle where
Snake-dancers, stripèd, brown, and bare,
With pouch in waving hand and horns on hair,
In old times swayed and swung
And called on Tunga-Tung,
With nasal *ang* and gutteral *unk*
Around a lightning-blasted trunk,
Or hissed in chorus with a serpent-stare.
Yet nothing like this there—
It's only the sign-board of the town's,
And crossroads cottonwood by Farmer Brown's.

IV

It's only twelve true men in pants and coats
(The sort who pay their bills, and cast their votes,
Or file to jury boxes on hot afternoons) . . .
Each with a finger on a trigger,
Dragging by ropes, around his gullet tied,
With hobbled legs and arms well lashed to side,

The best of all buffoons—
A banjo-boy and jigger,
A hovel-doorway bawler of coarse tunes.
Like Caliban he shuffles, only bigger;
Or ourang-outang, only larger-eyed—
A bandy-leggèd nigger,
Quite jerky, but all silent down inside.

V

They take the rope off at the tree—perhaps
Won't hang him after all?—These humorous chaps!
Just make him dance amid the glare
For women-folk and boys and girls back there,
Still in their seats?
Make him show off his feats?—
Stand on his head-piece while he eats
Hoe-cakes or possum sweets?
Or turn him up, and have him wag his ears;
Or wriggle and wrinkle scalp and brow,
Like a fly-bitten back of Holstein cow,
And throw from pate a bowl or plate,
While underneath he grins and leers?—
He'll butt his thick skull 'gainst the trunk, I think,
And then draw back, guffaw, and wink.

VI

Not so. They pay a chain out link by link.
Hear it rattle, hear it clink!
A good stout chain so much can do!—
As dancing bear and old-time showman knew,
Or bloodhound leashed at kennel door in straw.
And down along the Nile,
With Pharaoh's Sphinx in view,
The Coptic coolies, with a chain or two
Around his belly, tail, and jaw,

Aboard the freighter hoist the crocodile
For Circus or for Zoo—
A stout chain holds,
Come fear or fire, whatever's in its folds.

VII

They strip him, overalls and shirt,
They set his back against the tree,
They wind the links so tight about,
In girdles two and three. . . .
And yet it hardly seems to hurt,—
For not a word says he.
Honk! Honk!

VIII

He stands five fathoms deep in glare agrin.
Honk, Honk! Honk, Honk!
His skin-bark on the tree bark-skin,
Trunk grafted on to trunk.
Honk! Honk! . . .
The graft should take, for they are close of kin,—
Both sprung of one old soil of earth,
Both fed on rain and air and dirt from birth,
Both tough and stark and thin . . .

IX

One steps with jack-knife up. And he
Will cut the bark—of which dark tree?
Nigger or cottonwood?—With that
He gelds him like a colt or cat!
But the coon's caterwauls and wails
(Honk, Honk! Honk, Honk!)
Fall thin and blurred and flat—
While every conch-horn at him rails:

"No more he'll spawn in bush or bed,
With cocaine crazed, with whiskey drunk,
A charcoal woolly head,
Or yellow half-breed brat!"
Honk, Honk!

X

Another comes with brush and pot,
And smears him over, as with ointment hot.
Honk! Honk!
Good fellow, at your trellised house in town,
You boil the tar to indigo and brown,
Shimmering in sunshine, bubbling to the brim—
Why waste it at the crossroads here on him?
Tar on your driveway, rolled in grit,
Makes you a roadbed firm and fit;
Tar on your upturned row-boat sinks
In all the nail-holes, joints, and chinks;
Tar on your gadding daughter's white kid shoe
Was black, and tickled you all through;
But, brother, with the brush and pot,
Tar does no good on hide of Hottentot—
Or have you feathers in a bag or two?—
If so, by now, he'd just as lief as not.
Honk! Honk!

XI

With rags, and straw, and sticks, and other toys,
In run the women-folk and girls and boys.
They'll prod his ribs? tickle his arm-pits? sop
His sweating cheeks, as with a pantry mop?
Such crossroads pranks are not just right
For decent town-folk, it would seem. . . .
(Or is this only a midsummer dream
In innocent midnight?) . . .

Besides they haven't the heart. They drop
Their knickknacks at black ankles and bare feet,
And cool him from the spouts of cans
(Fetched from below-stairs, under washing pans
Porcelain-lined and scoured so white.)
And then they all, excepting one, retreat,
Back through the length of light.

XII

This one is honored over every other,—
She is the dead child's Mother.

And the two glare and glare
At one another
In two eternities of hate and pain,
Yet with such monstrous union in despair,
Such hideous sameness in their haggard shapes,
The one, the other,
That you would say the twain
Seemed like a savage sister and twin-brother
Dying of hunger out among the apes.

XIII

Her hand is clutching her unsuckled breast—
You know the rest:
The bloody curls, the dainty skirt a shred,
The sprawling hand-prints on the legs and head,
Her body's little body in a shed. . . .
Then down she kneels;
You see her hunched back and her upturned heels. . . .
But not the scratch and scratch,
Not the small flame that tips the second match. . . .
And not her hands, her face, her hank of hair,—
As when a Java woman kneels in prayer,
Under a temple-hut of thatch,
Before some devil-idol standing lone,—
Not far from jungles and the tiger's lair,—

Carved from the teak-wood to a jet-black face,
With Pagan wrinkles, curving pair by pair,
With set grimace,
And two great eyeballs, staring white in stone. . . .
Whilst smoke curls roofward from its hidden base . . .
The Mother rises . . . will depart . . .
Her duty done . . . and her desire. . . .
And as she turns, you see a strange
And quiet rapture of most uncouth change.
For from her burning marrow, her crazed heart,
She has transferred the fire
Of horror and despair
To the dumb savage there. . . .
She has transferred, she thinks, the fire to him.
Honk, Honk! let lights be dim!
(And now the lights are dim.) . . .

XIV

And for a moment is the night so black
It swallows tree and coon and all the pack,
And lets the sickle of the new moon hang,
Keen as a knife, bent like a boomerang,
A witch's bangle in the Zodiac.

XV

Gone is the light that played upon the tree,
But at the cottonwood's own base
Another light now takes its place—
And there is still so much for us to see.
Honk! Honk!
There have been many bonfires on the earth,
Born out of many moods and needs of men:
As when the maskers, in their twilight mirth
On Wessex heaths, would burn Guy Fawkes again;
As when the bustling country-side in dread
Against the Armada's coming set the beacons,

In the heroic English days, on Beachy Head,
When the midsummer sea-winds blew;
As when the village dames and Yankee deacons
Out on the common had a barbecue;
As when the boys in South and North
Still make the boxes blaze and crackle on the Fourth.
The ghouls and witches too
In olden times and regions far away
Danced at their wonted rendezvous
Upon the Brocken on the first of May,
Screaming round the bonfire's light
All through Walpurgis Night.—
Honk! Honk!

There is much fascination in a flame,—
Not least, whenever it has sprung
In intertwining tongue and tongue,
And left the one small spot from whence it came—
Faster, faster, higher, higher,
Shapes of wing, and wave, and lyre,
Shapes of demon-heads and peaked caps
And flying smocks, and shreds and scraps
Of all fantastic things without a name.
Tongue after tongue in middle air—
Snatched from existence, how and where?—
There is much fascination in a flame—
Not least, when it is yellow, blue, and red,
With blackness for a background and a frame,
Still fuel-fed
With straw and wood and tar and kerosene,
And some organic matter still alive.—
Its witcheries of color, how they strive!—
Even though some smudge and smoke may get between.

XVI

Yet two vast bloodshot eyeballs by their might
Out-top the flame, though from the flame their light—

Two eyeballs wrought (like eyeballs of the steer's
Or dog's, or cat's, or woodchuck's, or a deer's)
By one blind Nature in a mammal's womb,—
By one Herself with neither eyes nor ears,
Nor birth, nor breath, nor doom.

The two vast eyeballs grow and grow,
Till, to the masters of the revels,
They seem the eyeballs of the devil's
Ascending from hell-fire down below.
The masters will not have it so:
A pole, all glowing charcoal at the tip,—
Zip, Zip! Zip, Zip!
Honk, Honk! Honk, Honk!
And the blind savage at the flaming tree
No more will glare so monstrously.

XVII

But on the crossroads our midsummer dream
Converts each flame into a scream, a scream—
A shriek, a shriek!
The horns honk at them as a hose at fire;
But still with every honk they come,
Shriek after shriek,
But fiercer, faster, higher!
(And all the while before, he was as dumb
As Roman martyr, schooled to turn the cheek.)
Honk, honk, away to left and right!—
Between the honking and the shrieking black
The odds (awhile) are ten to one to-night
In favor of the blazing maniac!
All ancient Africa is in his yells:
The wounded zebra's neighing, the gazelle's
Fierce whinny at the salt-lick, and the goat's;
The roars of lions, with distended throats,
Over the moonlit rocks for hollow hunger;
The bellowing elephants, with jaws agape,

And lifted trunks that thrash across their backs
Like writhing pythons or the great sea-conger,
Their monstrous hindlegs bogged beyond escape
In fire-swept jungles off their beaten tracks.
All Africa is in the Negro's shrieks:
The forests with their thousand parrot-beaks,
From Nile and Congo to the Cape;
But the Gorilla, the man-ape,
With his broad, hairy, upright chest,
Seems to out-scream the rest.
All Africa is in his agony:
The human ladings at the western coast,
The slave-ship, and the storm at sea,
The naked bodies (never very old)—
Dragged, sick and crippled, from the fetid hold
And over the pitching gunwales tossed,
Both male and female, overboard,
While sharks, careening on their backs,
In the green swells with scudding foam astreak,
Ate up the blacks,
And crew and captain prayed the Lord,
Or crammed fresh oakum in the leak.
All Africa is on his lips:
The million sweats, the million bloody whips,
The million ankles festering in a cord—
The unborn baby still between the hips,
The bent gray head along the rice-swamp humming,
"O Massa Gawd, I'se coming."

XVIII

His voice has come from other times and places. . . .
And hence away it carries far and far. . . .
For in mid-darkness, level with a limb,
Above the flames and smoking tar,
Ride feather-crested heads that bob at him,
With peering faces,
There—and—there—and there!

Faces, Faces,
Sudden and weird as those that loom and peep
Upon us nightly just before we sleep.
No hands, nor arms, nor tomahawks you see,
No thighs in buck-skins dyed and slashed,
No moccasin, no foot, no knee,
Not even a copper torso brave and bare
From many a war-path scarred and gashed—
But only faces, faces, faces,
Riding in the air—
Faces, faces, faces, faces,
Feather-crested with long braided hair,
Peering with an old desire
From the gloom upon the fire,
Summoned back from Otherwhere. . . .
Summoned back from What-has-been:
"Is that a Jesuit father at the stake
Burning for his Jesus' sake?—
He hung us crosses round our necks to save—
But when the Mohawks to our village came
They killed both squaw and brave;
We Hurons put the Mumble-Jumble to the flame.
The cross it was no good to make us win—
It was bad medicine!"
And Seminole, Pawnee, and Sioux,
Apache, Blackfoot, Chippewa, and Crow,
Each gloats as if he saw anew
His own best captive of the long ago. . . .

XIX

The faces fade away. . . .
The Negro's cries
Have joined the uncouth sounds of Yesterday—
The incantations to the blood-red moon,
The ululations in the eclipse at noon,
The old palm-island lullabies
That ring-nosed crones were used to croon,
Squatting circle-wise. . . .

And the twelve Shadows to the fire fling
Great logs with fungus, spines, and rotted pith,
And great dead boughs with thin and sprawling arms
(Fetched from about a long-abandoned spring,
And toad-stool woodlots of surrounding farms)
As if to cage in wickerwork therewith
(Like the wild people of a South-sea myth)
The Demon-in-fire from everything it harms. . . .
The Negro's corpse will take strange shapes,
As the flames gnaw it, flesh and bone;
But neither men shall see, nor apes,
For it shall burn from now alone. . . .

Alone . . . and up and up . . . and down and down. . . .
While honkers honk it back to town.

XX

At last the stench, or glow of embers, brings
The wolves, or wolf-like things. . . .
Such as on earthquake midnights prowl around
Smoulder of fallen beams and littered ground,
And tear from dead hands golden finger-rings.
But though they crouch in slow two-leggèd stealth,
Their hunt is not for wealth.
They paw into the cinders, as with hooks. . . .
Snatch something out,
With gloating, starveling looks . . .
A bit of rib . . . or skull . . . or crup . . .
Hot ash and finger knuckle . . .
They wrap them up,
And putter round about . . .
And chuckle . . .
And foot it off and down the road,
Past the weasel, skunk, and toad,
The barnyard rat,
The hooting owl and the whirring bat.

XXI

But over the spot of glowing embers, listen,
The poplar's leaves are rustling like the rain
That patters on my garden-shrubs by night. . . .
The dew may glisten,
The south-wind come this way again,
And wander thither,
But the charred cottonwood has caught the blight. . . .
Its leaves shall wither.
Here on the fork, except that spot of red
(Still fierce as some primordial desire),
All lust is dead:
The lust to breed, the lust to burn;
The rut of flesh, the glut of fire. . . .
Lift up the head,
If still you can, and turn
To the great spaces of the skies.
Black . . . black . . . all black . . .
The moon has set,—perhaps elsewhere to hang,
Keen as a knife, bent like a boomerang,
A witch's bangle in the Zodiac . . .
Black . . . black . . . all black . . .
Though dawn be pregnant with her enterprise,
And stars perhaps will keep . . .
Black . . . black . . . and over yonder,
The glow is gone from all the town thereunder . . .
And all the people sleep . . . and sleep . . . and sleep.*

    *(You cringe and shrink?—
    It makes your own eyes in their sockets ache?—
    O squeamish listener, but think
    It's all a midnight dream, and no one is awake;
    And in the morning, with the bobolink,
    We'll see together, you and I,
    The flowers, the fields, the sun, the sky,
    And the magnolia blossoms, white and pink.)

NICE DAY FOR A LYNCHING[15]
by Kenneth Patchen

The bloodhounds look like sad old judges
In a strange court. They point their noses
At the Negro jerking in the tight noose;
His feet spread crow-like above these
Honorable men who laugh as he chokes.

I don't know this black man.
I don't know these white men.

But I know that one of my hands
Is black, and one white. I know that
One part of me is being strangled,
While another part horribly laughs.

Until it changes,
I shall be forever killing; and be killed.

NEGROES[16]
by Maxwell Bodenheim

The loose eyes of an old man
Shone aloof upon his boyish face;
And a sluggish innocence
Hugged his dull, brown skin.
He sang a hymn borrowed from his elders
And his voice resembled
A quavering, feverish laugh
Softened in a swaying cradle.
His life had found a refuge in his voice,
And the rest of him was under-nourished flesh
Ignorant of life and death.

[15]By permission of New Directions.
[16]By permission of author.

Centuries of oppression
Became a mute, infinitely compassionate
Background for this child's refrain.
His mother shuffled out upon the porch.
Slowly her dark brown face resolved
Into the hushed and sulky look
Of one who stands within a dim-walled trap.
Lazily uncertain,
She raised the boy into her arms.
Then her voice swung in the air
Like a quavering, feverish laugh
Softened in a long-forgotten cradle.

LYNCHED NEGRO[17]
by Maxwell Bodenheim

Your downcast, harlequin, defenceless face
Was turned to ashen flakes, and wavered up
In lightly shapeless impotence upon
The sprightly scandals of a morning wind,
The hands of other men fell on your breast,
Like scores of scorpions instinctively
Expelled from jungle-spots within their hearts.
Your blood, in fine quick problems, spattered out
Upon the morning air that studied them
And left complete, dry answers on your skin.
(Oh, what is life but cold arithmetic
Where fractions serve as subtleties and add
Refinement to the rise and fall of dull,
Blunt numbers shuffled indisputably:
And what is death but mathematics where
The numbers graduate to higher planes
And leave a "terrifying" interest?)

[17]From *Return to Emotion*, by Maxwell Bodenheim. Reprinted by permission of
Liveright Publishing Corporation.

Yet, something beyond pain within your shriek
Would indicate, black man, that sky-large brains
Can stumble in their count and recognize
An eerie, unrelenting quality
Forever in revolt against their plans.
Emotion and its choking metaphors
Insist that two times two is never quite
The four that "life" methodically brands
On nations and the ceaseless pain of men.
You were accused of tendering a strong,
Experimental hatred to the frail,
Intense obstruction of a woman's flesh,
And endlessly you squawked your innocence.
But crime and justice do not live beyond
The point where death, with one, efficient whim,
Corrects the tongues of bungling, churlish men.

POEM TO NEGRO AND WHITES[18]
by Maxwell Bodenheim

The elevator rises, Negro men
Receive from Whites a condescending, slight,
Forever draped removal—voice and pen
Intensifying sugar half-contrite.
A quiet, level spontaneity
Springs only where familiar burdens pile,
Far from the hired, night-club gaiety,
The inexpensive speech, the tactful smile.
The radio commentator rolls his trite
Evasions, taste of soap within his mouth.
Newspapermen who know the truth must write:
"The delicate race question of the South."
The South!—for years, astute, coarse, windy bands
Of men with venom blackening their lips
Have ruled the South, but they are not the lands,
The loads, the common, homely needs and whips.

[18]By permission of author.

They are the ones who spur the lynchers' feet:
They scurry out to spread old lie and smear.
Without them, southern Negroes, Whites could meet
And plan sane compromise within one year.
The soldiers in the fox-holes, black and white,
Must function with reliance and respect,
And some who march back from pain-welded night
Will shoulder memories close and erect.
For in the centuries that seem to lift
Almost too imperceptibly for hope,
Equalities have been a threatened gift
Wrenched from the dim light where men thrash and grope.
This much we know—a solid meeting sheers
From arduous, scarcely noticed brotherhood:
The bread, the stumbling labor shared for years,
The mutual rescues, quiet, understood.

A COMMUNICATION TO NANCY CUNARD[19]
by Kay Boyle

These are not words set down for the rejected
Nor for outcasts cast by the mind's pity
Beyond the aid of lip or hand or from the speech
Of fires lighted in the wilderness by lost men
Reaching in fright and passion to each other.
This is not for the abandoned to hear.

It begins in the dark on a box-car floor, the groaning timber
Stretched from bolt to bolt above the freight-train wheels
That grind and cry aloud like hounds upon the trail, the breathing
    weaving
Unseen within the dark from mouth to nostril, nostril to speaking mouth.
This is the theme of it, stated by one girl in a box-car saying:
"Christ, what they pay you don't keep body and soul together."
"Where was you working?" "Working in a mill-town."

The other girl in the corner saying: "Working the men when we could
    get them."
"Christ, what they pay you," wove the sound of breathing, "don't keep
    shoes on your feet.
Don't feed you. That's why we're shoving on."
(This is not for Virginia Price or Ruby Bates, the white girls dressed
like boys to go; not for Ozie Powell, six years in a cell playing the harp
he played tap-dancing on the box-car boards; not for Olen Montgomery,
the blind boy travelling towards Memphis that night, hopping a ride to
find a doctor who could cure his eyes; not for Eugene Williams or
Charlie Weems, not for Willie Robertson nor for Leroy and Andy
Wright, thirteen years old the time in March they took him off the train
in Paint Rock, Alabama; this is not for Clarence Norris or Haywood
Patterson, sentenced three times to die.)

    This is for the sheriff with a gold lodge pin
    And for the jury venireman who said: "Now, mos' folk don't go on
    And think things out. The Bible never speaks
    Of sexual intercourses. It jus' says a man knows a woman.
    So after Cain killed Abel he went off and knew a woman
    In the land of Nod. But the Bible tells as how
    There couldn't be no human folk there then.
    Now, jus' put two and two together. Cain had off-spring
    In the land of Nod so he musta had him a female baboon
    Or chimpanzee or somethin' like it.
    And that's how the nigger race begun."
This is for the Sunday-school teacher with the tobacco-plug
Who addressed the jury, the juice splattering on the wall,
Pleading: "Whether in overalls or furs a woman is protected by the
    Alabama law
Against the vilest crime the human species knows. Now, even dogs
    choose their mates,
But these nine boys are lower than the birds of the air,
Lower than the fish in the sea, lower than the beasts of the fields.
There is a law reaching down from the mountain-tops to the swamps
    and caves——
It's the wisdom of the ages, there to protect the sacred parts of the
    female species
Without them having to buckle around their middles
Six-shooters or some other method of defense."

This is set down for the others: people who go and come,
Open a door and pass through it, walk in the streets
With the shops lit, loitering, lingering, gazing.
This is for two men riding, Deputy Sheriff Sandlin, Deputy Sheriff
    Blacock,
With Ozie Powell, handcuffed. Twelve miles out of Cullman
They shot him through the head.

THE TESTIMONY

Haywood Patterson:	Victoria Price:
"So here goes an I shell try	
Faithfully an I possibly can	"I
Reference to myself in particularly	cain't
And concerning the other boys personal pride	remember."
And life time upto now.	
You must be patience with me and remember	"I
Most of my English is not of much interest	cain't
And that I am continually	remember."
Stopping and searching for the word."	

So here goes and I shall try faithfully as possible to tell you as I understand if not mistaken that Olen Montgomery, who was part blind then,
kept saying because of the dark there was inside the box-car and outside it: "It sure don't seem to me we're getting anywheres. It sure don't
seem like it to me." I and my three comrades whom were with me,
namely Roy Wright and his brother Andy and Eugene Williams, and
about my character I have always been a good natural sort of boy, but
as far as I am personally concerned about those pictures of me in the
papers, why they are more or less undoubtedly not having the full likeness of me for I am a sight better-looking than those pictures make me
out. Why all my life I spent in and around working for Jews in their
stores and so on and I have quite a few Jew friends whom can and
always have gave me a good reputation as having regards for those
whom have regards for me. The depression ran me away from home,
I was off on my way to try my very best to find some work some else-

where but misfortune befalled me without a moving cause. For it is events and misfortune which happens to people and how some must whom are less fortunate have their lives taken from them and how people die in chair for what they do not do.

THE SPIRITUAL FOR NINE VOICES

I went last night to a turkey feast (Oh, God, don't fail your children now!)
My people were sitting there the way they'll sit in heaven
With their wings spread out and their hearts all singing
Their mouths full of food and the table set with glass
(Oh, God, don't fail your children now!)
There were poor men sitting with their fingers dripping honey
All the ugly sisters were fair. I saw my brother who never had a penny
With a silk shirt on and a pair of golden braces
And gems strewn through his hair.

(Were you looking, Father, when the sheriffs came in?
Was your face turned towards us when they had their say?)

There was baked sweet potato and fried corn pone
There was eating galore, there was plenty in the horn.
(Were you there when Victoria Price took the stand?
Did you see the state attorney with her drawers in his hand?
Did you hear him asking for me to burn?)

There were oysters cooked in amplitude
There was sauce in every mouth.
There was ham done slow in spice and clove
And chicken enough for the young and the old.

(Was it you stilled the waters on horse-swapping day
When the mob came to the jail? Was it you come out in a long tail coat
Come dancing high with the word in your mouth?)

I saw my sister who never had a cent
Come shaking and shuffling between the seats.
Her hair was straight and her nails were pointed
Her breasts were high and her legs double-jointed.

(Oh, God, don't fail your children now!)

THE SENTENCE

Hear how it goes, the wheels of it travelling fast on the rails
   The box-cars, the gondolas running drunk through the night.
Hear the long high wail as it flashes through stations unlit
   Past signals ungiven, running wild through a country
A time when sleepers rouse in their beds and listen
   And cannot sleep again.
Hear it passing in no direction, to no destination
Carrying people caught in the box-cars, trapped on the coupled chert-
   cars
(Hear the rattle of gravel as it rides whistling through the day and
   night.)
Not the old or the young on it, nor people with any difference in their
   color or shape,
Not girls or men, negroes or white, but people with this in common:
People that no one had use for, had nothing to give to, no place to offer
But the cars of a freight-train careening through Paint Rock, through
   Memphis,
Through town after town without halting.
The loose hands hang down, and swing with the swing of the train in
   the darkness,
Holding nothing but poverty, syphilis white as a handful of dust, taking
   nothing as baggage
But the sound of the harp Ozie Powell is playing or the voice of Mont-
   gomery
Half-blind in oblivion saying: "It sure don't seem to me like we're
   getting anywheres.
It don't seem to me like we're getting anywheres at all."

(1937)

THE TRIAL[20]
by Muriel Rukeyser

The South is green with coming spring; revival
flourishes in the fields of Alabama. Spongy with rain,
plantations breathe April: carwheels suck mud in the roads,
the town expands warm in the afternoons. At night the black boy
teeters no-handed on a bicycle, whistling The St. Louis Blues,
blood beating, and hot South. A red brick courthouse
is vicious with men inviting death. Array your judges; call your jurors;
    come,
here is your justice, come out of the crazy jail.
Grass is green now in Alabama; Birmingham dusks are quiet
relaxed and soft in the park, stern at the yards:
a hundred boxcars shunted off to sidings, and the hoboes
gathering grains of sleep in forbidden corners.
In all the yards: Atlanta, Chattanooga,
Memphis, and New Orleans, the cars, and no jobs.

Every night the mail-planes burrow the sky,
carrying postcards to laughing girls in Texas,
passionate letters to the Charleston virgins,
words through the South: and no reprieve,
no pardon, no release.
A blinded statue attends before the courthouse,
bronze and black men lie on the grass, waiting,
the khaki dapper National Guard leans on its bayonets.
But the air is populous beyond our vision:
all the people's anger finds its vortex here
as the mythic lips of justice open, and speak.

Hammers and sickles are carried in a wave of strength, fire-tipped,
swinging passionately ninefold to a shore.
Answer the back-thrown Negro face of the lynched, the flat forehead
    knotted,

[20]From *Theory of Flight,* by Muriel Rukeyser. Reprinted by permission of Yale University Press.

the eyes showing a wild iris, the mouth a welter of blood,
answer the broken shoulders and these twisted arms.
John Brown, Nat Turner, Toussaint stand in this courtroom,
Dred Scott wrestles for freedom there in the dark corner,
all our celebrated shambles are repeated here: now again
Sacco and Vanzetti walk to a chair, to the straps and rivets
and the switch spitting death and Massachusetts' will.
Wreaths are brought out of history
here are the well-nourished flowers of France, grown strong on blood,
Caesar twisting his thin throat toward conquest,
            turning north from the Roman laurels,
the Istrian galleys slide again to sea.
How they waded through bloody Godfrey's Jerusalem!
How the fires broke through Europe, and the rich
and the tall jails battened on revolution!
The fastidious Louis', cousins to the sun, stamping
those ribboned heels on Calas, on the people;
the lynched five thousand of America.
Tom Mooney from San Quentin, Herndon: here
is an army for audience
            all resolved
to a gobbet of tobacco, spat, and the empanelled hundred,
a jury of vengeance, the cheap pressed lips, the narrow eyes like hard-
            ware;
the judge, his eye-sockets and cheeks dark and immutably secret,
the twisting mouth of the prosecuting attorney.

Nine dark boys spread their breasts against Alabama,
schooled in the cells, fathered by want.
    Mother: one writes: they treat us bad. If they send
    us back to Kilby jail, I think I shall kill myself.
    I think I must hang myself by my overalls.

Alabama and the South are soft with spring;
in the North, the seasons change, sweet April, December and the air
loaded with snow. There is time for meetings
during the years, they remaining in prison.

                              In the Square
a crowd listens, carrying banners.
Overhead, boring through the speaker's voice, a plane
circles with a snoring of motors revolving in the sky,
drowning the single voice. It does not touch
the crowd's silence. It circles. The name stands:
Scottsboro.

THEY ARE OURS[21]
On the Scottsboro Boys
by A. B. Magil

They are ours; we claim them and we claim
what they have suffered, upon our backs is laid
the stone of their dark days, and we have made
their name our name.

These are the nine black boys, the stubborn fruit
sprung from a sour soil manured with blood;
these are the lives covered with lynchers' mud,
withered at the root.

But withered root becomes seed, and death becomes birth,
and over all the Southland, on every farm
the nine black boys are planted, rise ripe and warm
through the bleeding earth.

You who have lynched three years of their lives, who have taken
the sun from their sky and buried their young strength away,
see; on our shoulders we bear a new sun, a new day
that shall not darken.

Though you have drawn your noose around their throat,
we come, the millions that do not beg or haggle,
to bind them to us with the flesh of struggle
and revolt.

[21]Originally published in *International Literature* magazine.

RECAPITULATIONS[2]-
by Karl Shapiro

XI

We waged a war within a war,
 A cause within a cause;
The glory of it was withheld
 In keeping with the laws
Whereby the public need not know
The pitfalls of the status quo.

Love was the reason for the blood:
 The black men of our land
Were seen to walk with pure white girls
 Laughing and hand in hand.
This most unreasonable state
No feeling White would tolerate.

We threw each other from the trams,
 We carried knives and pipes,
We sacrificed in self-defense
 Some of the baser types,
But though a certain number died
You would not call it fratricide.

The women with indignant tears
 Professed to love the Blacks,
And dark and woolly heads still met
 With heads of English flax.
Only the cockney could conceive
Of any marriage so naïve.

Yet scarcely fifty years before
   Their fathers rode to shoot
The undressed aborigines,
   Though not to persecute.
A fine distinction lies in that
They have no others to combat.

By order of the high command
   The black men were removed
To the interior and north;
   The crisis thus improved,
Even the women could detect
Their awful fall from intellect.

THE SOUTHERNER[23]
by Karl Shapiro

He entered with the authority of politeness
And the jokes died in the air. A well-made blaze
Grew round the main log in the fireplace
Spontaneously. I watched its brightness
Spread to the altered faces of my guests.
They did not like the Southerner. I did.
A liberal felt that someone should forbid
That soft voice making its soft arrests.

As when a Negro or a prince extends
His hand to an average man, and the mind
Speeds up a minute and then drops behind,
So did the conversation of my friends.
I was amused by this respectful awe
Which those hotly deny who have no prince.
I watched the frown, the stare, and the wince
Recede into attention, the arms thaw.

[23]Copyright, 1947, by The New Yorker Magazine, Inc. From *Trial of a Poet and Other Poems,* copyright, 1947, by Karl Shapiro. Reprinted by permission of Reynal and Hitchcock, Inc.

I saw my southern evil memories
Raped from my mind before my eyes, my youth
Practicing caste, perfecting the untruth
Of staking honor on the wish to please.
I saw my honor's paradox:
Grandpa, the saintly Jew, keeping his beard
In difficult Virginia, yet endeared
Of blacks and farmers, although orthodox.

The nonsense of the gracious lawn,
The fall of hollow columns in the pines,
Do these deceive more than the rusted signs
Of Jesus on the road? Can they go on
In the timeless manner of all gentlefolk
There in a culture rotted and unweeded
Where the black yoni of the South is seeded
By crooked men in denims thin as silk?

They do go on, denying still the fall
Of Richmond and man, who gently live
On the street above the violence, fugitive,
Graceful, and darling, who recall
The heartbroken country once about to flower,
Full of black poison, beautiful to smell,
Who know how to conform, how to compel,
And how from the best bush to receive a flower.

UPSTAIRS DOWNSTAIRS[24]
by Hervey Allen

The judge, who lives impeccably upstairs
With dull decorum and its implication,
Has all his servants in to family prayers,
And edifies *his* soul with exhortation.

[24]From *Carolina Chansons, Legends of the Low Country,* by Du Bose Heyward
and Hervey Allen, copyright, 1922, by Rinehart & Company, Inc.

Meanwhile his blacks live wastefully downstairs;
Not always chaste, they manage to exist
With less decorum than the judge upstairs,
And find withal a something that he missed.

This painful fact a Swede philosopher,
Who tarried for a fortnight in our city,
Remarked, one evening at the meal, before
We paralyzed him silent with our pity——

Saying the black man living with the white
Had given more than white men could requite.

PORGY, MARIA, AND BESS[25]
by Du Bose Heyward

Porgy, Maria, and Bess,
Robbins, and Peter, and Crown;
Life was a three-stringed harp
Brought from the woods to town.

Marvelous tunes you rang
From passion, and death, and birth,
You who had laughed and wept
On the warm, brown lap of the earth.

Now in your untried hands
An instrument, terrible, new,
Is thrust by a master who frowns,
Demanding strange songs of you.

God of the White and Black,
Grant us great hearts on the way
That we may understand
Until you have learned to play.

[25]By permission of Mrs. Du Bose Heyward.

MAMMY HUMS[26]
by Carl Sandburg

This is the song I rested with:
The right shoulder of a strong man I leaned on.
The face of the rain that drizzled on the short neck of a canal bcat.
The eyes of a child who slept while death went over and under.
The petals of peony pink that fluttered in a shot of wind come and gone.

This is the song I rested with:
Head, heels, and fingers rocked to the mammy humming of it, to the
    mile-off steamboat landing whistle of it.

The murmurs run with bees' wings
                    in a late summer sun.
They go and come with white surf
                      slamming on a beach all day.

  Get this.
And then you may sleep with a late afternoon slumber sun.
Then you may slip your head in an elbow knowing nothing—only sleep.
If so you sleep in the house of our song,
If so you sleep under the apple trees of our song,
Then the face of sleep must be the one face you were looking for.

JAZZ FANTASIA[27]
by Carl Sandburg

        Drum on your drums, batter on your banjoes,
        sob on the long cool winding saxophones.
        Go to it, O jazzmen.

Sling your knuckles on the bottoms of the happy
tin pans, let your trombones ooze, and go husha-
husha-hush with the slippery sand-paper.

Moan like an autumn wind high in the lonesome tree-
tops, moan soft like you wanted somebody terrible,
cry like a racing car slipping away from a motorcycle
cop, bang-bang! you jazzmen, bang altogether drums,
traps, banjoes, horns, tin cans—make two people fight
on the top of a stairway and scratch each other's eyes
in a clinch tumbling down the stairs.

Can the rough stuff . . . now a Mississippi steamboat
pushes up the night river with a hoo-hoo-hoo-oo . . .
and the green lanterns calling to the high soft stars
. . . a red moon rides on the humps of the low river
hills . . . go to it, O jazzmen.

SONGS FOR A COLORED SINGER[28]
by Elizabeth Bishop

I

A washing hangs upon the line,
     but it's not mine.
None of the things that I can see
     belong to me.
The neighbors got a radio with an aerial;
     we got a little portable.
They got a lot of closet space;
     we got a suitcase.

I say, "Le Roy, just how much are we owing?
Something I can't comprehend,
the more we got the more we spend. . . ."

He only answers, "Let's get going."
Le Roy, you're earning too much money now.

I sit and look at our back yard
   and find it very hard
that all we got for all his dollars and cents
   's a pile of bottles by the fence.
He's faithful and he's kind
   but he sure has an inquiring mind.
He's seen a lot; he's bound to see the rest,
   and if I protest
Le Roy will answer with a frown,
"Darling, when I earns I spends.
The world is wide; it still extends. . . .
I'm going to get a job in the next town."
Le Roy, you're earning too much money now.

II

The time has come to call a halt;
   and so it ends.
     He's gone off with his other friends.
     He needn't try to make amends,
'cause this occasion's all his fault.
     Through rain and dark I see his face
     across the street at Flossie's place.
     He's drinking in the warm pink glow
     to th' accompaniment of the piccolo.

The time has come to call a halt.
I met him walking with Varella
and hit him twice with my umbrella.
Perhaps that occasion was my fault,
but the time has come to call a halt.

Go drink your wine and go get tight.
   Let the piccolo play.
   I'm sick of all your fussing anyway.
   Now I'm going to go and take the bus
   and find someone monogamous.

The time has come to call a halt.
I've borrowed fifteen dollars fare
and it will take me anywhere.
For this occasion's all his fault.
The time has come to call a halt.

III

Lullaby.
Adult and child
sink to their rest.
At sea the big ship sinks and dies,
lead in its breast.

Lullaby.
Let nations rage,
let nations fall.
The shadow of the crib makes an enormous cage
upon the wall.

Lullaby.
Sleep on and on,
war's over soon.
Drop the silly, harmless toy,
pick up the moon.

Lullaby.
If they should say
you have no sense,
don't you mind them; it won't make
much difference.

Lullaby.
Adult and child
sink to their rest.
At sea the big ship sinks and dies,
lead in its breast.

IV

What's that shining in the leaves,
the shadowy leaves,
like tears when somebody grieves,
shining, shining in the leaves?

Is it dew or is it tears,
dew or tears,
hanging there for years and years
like a heavy dew of tears?

Then that dew begins to fall,
roll down and fall.
Maybe it's not tears at all.
See it, see it roll and fall.

Hear it falling on the ground,
hear, all around.
That is not a tearful sound,
beating, beating on the ground.

See it lying there like seeds,
like black seeds.
See it taking root like weeds,
faster, faster than the weeds,

all the shining seeds take root,
conspiring root,
and what curious flower or fruit
will grow from that conspiring root?

Fruit or flower? It is a face.
Yes, a face.
In that dark and dreary place
each seed grows into a face.

Like an army in a dream
the faces seem,
darker, darker, like a dream.
They're too real to be a dream.

SINGING IN THE DARK[29]
by Irma Wassall

A blind girl singing on the radio.
A blind young man "blacked on" the stage
        and guided off by a voice from the wings,
        unheard by the audience through the applause.
A blind beggar in the City of Mexico,
        sitting with his guitar on the sidewalk,
        singing *"Cielito Lindo"* with his unseeing face
        lifted to the beautiful heaven of his song,
        in the warm sun that was black to him.
All these—
Then others deliberately closing their brilliant eyes,
        looking inward, withdrawing: Roland Hayes,
                seeming almost to float across the dim
                stage to the dark polished piano;
        and Marian Anderson, at the Lincoln Memorial,
                before that enthralled, tremendous throng,
        singing in the darkness behind their own eyelids.

ON A PICTURE BY PIPPIN, CALLED "THE DEN"[30]
        To William Calfee
by Selden Rodman

Here is the way the white man's heaven felt
That day in Paoli in Jane's château,

[29]By permission of author. Originally published in *The Kansas Magazine*, 1948.
[30]From *The Amazing Year*, by Selden Rodman. Charles Scribner's Sons, publishers.

A drink or two, or three, under your belt.
Inside, the fire, and outside, the snow
Reflected what was there: a wire screen,
A bearskin and two leopard chairs, a flock
(Along the mantelpiece) of European
Porcelain dogs ascending to a clock.

But what is *here* did not exist until
Your art recalled what only children learn:
That leopards have a thousand eyes; a grill
Containing fire warms, but need not burn;
Bears can be guardians; and on a sill
Whose dogs deploy, the hands of Time are still.

DAPHNE[31]
by Selden Rodman

The god spoke once that made your girdle fall
And then was gone. Whatever magic mastered
That night your heart until its unscaled wall
Caught fire on the frozen ground, was blasted
When morning slew the dark and winter hung
On every amorous curve its classic scaffold.
Now here, now there, I watched you pose among
Desires like a marble, and was baffled
Till in a land too hot for stratagems,
Where only priests and white men are immoral,
I saw your lips sprout leaves and fingers stems;
How floating in the sea your breasts were coral,
Your eyes still brilliant but as hard as gems,
And your hair that the god had breathed upon turned laurel.

[31]From *The Amazing Year*, by Selden Rodman. Charles Scribner's Sons, publishers.

NORRIS DAM[32]
by Selden Rodman

Liberals raised this in their finest hour
  Thinking, between two worlds, to build a bridge;
The doors say "WHITE" and "COLORED," and the power
  Stokes the atomic ovens at Oak Ridge.

THE CASTLE[33]
by Sidney Alexander

I watched them playing there upon the sand:
the little white boy and the little black,
their hands happy as the hands of artists
shaping a castle of their dreams together.
And as each turret grew, each battlement—
exultant cries burst from one throat:
They danced like prospectors striking oil
at the wink of water in the tiny moat.

And then the tide, the hateful tide rolled in.
The boyhood castle crumbled. Innocence fled.
A cloud coiled and struck like a cobra.
The beach was starred with devils and with wrack.
I saw them clutched in murder before my eyes—
the grown-up white man and the grown-up black.

[32]From *The Amazing Year*, by Selden Rodman. Charles Scribner's Sons, publishers.
[33]By permission of author.

DEFEAT[34]
by Witter Bynner

> On a train in Texas German prisoners eat
> With white American soldiers, seat by seat
> While black American soldiers sit apart—
> The white men eating meat, the black men heart.
> Now, with that other war a century done,
> Not the live North but the dead South has won:
> Not yet a riven nation comes awake.
> Whom are we fighting this time, for God's sake?
> Mark well the token of the separate seat—
> It is again ourselves that we defeat.

THE STRONG SWIMMER[35]
by William Rose Benét

> I have a story fit to tell,
> In head and heart a song;
> A burning blue Pacific swell;
> A raft that was towed along.
>
> Out in the bloody Solomon Isles
> Destroyer *Gregory* gone;
> Ocean that kills for all her smiles,
> And darkness coming on.
>
> The *Gregory's* raft bobbed on the tide
> Loaded with wounded men.
> Ensign and seaman clung her side.
> Seaward she drifted then.

[34]From *Take Away the Darkness*, copyright, 1944, 1947, by Witter Bynner. Reprinted by permission of Alfred A. Knopf, Inc.

[35]From *Day of Deliverance*, copyright, 1944, by William Rose Benét. Reprinted by permission of Alfred A. Knopf, Inc.

A mess-attendant, a Negro man,
Mighty of chest and limb,
Spoke up: "I'll tow you all I can
As long as I can swim."

Naked, he wound his waist with a line;
Slipped smoothly overside,
Where the red bubble tells the brine
That sharks have sheared the tide.

"I'm goin' to tow this old craft in
Since we ain't got not one oar,"
He breathed, as the water lapped his chin;
And he inched that raft ashore.

Strongly he stroked, and long he hauled—
No breath for any song.
His wounded mates clung close, appalled.
He towed that raft along.

Clear to the eye the darkening swell
Where glimmering dangers glide;
The raft of sailors grimed from Hell
Afloat on a smoky tide—

And a dark shoulder and muscled arm
Lunging, steady and strong.
The messman, their brother, who bears a charm,
Is towing their raft along.

He gasped, *"Just say if I'm goin' right!"*
Yes, brother, right you are!
Danger of ocean or dark of night,
You steer by one clear star.

Six hours crawled by. . . . A barge in sight
With the raft just off the shore. . . .
The messman coughed, "Sure, I'm all right."
He was just as he was before.

And all that they knew was they called him "French"—
Not quite a name to sing.
Green jungle hell or desert trench,
No man did a braver thing.

He's burned a story in my brain,
Set in my heart a song.
He and his like, by wave and main,
World without end—*and not in vain*—
Are towing this world along!

MY SOUTH
by Don West

Oh soft flowing rivers
With slender willows
Clutched hungrily
To your bosom—
And red Georgia hills
Where cotton patches
Speckle the ground
With downy snow balls
Like a spotted hound's back,
And lazy pools
The deep green of corn blades
In June
Glisten under a Southern moon—
You are my South.
I found life deep in your womb
And I love you . . .

I love the sad solemn beauty
In your mountains—
The great Blue Ridge,
Cumberlands
Smokies
Unakas—

That stand like sentinels
To witness the surge
Of human passion
Flowing through your ribs,
Laughter and hate
Of Southern toilers . . .

And I love you who toil
In the dirt
And factories
And mines—
You whose skin is ebony
From a tropic sun
And my own bleached brothers . . .
I love the slow soft drawl
Of your Southern voice,
The way you love the sound
Of silence
And the easy swing
Of your bent shoulders . . .

I've felt your deep sorrow
In songs you sing
And I've wanted to sing
With you,
To tune your songs
Into keen blue blades
Slashing at your chains,
The cruel chains of hunger!

But your eyes were blind
And your hate was old
Your brain was warped
And your heart was cold . . .

Oh, my South,
My cold-blooded South
With a Negro's blood
Smeared over your mouth

And a Negro's bones
Which you blindly make
A few charred coals
By a burnt-off stake—

You have drunk poison
And it turns you mad
Like a rotten cancer
Gnawing at your brain.

And am I grinding
The blades of my songs
To a tempered edge
To whittle on
Your cancerous brain . . .

Tomorrow you must wake
And white hands will clasp
Ebony
Bowed over a few charred bones.
By a burnt-off stake . . . !

You are my South;
I'll hammer you
Into a beautiful song
For I love you . . .

STREET SCENE—1946[86]
by Kenneth Porter

On a street in Knoxville—
bless these eyes of mine!—
white man and a Negro
form a picket line!

Rankin and McKellar
rant in Washington:

[86]Originally published in *Common Ground*.

over eastern Tennessee
shows a streak of sun!

Storms and shadows thicken.
Here is fairing weather!
Negro and a white man
picketing together!

GOVERNMENT INJUNCTION[37]
Restraining Harlem Cosmetic Co.
by Josephine Miles

They say La Jac Brite Pink Skin Bleach avails not,
They say its Orange Beauty Glow does not glow,
Nor the face grow five shades lighter nor the heart
Five shades lighter. They say no.

They deny good luck, love, power, romance and inspiration
From La Jac Brite ointment and incense of all kinds,
And condemn in writing skin brightening and whitening
And whitening of minds.

There is upon the federal trade commission a burden of glory
So to defend the fact, so to impel
The plucking of hope from the hand, honor from the complexion,
Sprite from the spell.

BOOGIE-WOOGIE BALLADS[38]
by St. Clair McKelway

The Touchin' Case of Mr. and Mrs. Massa

Oh, let's fix us a julep and kick us a houn'
(Sing "Yassah! Yassah! Yassah!")

[37]From *Poems of Several Occasions*, by Josephine Miles, copyright, 1941. Reprinted by permission of New Directions.

[38]By permission of the author. Copyright, 1943, *The New Yorker* magazine, Inc.

And let's dig a place in de col', col' groun'
For Mr. and Mrs. Massa!

(Boogie-woogie)

Oh, this Mr. and Mrs. Massa have always lived in old Virginia and old North Carolina and old South Carolina and old Alabama and old Kentucky and old So Forth and old So On and nobody has ever understood the colored people the way they do because down in old So Forth and old So On is where the white folks understand the colored folks like no other white folks on earth understand colored folks. Yassah, Massa! Yassah!

(Boogie-woogie)

Oh, before the war and for some time afterward Mr. and Mrs. Massa understood the colored folks so well that they had a washerwoman they paid $1.50 a week and a cook they paid $1.75 a week and a butler they paid $2.25 a week and it was mighty lucky for these colored folks that the washerwoman was the cook's mother and the butler was the cook's husband because this enabled the three of them to live cozily in the fifth one-room shack from the left on the other side of the railroad tracks and thus pay $0.85 less a week for rent than the total of their combined salaries.

(Boogie-woogie)

Oh, and over and above the total of their combined salaries Mrs. Massa every other week gave the cook a ham bone outright and Mr. Massa every other month gave the butler a whole quarter of a dollar extra right out of a clear sky. It was manna, Mammy! Manna!

(Boogie-woogie)

Oh, but after the war had been going along for a while the butler, whose name was Charles F. Parker, came to Mr. Massa and told him he was going to quit because he had been offered a job as a counterman in the cafeteria of a defense plant at a salary of $15 a week plus three meals a day and Mr. Massa understood the colored folks so well he told Charles F. Parker that up to then he (Mr. Massa) had been able through influence to persuade the local draft board not to draft him (Charles F. Parker) but that if he (Charles F. Parker) quit his job as butler he (Mr. Massa) would have to persuade the draft board to go ahead and draft him (Charles F. Parker). Swing low, sweet Lincoln!

(Boogie-woogie)

Oh, but then Charles F. Parker told Mr. Massa that as he (Charles F. Parker) understood the situation after conversations with the draft board he (Charles F. Parker) had already been classed as 4-F owing to a number of physical disabilities, including chronic hoecake poisoning, and that therefore he thought he would take the job at the defense-plant cafeteria but with all due respect to Mr. Massa, etc. and etc. Hit that hoecake, boys! Hit it!

(Boogie-woogie)

Oh, so Mr. and Mrs. Massa saw the straws in the wind, saw which way the wind was blowing, and also recognized the trend of the time, so they took another tack, changed face, turned over new leaves, and each gave Charles F. Parker fifteen cents as a bonus and wished him success in his new job and raised the washerwoman (Esther G. Henderson) from $1.50 a week to $1.75 a week and raised the cook (Mrs. Charles F. Parker) from $1.75 a week to $1.85 a week with the understanding that Mrs. Esther G. Henderson would help out Mrs. Charles F. Parker in the kitchen and that Mrs. Charles F. Parker would wait on the table. Pass the hominy grits, boys! Pass it!

(Boogie-woogie)

Oh, but at the end of the first week under the new arrangement Mrs. Charles F. Parker came to Mrs. Massa and said she was going to quit because she had been offered a job as cook at the defense-plant cafeteria at a salary of $22.50 per week plus three meals a day and Mrs. Massa jus' had to cry. Weep some mo', my lady, oh, weep some mo'!

(Boogie-woogie)

Oh, and then the washerwoman (Esther G. Henderson) came to Mrs. Massa and said she was going to quit because she was eighty-two years old and her back ached and her daughter and son-in-law were going to support her for nothing, and Mrs. Massa jus' had to cry some mo'!

(Boogie-woogie)

Oh, and then one day a week after that Mr. and Mrs. Massa were walking back home after a dinner at the Old Southern Greek Chophouse and they saw Charles F. Parker and Mrs. Charles F. Parker and Esther G. Henderson coming out of the colored section of a movie house after having seen a Technicolored feature featuring Jack Benny and Mr. and Mrs. Massa noticed that Charles F. Parker had on a new suit and looked happy and that Mrs. Charles F. Parker had on a new dress and looked happy and that Esther G. Henderson had on a new shawl and looked happy and moreover was still laughing at the jokes Jack Benny had made inside the movie house and Mr. and Mrs. Massa saw the three of them go into a three-room stucco bungalow where Esther G. Henderson had a room all to herself and Mr. and Mrs. Charles F. Parker had a room all to themselves and then Mr. and Mrs. Massa looked at each other understandingly and tears came into the eyes of Mrs. Massa and Mr. Massa put his hand on her shoulder and said to her softly, "Nevah you mind, there'll be a reckonin' one of these days!"

(Boogie-woogie)

Oh, and so Mr. and Mrs. Massa finally closed up the house in old So Forth and old So On and came to New York and leased a suite at the Savoy-Plaza and the Savoy-Netherlands and the Savoy-So Forth and the Savoy-So On and any time you want to listen day or night as well as any time you don't want to listen day or night they will tell you for hours without stopping how they understand the colored people like no other white folks on earth understand colored folks and how the war and high wages are jus' ruinin' everything down in old So Forth and old So On and how never you mind there's goin' to be a reckonin' one of these days. Reckon twice and hit it again, boys! Hit it!

(Boogie-woogie)

Oh, and the bones of Mr. and Mrs. Massa are not growing cold and their heads are not bending low and no angel voices are calling to them and if nobody will carry them back to old So Forth and old So On, oh, then. . . .

(Boogie-woogie)

> Let's fix us a julep and kick us a houn'
> (Sing "Yassah! Yassah! Yassah!")
> And let's dig a place in de col', col' groun'
> For Mr. and Mrs. Massa!

LENOX AVENUE[89]
by Sidney Alexander

> *And it came to pass,*
> *when Joseph was come unto his brethren,*
> *that they stripped Joseph out of his coat,*
> *his coat of many colors that was on him;*
> *And they took him, and cast him into a pit:*
> *and the pit was empty,*
> *there was no water in it.*
>
> GENESIS XXXVII

With the hooves of a doe
my eye has wandered into this strange forest:
Soft-footed, break no twigs, stir no grass;
the underfoot of last year's death is here—

Cactuses of men
weird against the sky . . .
Fantastic shapings of the poor . . .
Waste of seed . . .

And swaying to the icy air of flutes
the chorus of the prostitutes
led by hunger to the act of dogs—

[89]Originally published in *The Negro Quarterly*, fall 1942.

The palm-leaf is your mouth,
And sinuous as rivers down the perfumed banks
Your hips before me on the avenue.

And you, O bronze boy, playing at the curb,
Why do you stare with eyes of a mountain-pool
suddenly freezing over at my step?
What is there in the pinkness of my skin
makes me an interloper in your home?
A lost stag in a lost valley,
startled at the muttering horizons,
hemmed by the pointing of fingers—

The questions whirl, the mind sees
the shadow hanging from the trees;
green by day and purple by night;
The wind kissing the innocent leaves,
And ever behind me is the tread
of guilt creeping toward my bed . . .

For though I have not sown, yet I must reap:
The harvests of hatred are shared;
The galley-slave is chained to my oar;
The cotton is bloodied at my door;
The storm breaks. No one is spared.

When freedom's rose blooms in the senator's mouth
Does he hear the beating of that drum?
the tomtom stretched of his failure?
the seamstress and the shoeshine boy
whirling round the cauldron of his bones?

When the statue bleeds
When the motionless move
When the tiger leaps from the cates of these eyes—?

So before me, Lenox Avenue,
you pass like a dream half-realized,
Twisted by anger and fear. . . .

Your loungers of a jungle grace
Your numbers on the flung dice
Your exclamations of cigars
Your marijuana and your bread.

Those who cast you in the pit have fled.
The caravan has come. Give me your hand!
In that embrace stars shall explode,
And brotherhood like a coat of many colors
Cover the nakedness of man.

3 THE CARIBBEAN

THE CARIBBEAN[1]
by Stephanie Ormsby

Here where the pirate chieftains sailed
In quest of gore and gold,
Where brutal, bloody Might prevailed
We pass, with none to hold.

Thought dreams behind, Hope flies before
The sea knows naught of years.
The white foam flashes as of yore,
And melts in pearls and tears.

SAN GLORIA
by Tom Redcam

Oh, Captain of wide western seas,
Where now thy great soul lives, dost thou
Recall San Gloria's spice-'censed breeze?

White-sanded curves where serried trees
Filed backward as thy sharpened prow
Sheared into foam the racing seas?

San Gloria's wood-carved mountain frieze
In the blue bay is mirrored now,
As when thy white sail wooed the breeze.

The thunder of insurgent seas
Beats yet the rough reef's ragged brow,
Roaring by green, far-stretching leas;

[1]By permission of author.

Yet through the wood the peony flees,
And frets with gold the night-dark bough
Down the long avenue of trees.

Still flowering gyneps tempt the bees,
The yellow guave ripens now,
Rich-hearted ipomes please.

Dost thou remember things like these,
Hear yet the dark-robed woodlands sough,
Oh, Captain of wide western seas,
Dost thou remember things like these
Where thy great soul inhabits now?

JAMAICA MARKET
by Agnes Maxwell-Hall

Honey, pepper, leaf-green limes,
Pagan fruit whose names are rhymes,
Mangoes, breadfruit, ginger-roots,
Granadillas, bamboo-shoots,
Cho-cho, ackees, tangerines,
Lemons, purple Congo-beans,
Sugar, okras, kola-nuts,
Citrons, hairy cocoanuts,
Fish, tobacco, native hats,
Gold bananas, woven mats,
Plantains, wild-thyme, pallid leeks,
Pigeons with their scarlet beaks,
Oranges and saffron yams,
Baskets, ruby guava jams,
Turtles, goat-skins, cinnamon,
Allspice, conch-shells, golden rum.
Black skins, babel—and the sun
That burns all colours into one.

LIZARD
by Agnes Maxwell-Hall

O, what would people say if you
Ate bitter-tasting ants, drank dew,
Caught gnats as blue as summer skies,
And swallowed painted butterflies?

And what would people think, if then
You laid eggs—just like any hen—
Forgot them in a windy nest,
And left the sun to do the rest?

Leave everyone—come sit with me
In trees; the things you'll hear and see!
And lead a lizard-life—I'm one!
A pocket-dragon in the sun!

BOYHOOD ETCHINGS[2]
by Walter Adolphe Roberts

I: Tropic Sunset

Oh, full and soft, upon the orange trees,
   Flamed forth bright beams of glory from the West!
And through the boughs there sighed a gypsy breeze,
   Bearing a thousand perfumes on its breast.

For it had kissed the coffee's starry spray,
   Had stolen sweetness from the lily's bell,
And I had seen the stephanotis sway
   Before its breath, as it swept up the dell.

[2]Reprinted by permission of Walter Adolphe Roberts.

The feathery bamboos pencilled on the sky,
　　The cedar's branches garbed in August green,
The palms that stirred storm-tattered fronds on high—
　　All breathed the languor of the hour serene.

II: *Tropic Storm*

The scent of jasmines in the sultry air,
　　A deathly stillness hanging over all,
Great sombre clouds, which float across the sky
　　And hide the sun, as with a funeral pall.

The birds' sweet voices silenced in the trees,
　　As if they had not got the heart to sing,
As on some twig, close-sheltered by the leaves,
　　Each sits with ruffled plumes and drooping wing.

But now a sullen murmur breaks the calm,
　　The gathering East wind stirs the vapors warm,
The roll of thunder smites upon the ear,
　　The lightning flashes red—and bursts the storm.

THE CAPTAINS[3]
by Walter Adolphe Roberts

A glamor of regret is on the brown
And placid streets of this old harbor town,
That wear their pride like a Victorian gown.

They mourn the vanished captains and their fleets,
Whose cargoes once were spices and strange sweets,
Parrots, and marmosets, and parakeets.

*Reprinted by permission of Walter Adolphe Roberts.

SAN FRANCISCO[4]
by Walter Adolphe Roberts

My galleon of adventure
    Beat through the Golden Gate.
The sailors said it was a ship
    With passengers and freight.

But I was young and dreamful.
    Dreams were the best of me.
And I, to San Francisco,
    Came dreaming from the sea.

I found a woman city,
    Suave as a cooing dove.
I sought her as a lover,
    But was too young for love.

Draped on her like a mantle,
    Her fog was cool and gray;
But since her girdle baffled me,
    She sent me on my way.

Now I have learned that poets
    When youth is gone kiss best,
I think, if I went back, that she
    Would take me to her breast.

VILLANELLE OF WASHINGTON SQUARE[5]
by Walter Adolphe Roberts

The starshine on the Arch is silver white;
    Elves, April elves, are dancing in the Square;
The green-robed Spring has come to town tonight.

[4,5]Reprinted by permission of Walter Adolphe Roberts.

Jasmines are in her arms and clouded quite
    With lilac is the nimbus of her hair;
The starshine on the Arch is silver white.

With sap at floodtide and pale leaves bedight,
    Ghosts of gray trees assume a vernal air;
The green-robed Spring has come to town tonight.

Young lovers' lips seek for the old delight,
    On the park bench that winter-long was bare——
The starshine on the Arch is silver white——

And they who hear her primal call aright
    Rejoice that, deathless, virginal and fair,
The green-robed Spring has come to town tonight.

Dreamers whose windows on the Square are bright,
    Know that your dreams may not with this compare;
The starshine on the Arch is silver white,
The green-robed Spring has come to town tonight.

VILLANELLE OF THE LIVING PAN[6]
by Walter Adolphe Roberts

Pan is not dead, but sleeping in the brake,
    Hard by the blue of some Aegean shore.
Ah, flute to him, Belovèd, he will wake.

Vine leaves have drifted o'er him, flake by flake,
    And with dry laurel he is covered o'er.
Pan is not dead, but sleeping in the brake.

The music that his own cicadas make
    Comes to him faintly, like forgotten lore.
Ah, flute to him, Belovèd, he will wake.

[6]Reprinted by permission of Walter Adolphe Roberts.

Let not the enemies of Beauty take
   Unction of soul that he can rise no more.
Pan is not dead, but sleeping in the brake,

Dreaming of one that for the goat god's sake
   Shall pipe old tunes and worship as of yore.
Ah, flute to him, Belovèd, he will wake.

So once again the Attic coast shall shake
   With a cry greater than it heard before:
"Pan is not dead, but sleeping in the brake!"
Ah, flute to him, Belovèd, he will wake.

PEACOCKS[7]
by Walter Adolphe Roberts

They came from Persia to the Sacred Way
   And rode in Pompey's triumph, side by side
   With odalisques and idols, plumes flung wide.
A flame of gems in the chill Roman day.
They that were brought as captives came to stay,
   To flaunt in beauty, mystery and pride,
   To preen before the emperors deified,
Symbols of their magnificent decay.

Then there was madness and a scourge of swords.
   Imperial purple mouldered into dust.
But the immortal peacocks stung new lords
   To furies of insatiable lust.
Contemptuous, they loitered on parade—
Live opals, rubies, sardonyx and jade.

VIEUX CARRÉ[8]
by Walter Adolphe Roberts

This city is the child of France and Spain,
  That once lived nobly, ardent as the heat
  In which it came to birth. Alas, how fleet
The years of love and arms! There now remain,
Bleached by the sun and mouldered by the rain,
  Impassive fronts that guard some rare retreat,
  Some dim, arched salon, or some garden sweet,
Where dreams persist and the past lives again.

The braided iron of the balconies
  Is like locked hands, fastidiously set
To bar the world. But the proud mysteries
  Showed me a glamour I may not forget:
Your face, camellia-white upon the stair,
Framed in the midnight thicket of your hair.

ON A MONUMENT TO MARTI[9]
by Walter Adolphe Roberts

Cuba, disheveled, naked to the waist,
Springs up erect from the dark earth and screams
Her joy in liberty. The metal gleams
Where her chains broke. Magnificent her haste
To charge into the battle and to taste
Revenge on the oppressor. Thus she seems.
But she were powerless without the dreams
Of him who stands above, unsmiling, chaste.

Yes, over Cuba on her jubilant way
Broods the Apostle, José Julian Marti.

[8],[9]Reprinted by permission of Walter Adolphe Roberts.

He shaped her course of glory, and the day
The guns first spoke he died to make her free.
That night a meteor flamed in splendid loss
Between the North Star and the Southern Cross.

THE MAROON GIRL[10]
by Walter Adolphe Roberts

I see her on a lonely forest track,
  Her level brows made salient by the sheen
  Of flesh the hue of cinnamon. The clean
Blood of the hunted, vanished Arawak
Flows in her veins with blood of white and black.
  Maternal, noble-breasted is her mien;
  She is a peasant, yet she is a queen.
She is Jamaica poised against attack.

Her woods are hung with orchids; the still flame
  Of red hibiscus lights her path, and starred
  With orange and coffee blossoms in her yard.
Fabulous, pitted mountains close the frame.
  She stands on ground for which her fathers died;
  Figure of savage beauty, figure of pride.

LITANY
by George Campbell

I hold the splendid daylight in my hands
Inwardly grateful for a lovely day.
Thank you life.
Daylight like a fine fan spread from my hands
Daylight like scarlet poinsettia
Daylight like yellow cassia flowers
Daylight like clean water
Daylight like green cacti

[10]Reprinted by permission of Walter Adolphe Roberts.

Daylight like sea sparkling with white horses
Daylight like sunstrained blue sky
Daylight like tropic hills
Daylight like a sacrament in my hands.
Amen.

LIZARD[11]
by K. E. Ingram

In the tender spreading tropical mornings
The collandium leaves extend themselves
To the quivering flaming light
Spread out so open and so wide
Like giant red spiders with their feet webbed together.
O webbed so very neatly;
And forming such cool soft divans for the lizard's belly,
For lizards lie belly-leafed in the early dawning.
One little fellow lies reared on his fore-legs
Upright and aware towards the leaping light,
For lizards are very aware little creatures seldom caught off guard:
As I turned the corner this little fellow
Had cocked his head inquiringly
Demanding of me the password.

"Who goes?"

And when I still have made no motion, friendly or hostile,
He still with head question-wise insists,

"Who goes?"

And then I put my question to him,
What was he doing out there in the spreading, flaming light
In the burning gold of the new-risen sun,
When I had always thought that the lizard's world

[11]By permission of author. First published in the Jamaican weekly, *Public Opinion.*

Was a green-world, gloom-world,
Beneath the mysterious shade of leaf and fern
Where stalk knows root on the hard earth's lip;
Had he deserted his unknowable world of
Lizard-leap, lizard-dive and lizard-chase.
And then, just as I turned,
Just as I couldn't stand his impertinent slow-eyed stare,
He jumped, jumped into the deep gloom of the leaf-shade,
As if to show me how superior he was
For he was able to experience my world and his own.
And I was left wondering what new blood was now creeping through
    his veins,
Through his limpid green veins,
This cold-blooded, cool-world creature
That had ventured forth into the spilling morning light.

NINE O'CLOCK
by Louis Simpson

At nine o'clock the bus snouts cityward
Surfeited, and groaning at every start;
The passengers, in lulls of being tossed,
With relish chew their misanthropic cud.

Reluctantly agreed, their bodies sway,
While, clogged with too much marmalade at heart,
Again they pick up pins of grievance lost,
Nudge room from neighbours going the same way.

They scan the usual banners of world hate.
A girl clutching her purse conjures the cost
Of daily lunch, or shoes that might be smart,
Or matinees . . . she strokes a perfumed pate. . . .

And Charon, coming round for his due fare,
Collects all men's frustrations in a stare.

DINNER PARTY, 1940
by P. M. Sherlock

Do you mind the news while we eat?
  So, guests assenting,
The well-bred voice from Daventry
Mingled with sounds from the pantry
And slowly through the ether spilled
Its syllables—not silencing—augmenting
The show of wit which never fails
Thanks to 7:30 cocktails . . . "and at
Narvik where for 5 days a storm has raged a few were killed"
More mutton Alice? Yes, it's delicious dear
Yesterday at bridge I held three aces, three——
  "In the Baltic
It is reported from Stockholm that the soldiers fled
Leaving a number of dead."

But don't you like it cold with guava-jelly?
The well-bred voice from Daventry
Did not grow less well-bred,
And did not speak of more than 3 or 400 dead,
And did not really silence the sounds from the pantry
Or the show of wit which never fails
Thanks to 7:30 cocktails.
Cold mutton is delicious with guava-jelly
And does not seriously incommode
Like cold lead in the belly.

THE FINAL MAN
by Basil McFarlane

This is the final man;
Who lives within the dusk,
Who is the dusk
Always.

To know birth and to know death
In one emotion,
To look before and after with one eye,
To see the Whole,
To know the Truth,
To know the World and be without a World:
In this light that is no light,
This time that is no time, to be
And to be free:
This is the final man,
Who lives within the dusk,
Who is the dusk
Always.

ON NATIONAL VANITY
by J. E. Clare McFarlane

Slowly we learn; the oft repeated line
Lingers a little moment and is gone;
Nation on Nation follows, Sun on Sun;

But we are blind and see not. In our pride
We strain toward the petrifying mound
To sit above our fellows, and we ride
The slow and luckless toiler to the ground.

Fools are we for our pains! Whom we despise,
Last come, shall mount our withered vanities,
Topmost to sit upon the vast decay
Of time and temporal things; for, last or first,
The proud array of pictured bubbles burst;
Mirages of their glory pass away.

THE CAGED MONGOOSE
by Constance Hollar

Within the cage he ramped and raged!
His jailer, proud, exultant, stood before him,
The while he hissed and spat
Forth fury. His tail, all reddish silver,
Coiled high in bristling anger, flashed
Upon his back. His sleek grey sides
Like ribbon gleamed. His eyes,
Keen steel-bright rapiers,
Cut the distance as a Damasc blade
A skein of silk.
His white teeth gleamed like daggers,
As he flew and bit the wooden bars,
As in old days he slew the snake,
Or cracked the bones of juicy chickens
Or stole the red gold
From the crystal fountain of the egg.
No prayer for pity crossed his lips,
But curses deep, rage and despair.

I turned aside—I could not bear
To see him drowned.—To see the light
Go out from those bright eyes—
But, fascinated, turned and looked
Just as he went beneath the pool—
And saw two fore-feet
High-uplifted, clenched,
As if in prayer.
A gurgling sound! A hissing breath!—
The problem of both Life and Death
Was solved for him.
His race was run.

.   .   .

Beneath the bamboo tree
His brown mate waited till the dusk:

She and her little ones,
And oft she raised her eyes and peered,
Or nosed the ground.
Then with half-sigh she settled
'Midst the leaves again.
In that blind patience of dumb animals
She made her prayer.

And I pray too
For all the chased and hunted "little ones" of earth,
For cattle with black fear within their hearts,
Imprisoned in the cruel slaughter-yards,
For patient sheep and goats
Led to the Sacrifice.
For foxes hunted by the loud-voiced pack,
For hares fast coursing down the wind,
Also for barn-yard fowls
In feathers clean and neat,
For all the graceful birds on wing
Now airy joys—then broken bones and blood,
To "make a Roman holiday":
For all who yield the sweet delights of Life
Unasked, unwilling and with grievous fear
And voiceless agony,
I make my prayer to God and man.

I, REMEMBERING
by Roger Mais

I, remembering how light love
Has a soft footfall, and fleet,
That goes clicking down
The heart's lone
And empty street
In a kind
Of spread twilight-nimbus of the mind,

And a soft voice of shaken laughter
Like the wind . . .

I, remembering this,
And remembering that light love is
As fragile as a kiss
Lightly given,
And passes like the little rain
Softly down-driven;

Bade love come to you
With rough male footsteps—
Deliberate—
That hurt to come,
And hurt to go. . . .
And bade love speak to you
With accents terrible, and slow.

HUNTED
by Una Marson

The hunted hare seeks out some dark retreat
And hopes the pulsing pack will pass him by
His body quivers, fast his heart must beat
As oft he hears the heartless huntsmen's cry:
So hunted still by love's relentless might
With heart convulsing and with hasty tread
I seek some refuge, hidden from his sight
So he might pass whom I so darkly dread;
Pass on, and leave me there to die of grief
Or solaced back to life in Nature's arms
On her soft soothing breast to find relief
And half forget the sorrow of love's charms:
But lo! he comes with his own cruel dart
To find me out and wound for sport my heart.

NIGHTFALL
by Una Marson

How tender the heart grows
At the twilight hour,
More sweet seems the perfume
Of the sunless flower.

Come quickly, wings of night,
The twilight hurts too deep;
Let darkness wrap the world around,
My pain will go to sleep.

THE GLEANER
by Vivian L. Virtue

". . . And Ruth the Moabitess . . .
came to Bethlehem
in the beginning of barley harvest."

Gleaning she goes down the far golden ways,
Longing her garment, with Loneliness shod,
Lift up your hearts, all ye sons, in her praise!

Bethlehem fields are with harvest ablaze:
Fairer than she not among them has trod;
Gleaning she goes down the far golden ways.

Daughter most dutiful, lo, in her gaze
Faith that not Sorrow could break with its rod!
Lift up your hearts, all ye sons, in her praise!

Hark the rare words that she steadfastly says,
All thine be mine till we home to the clod. . . .
Gleaning she goes down the far golden ways.

Binding the sheaves of ripe barley she prays;
Answer her, Heaven! raise her hope from the sod!
Lift up your hearts, all ye sons, in her praise!

Cometh fulfilment . . . O joy and amaze!
Out of her faithfulness flowers our God.
Gleaning she goes down the far golden ways,
Lift up your hearts, all ye sons, in her praise!

ATLANTIC MOONRISE
by Vivian L. Virtue

The new-washed moon drew up from the sea's dark rim.
Naked, and unsuspecting, on my sight
Her bosom dripped, till, struck with virgin fright,
Catching my gaze, she snatched a cloud-fold dim
Across the delightsome shame that flushed each limb,
Mocking the hunger in me to possess her bright
Divinity with proper, prudish spite,
With beauty's conscious sovereignty and whim.

Baffled I waited, burning with desire;
Then with such slow magnificent pretence,
As though I were not there, she stripped again. . . .
I stood like David on the roof, the fire
Of young Bathsheba torturing his sense,
Bartered, like him, my peace for Beauty's pain.

TO CLAUDE McKAY
by Vivian L. Virtue

Far from your native hills although you roam,
How would your heart rejoice this picnic day
With rustic fiddle and flute and roundelay
To welcome August, from the dawning gloam'

Until the new moon climbed the dewy dome,
Lingered above your village, went her way,
Leaving, night long, dusk limbs to trip and sway
To rhythmic dance and song in fields of home!

These have not changed, old loves you left behind;
The rural sights and sounds are lovely yet
And times and seasons that would make you yearn
With lyrical remembrance and regret
For pathways waiting your delayed return
Of long, long years of pain to ease your mind.

THE TROPICS IN NEW YORK[12]
by Claude McKay

Bananas ripe and green, and ginger-root,
Cocoa in pods and alligator pears,
And tangerines and mangoes and grapefruit,
Fit for the highest prize at parish fairs,

Set in the window, bringing memories
Of fruit-trees laden by low-singing rills,
And dewy dawns, and mystical blue skies
In benediction over nun-like hills.

My eyes grew dim, and I could no more gaze;
A wave of longing through my body swept,
And, hungry for the old, familiar ways,
I turned aside and bowed my head and wept.

AFTER THE WINTER[13]
by Claude McKay

Some day, when trees have shed their leaves
    And against the morning's white
The shivering birds beneath the eaves
    Have sheltered for the night,

We'll turn our faces southward, love,
　　Toward the summer isle
Where bamboos spire to shafted grove
　　And wide-mouthed orchids smile.

And we will seek the quiet hill
　　Where towers the cotton tree,
And leaps the laughing crystal rill,
　　And works the droning bee.
And we will build a cottage there
　　Beside an open glade,
With black-ribbed blue-bells blowing near,
　　And ferns that never fade.

HERITAGE[14]
by Claude McKay

Now the dead past seems vividly alive,
　　And in this shining moment I can trace,
Down through the vista of the vanished years,
　　Your faun-like form, your fond elusive face.

And suddenly some secret spring's released,
　　And unawares a riddle is revealed,
And I can read like large, black-lettered print,
　　What seemed before a thing forever sealed.

I know the magic word, the graceful thought,
　　The song that fills me in my lucid hours,
The spirit's wine that thrills my body through,
　　And makes me music-drunk, are yours, all yours.

I cannot praise, for you have passed from praise,
　　I have no tinted thoughts to paint you true;
But I can feel and I can write the word;
　　The best of me is but the least of you.

[14]From *Harlem Shadows,* by Claude McKay, copyright. 1922. Harcourt, Brace
& Co., publishers.

SPRING IN NEW HAMPSHIRE[15]
by Claude McKay

Too green the springing April grass,
  Too blue the silver-speckled sky,
For me to linger here, alas,
  While happy winds go laughing by,
Wasting the golden hours indoors,
Washing windows and scrubbing floors.

Too wonderful the April night,
  Too faintly sweet the first May flowers,
The stars too gloriously bright,
  For me to spend the evening hours,
When fields are fresh and streams are leaping,
Wearied, exhausted, dully sleeping.

TO O.E.A.[16]
by Claude McKay

Your voice is the color of a robin's breast,
  And there's a sweet sob in it like rain—still rain in the night.
Among the leaves of the trumpet-tree, close to his nest,
  The pea-dove sings, and each note thrills me with strange delight
Like the words, wet with music, that well from your trembling throat.
  I'm afraid of your eyes, they're so bold,
  Searching me through, reading my thoughts, shining like gold.
But sometimes they are gentle and soft like the dew on the lips of the
    eucharis
Before the sun comes warm with his lover's kiss.
  You are sea-foam, pure with the star's loveliness,
Not mortal, a flower, a fairy, too fair for the beauty-shorn earth.

[15,16]From *Spring in New Hampshire*, by Claude McKay, copyright, 1920. Grant Richards, Ltd., publishers; from *Harlem Shadows*, by Claude McKay, copyright, 1922, Harcourt, Brace & Co., publishers.

All wonderful things, all beautiful things, gave of their wealth to your
    birth.
Oh I love you so much, not recking of passion, that I feel it is wrong!
    But men will love you, flower, fairy, non-mortal spirit burdened with
    flesh,
Forever, life-long.

A SONG OF THE MOON[17]
by Claude McKay

The moonlight breaks upon the city's domes,
And falls along cemented steel and stone,
Upon the grayness of a million homes,
Lugubrious in unchanging monotone.

Upon the clothes behind the tenement,
That hang like ghosts suspended from the lines,
Linking each flat to each indifferent,
Incongruous and strange the moonlight shines.

There is no magic from your presence here,
Ho, moon, sad moon, tuck up your trailing robe,
Whose silver seems antique and so severe
Against the glow of one electric globe.

Go spill your beauty on the laughing faces
Of happy flowers that bloom a thousand hues,
Waiting on tiptoe in the wilding spaces,
To drink your wine mixed with sweet drafts of dews.

HARLEM SHADOWS[18]
by Claude McKay

I hear the halting footsteps of a lass
  In Negro Harlem when the night lets fall
Its veil. I see the shapes of girls who pass
  To bend and barter at desire's call.
Ah, little dark girls who in slippered feet
Go prowling through the night from street to street!

Through the long night until the silver break
  Of day the little gray feet know no rest;
Through the lone night until the last snow-flake
  Has dropped from heaven upon the earth's white breast,
The dusky, half-clad girls of tired feet
Are trudging, thinly shod, from street to street.

Ah, stern harsh world, that in the wretched way
  Of poverty, dishonor and disgrace,
Has pushed the timid little feet of clay,
  The sacred brown feet of my fallen race!
Ah, heart of me, the weary, weary feet
In Harlem wandering from street to street.

AMERICA[19]
by Claude McKay

Although she feeds me bread of bitterness,
  And sinks into my throat her tiger's tooth,
Stealing my breath of life, I will confess
  I love this cultured hell that tests my youth!

Her vigor flows like tides into my blood,
Giving me strength erect against her hate.
Her bigness sweeps my being like a flood.
Yet as a rebel fronts a king in state,
I stand within her walls with not a shred
Of terror, malice, not a word of jeer.
Darkly I gaze into the days ahead,
And see her might and granite wonders there,
Beneath the touch of Time's unerring hand,
Like priceless treasures sinking in the sand.

WHITE HOUSES[20]
by Claude McKay

Your door is shut against my tightened face,
And I am sharp as steel with discontent;
But I possess the courage and the grace
To bear my anger proudly and unbent.
The pavement slabs burn loose beneath my feet,
A chafing savage, down the decent street;
And passion rends my vitals as I pass,
Where boldly shines your shuttered door of glass.
Oh, I must search for wisdom every hour,
Deep in my wrathful bosom sore and raw,
And find in it the superhuman power
To hold me to the letter of your law!
Oh, I must keep my heart inviolate
Against the potent poison of your hate.

[20]From A Long Way from Home, by Claude McKay, copyright, 1937. Lee Furman, Inc., publishers.

IF WE MUST DIE[21]
by Claude McKay

If we must die, let it not be like hogs
Hunted and penned in an inglorious spot,
While round us bark the mad and hungry dogs,
Making their mock at our accursed lot.
If we must die, O let us nobly die,
So that our precious blood may not be shed
In vain; then even the monsters we defy
Shall be constrained to honor us though dead!
O kinsmen! we must meet the common foe!
Though far outnumbered let us show us brave,
And for their thousand blows deal one deathblow!
What though before us lies the open grave?
Like men we'll face the murderous, cowardly pack,
Pressed to the wall, dying, but fighting back!

BAPTISM[22]
by Claude McKay

Into the furnace let me go alone;
Stay you without in terror of the heat.
I will go naked in—for thus 'tis sweet—
Into the weird depths of the hottest zone.
I will not quiver in the frailest bone,
You will not note a flicker of defeat;
My heart shall tremble not its fate to meet,
My mouth give utterance to any moan.
The yawning oven spits forth fiery spears;
Red aspish tongues shout wordlessly my name.
Desire destroys, consumes my mortal fears,
Transforming me into a shape of flame.

[21,22]From *Harlem Shadows*, by Claude McKay, copyright, 1922. Harcourt, Brace
& Co., publishers.

I will come out, back to your world of tears,
A stronger soul within a finer frame.

RUSSIAN CATHEDRAL[23]
by Claude McKay

Bow down my soul in worship very low
And in the holy silences be lost.
Bow down before the marble man of woe,
Bow down before the singing angel host.
What jewelled glory fills my spirit's eye!
What golden grandeur moves the depths of me!
The soaring arches lift me up on high
Taking my breath with their rare symmetry.

Bow down my soul and let the wondrous light
Of beauty bathe thee from her lofty throne,
Bow down before the wonder of man's might.
Bow down in worship, humble and alone;
Bow lowly down before the sacred sight
Of man's divinity alive in stone.

FLAME-HEART[24]
by Claude McKay

So much have I forgotten in ten years,
So much in ten brief years! I have forgot
What time the purple apples come to juice,
And what month brings the shy forget-me-not.
I have forgot the special, startling season
Of the pimento's flowering and fruiting;

[23]By permission of Mrs. Hope McKay Virtue.

[24]From *Spring in New Hampshire*, by Claude McKay, copyright, 1920. Grant Richards, Ltd., publishers; from *Harlem Shadows*, by Claude McKay, copyright, 1922. Harcourt, Brace & Co., publishers.

What time of year the ground doves brown the fields
And fill the noonday with their curious fluting.
I have forgotten much, but still remember
The poinsettia's red, blood-red in warm December.

I still recall the honey-fever grass,
But cannot recollect the high days when
We rooted them out of the ping-wing path
To stop the mad bees in the rabbit pen.
I often try to think in what sweet month
The languid painted ladies used to dapple
The yellow by-road mazing from the main,
Sweet with the golden threads of the rose-apple.
I have forgotten—strange—but quite remember
The poinsettia's red, blood-red in warm December.

What weeks, what months, what time of the mild year
We cheated school to have our fling at tops?
What days our wine-thrilled bodies pulsed with joy
Feasting upon blackberries in the copse?
Oh some I know! I have embalmed the days,
Even the sacred moments when we played,
All innocent of passion, uncorrupt,
At noon and evening in the flame-heart's shade.
We were so happy, happy, I remember,
Beneath the poinsettia's red in warm December.

NATURE[25]
by H. D. Carberry

We have neither Summer nor Winter
Neither Autumn nor Spring.

We have instead the days
When the gold sun shines on the lush green canefields—
Magnificently.

[25]By permission of author; originally published in the Jamaican weekly, *Public Opinion*.

The days when the rain beats like bullets on the roofs
And there is no sound but the swish of water in the gullies
And trees struggling in the high Jamaica winds.

Also there are the days when the leaves fade from off guango trees
And the reaped canefields lie bare and fallow to the sun.

But best of all there are the days when the mango and the logwood
  blossom

When the bushes are full of the sound of bees and the scent of honey,
When the tall grass sways and shivers to the slightest breath of air,

When the buttercups have paved the earth with yellow stars
And beauty comes suddenly and the rains have gone.

I SHALL REMEMBER[26]
by H. D. Carberry

>   And in strange lands
>   Where the fog presses down
>   And even the street lamps are faint and misty,
>   I shall remember
>   The beauty of our nights,
>   With stars so near
>   That one could almost stretch and touch them,
>   Stars winking and flashing
>   Magnificently in a sky of velvet blue.
>
>   I shall remember
>   Walking down long avenues of trees,
>   The black asphalt flecked with pale moonlight
>   Pouring through the acacia leaves—
>   And the soft laughter of girls
>   Leaning back, cool and inviting
>   Against the trunks of flaming poincianne trees.

[26]By permission of author; originally published in the Jamaican weekly, *Public
Opinion*.

And in the long day when rain falls sullenly
And no sun shines
And all the earth lies in a weary stupor
I shall remember
The splendour of our sun
The brightness of our days.

And how the rain poured down
Upon a passionate thirsty earth,
Swiftly, unrelenting with immeasurable power,
Then vanished suddenly in a peal of childlike laughter
And all the earth was green and light once more.

I shall remember
The warmth of our island seas,
The sparkling whiteness of the breaking waves
And the blue haze on our hills and mountains
With their noisy streams cascading down
Sheer cliffs in clouds of incandescent spray
And deafening sound.

And in strange cities
Among unaccustomed people
Who move palefaced with tired staring eyes
I shall remember
The warmth and gaiety of my people,
The polyglot colour and variety of their faces,
The happy fusion of our myriad races
In the common love that unites and binds us to this land.

And I shall yearn for the sight
Of faces black and bronzed,
People with dark sparkling eyes
With ready tongue
And laughter loud and unashamed.

RETURN[27]
by H. D. Carberry

> In the narrow street
> Of filthy kerosene box shacks
> He stands.
>
> There are dark sullen clouds above
> One star and the dim street lamp—
> Scars in his hands
>
> And in his eyes a deep pity
> And a great love
> For the earth that is man's.

BRITISH GUIANA

Passages from
OVER GUIANA, CLOUDS[28]
by A. J. Seymour

> Over Guiana, clouds.
>
> Little curled feathers on the back of the sky.
> —White, chicken-downy on the soft sweet blue—
> In slow reluctant patterns for the world to see.

[27]By permission of author; originally published in the Jamaican weekly, *Public Opinion.*

[28]By permission of author; originally published in *Over Guiana, Clouds,* by A. J. Seymour. Published in British Guiana, 1944.

Then frisky lambs that gambol and bowl along
Shepherded by the brave Trade Wind.

And glittering in the sun come great grave battleships
Ploughing an even keel across the sky.

In their own time, their bowels full of rain
The angry clouds that rage with lightning
Emitting sullen bulldog growls
And then they spirit themselves away in mist and rain.

Over Guiana, clouds.

And they go rushing on across the country
Staining the land with shadow as they pass.
Closer than raiment to the naked skin, that shadow,
Bringing a pause of sun, over and across
Black noiseless rivers running out to sea,
Fields, pieced and plotted, and ankle-deep in rice
Or waving their multitudinous hair of cane.

It scales the sides of mountains
Lifting effortlessly to their summits,
And fleets across savannahs, in its race,
But there are times that shadow falters
And hesitates upon a lake
To fix that eye of water in a stare,
Or use its burnished shield to search the sun,
Or yet as maids do,
To let the cloud compose her hurried beauty.

And then upon its way to Venezuela
Across vast stretches where trees huddle close
And throw liana arms around their neighbours.

Over Guiana, clouds.

Forest night full of drums
Death-throbbing drums
For shining-breasted invaders of the shores.

Immemorial feuds shake hands
And Indians come,
Death's harvests swinging in their quivers.

A cinema of rapid figures
Thrown by wood-torches on the trees,
Impassive faces with passion forcing through,
Then the hard treks, and the long full canoes
Rustling down the river-night.

A horror of nights for Spaniards
Keen arrows biting the throat above the steel
The Indians flitting like actors in the wings
The swamps, the heavy marching, the malaria.

A trail of burnt villages and tortured men and treacheries.

Wave after wave, the white-faced warriors
Then weary of war,
The Indians talk of trade.

.   .   .

Indians knew the bird calls in the woods
Before Columbus sailed
The swallow songs
—Arrows of longing for the northern Summer days—
The clamorous-winging wild ducks and the choughs
The merry kiskadees and the pirate hawks
The cries of little frightened doves,
The brilliant and unmusical macaws.
And they can tell the single hours to sunset
By the birds cheeping, cheeping overhead.

This wildwood and untroubled knowledge still
Cradles the dying tribes
For death has laid his hand upon the race.
They know the wisdom of all herbs and weeds
Which one to eat for sickness, which to shun
And which to crush into an oil that pulls
The cramping pains from out the marrow bones.

They hear the river as it courses down
And they can tell the rising of the tide
From river-water lapping, lapping softly
Slapping against the wooden landing-stage.

The impassivity of silent trees becomes their own
And they will watch the wheeling of white birds
For company.

But still they have their dances and at nights,
When the drums trouble the dark with rhythm
The violin takes a voice and patterns the air
And then the Indians find their tribal memories
Of victories and war and dim old journeys
That brought them from beyond the Bering Strait.

• • •

Raleigh comes to Guiana

The wind had dropped, the giant hand
Of night was shrouding up the land
From where the thick couridas stand
    On the Guiana shore.
And when the ships their anchors weighed
Men went below, but one man stayed
    The distant jungle's roar.
These musings fed on his far stare
"I have been bold the King to dare,
And will my expedition fare
    As falsely as of yore?

These secret forests left behind
Will I in that star-peopled south find
The image stamped upon my mind,
    The city built in gold?"
—Where golden streets threw back the light,
And roofs gleamed dully through the night
But like an auburn head blazed bright
    When earth to morning rolled—

But deep within the mountains' breast
The city lay; there was no rest
Until he and his men had pressed
        And won a conqueror's way
Through jungles where death stung and leapt
Or in the tree-black midnight crept
And claimed each tenth man as he slept
        And therefore could not pray.

And to Sir Walter came the thought
Perhaps the destiny he sought
Would never shine, be gold.
Perhaps this kindly fitful breeze
He'd no more feel, nor see these seas,
Perhaps his men would feed the trees
        Changed to a rotting mould.
He pulled his cloak around his knees
        Because the night was cold.

                    .   .   .

Slaves
Humming in the twilight by the shanty door
Oh Lord Jesus.

Slaves
Pouring out heart-music till it run no more
Oh Lord Jesus.

Slaves born in hot wet forestlands
Tend the young cane-shoots and they give
Brute power to the signal of the lash
It curls and hisses through the air
And lifts upon the black, broad backs
Roped wales in hideous sculpture
"Oh Lord Jesus."

Some slaves are whipped
For looking at the Master's grown-up daughters
Picking their way across the compound,
And other slaves for trying to run away.
"Oh Lord Jesus."

Some few found kindly-hearted owners
And they were used like human beings
But those were rare, Lord Jesus.

Before, it was the shining yellow metal
And now, the dark sweet crystal owned the land
And if the chattel and the cattle died
There always would be more to take their place.
Till, in its deep sleep
Europe's conscience turned
And strenuous voices
Broke chains and set the people free.
"Oh Lord Jesus."

But there were other chains and earth was not yet heaven
And other races came to share the work
And halve the pay.

                              . . .

So with a stride down to the modern times and
Random villages dawning between the plantations
The sea pounding away to break the dams.

And the railway pencils a line to the Berbice River
Villages broaden shoulders and, sugar booming,
Schools spring up suddenly to dot the coast.

Men get eager for the yellow metal, shooting
Down rapids for diamonds and quick wealth, returning
Bloated and drunk to paint the villages red.

Plantations thicken, spread, and they web together,
The angry sea batters the concrete defences
Scooping a grave for them to bury themselves.

Bustle and industry on the coasts but inland
Few echoes shake the forests from their silences
And nothing wakes their strong cathedral calm.

Their tops like plumes, the years grow old with forests
And sleep upon the broad, short-shrubbed savannahs
Patient and free from suffering like the stones.

The races fade into a brown-stained people
And the Guiana Spirit arises, stretching
As a young giant begins to open his eyes

And sees his country with its waiting promise
Fair and unraped, and lifts his head to the heavens

Over Guiana, clouds.

. . .

Over Guiana clouds still lift their beauty
And pace the sheer glad firmament by day
They seem to halt, lay anchor when the night
Distains the heavens and pours thick darkness in
Its bowl, but on their pilgrimage they go
And weave themselves strange pagan arabesques
Or subtle unimaginable shapes
Before they pass on to another land.
High symbols, that behind the brow of history
Dim objects brood and huge hands shape events
From here, a little actuated dust
And there, the blind collisions of the stars.

Over Guiana, clouds.

BRITISH HONDURAS

THERE IS A MYSTIC SPLENDOR
by Raymond Barrow

There is a mystic splendor that one feels
Walking this shore in the half-light of dawn,
Placing one's footprints on the sands where keels
Of ancient vessels must have beached and drawn.

For there are tales that speak of glorious days
When martial shouting rang within our Bay,
And cannons thundered, and black battle haze
Clouded this sickle isle with dark affray.

Those were the times when privateers fled
The predatory Brethren of the Coast;
Pirates and buccaneers—all these are dead,
And all their lordly sway seems but a ghost.

But even now the surf's loud thunder brings
Sounds strangely clear—like battle cries of old;
And palm trees murmur of deep-sunken things,
Of buried treasure-chests . . . and Morgan's gold. . . .

BARBADOS

NOCTURNE
by H. A. Vaughan

The wind is blowing from the hill,
The sky is robed in purest sheen,
The crickets' music, sweetly shrill,
Comes from the cane-brake and the green.

The pond is quivering with delight,
The pear tree nods. The jasmine fair
And gracious lady-of-the-night
With perfume load the dewy air.

The village sleeps. Only beyond
The brake two lovers linger still.
The moon with silver clothes the pond.
Silent and silver is the hill.

THE OLD CONVICT
by H. A. Vaughan

Look at me. I am Ishmael,
    Ham's heir, the spit and spawn of Cain,
    The outcast with the twisted brain,
Lord of Cats Castle, fit for Hell.

I got no chance. The social odds
    Were dead against me when they sent
    Me up The Hill because I went
For some forgotten prank to Dodds.

And so because they made me wince,
    And stretched me on the legal rack,
    I took an oath I would hit back,
And have been hitting ever since.

Maybe it *is* a foolish game
    Judged by the record. Who likes jail?
    But then I've fought them tooth and nail,
And surely that's no cause for shame.

Reform, you say? Reform indeed!
    Let's all reform. They must not quit
    The Golden Rule, and I from it
Will not stray once. That is our need.

IN MEMORIAM
by Frank A. Collymore

And so, when the time came,
And you kissed them all and went,
All your bills paid and your affairs wound up,
To the lonely waiting ward,
Though they thought you'd be afraid
And tried to smile as they fussed around you,
You could afford to smile back;
For you were not afraid:
You knew you were going to die.

You'd known this all along, hadn't you?
You'd always been afraid of the little things—
The toothache, the crowded theatre, the fire alarm;
But when it came to this
You could afford to smile back at them;
For this was no trivial matter,
This was the end; and now
There was no cause for fear:
You had worked out the answer.

And so, when they came to see you
And told you you'd soon be better . . .
You were looking much better . . .
You must get better . . .
There were so many important things to live for . . .
You could only smile.
What else could you do?
There might be important things to live for,
But death was just round the corner,
And death was more important just then.
Only it was no good trying to explain.

TRINIDAD

ROOTS
by Harold Telemaque

Who danced Saturday mornings
Between immortelle roots
And plays about his palate
The mellowness of cocoa beans,
Who felt the hint of the cool river,
In his blood,
The hint of the cool river,
Chill and sweet.

Who followed curved shores
Between two seasons,
Who took stones in his hands,
Stones white as milk,
Examining the Island in his hands;
And shells,
Shells as pink as frogs' eyes
From the sea.

Who saw the young corn sprout
With April rain
Who measured the young meaning
By looking at the moon
And walked roads a footpath's width,
And calling,
Cooed with the mountain doves
Come morning time.

Who breathed mango odour
From his polished cheek,
Who followed the cus-cus weeders
In their rich performance,
Who heard the bamboo flute wailing,
Fluting, wailing,
And watched the poui golden
Listening.

Who with the climbing sinews
Climbed the palm
To where the wind plays most
And saw a chasmed pilgrimage
Making agreement for his clean return,
Whose heaviness
Was heaviness of dreams,
From drowsy gifts.

ADINA
by Harold Telemaque

They hunt chameleon worlds with cameras.
Their guides avoid the virtue of our valleys,
They have not seen Adina's velvet figure
Swimming uncovered in our rivers' bubbles

They have not seen the bamboo's slow manoeuvre,
The light refracting round her shapely ankles:
They have not seen Adina's dancing beauty
Blazing effulgent in the Caribbean.

They stalk with telescopes the larger precincts
Their view ascends skyscrapers' hazy regions,
They have not seen the silver sun on green leaves,
Adina's basket starred with fruit and flowers,
The bird sung matinee, the dancing palm-trees,
Beside her rhythmic swinging arms
Storms do not strike
They have not seen Adina in the breezes
Blazing effulgent in the Caribbean.

HAITI
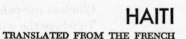
TRANSLATED FROM THE FRENCH

CHOUCOUNE[29]
by Oswald Durand

When I think of it all I am so sad,
In chains since that day my two feet I've had!

Choucoune—she is a *marabout*,
Her two eyes shine like candles too,
Her breasts stick straight out to view. . . .
Oh! if only Choucoune had been true!

We stood talking a long time there
Till the little wood-birds were all happy in air!

[29]From *Poets of Haiti*, translated by Edna Worthley Underwood; copyright, 1934.

I'd like to forget if I only could for it makes me sad,
In chains since that day my two feet I've had!

The little teeth of Choucoune as milk are white,
And her mouth is the color of our *caïmite,*
She's not a fat woman but plump and sweet,
The oldtime days are not these that we meet,
The little wood-birds every word they heard,
If they think of it now they must grieve and be sad,
In chains since that day my two feet I've had!

To the house of her mother we had to go,
An honest old woman and good you know.
She looked me over from shoes to hat,
Said I'm satisfied,—so that's all of that!

We drank nut-chocolate just as we should. . . .
Is it all settled now, Little Birds in the Wood?
But I'd like to forget it all I'm so sad,
In chains since that day my two feet I've had!

The furniture's ready; fine bed-*bateau,*
Rattan chair, table, and a *dodine,*
Mattress together with *porte-manteau,*
Table-spread, napkins, and shades *mousselines,*
And we had only fifteen days to go . . .
Little Birds of the Wood, hear, hear, for you know,
And you understand just why I'm so sad,
In chains since that day my two feet I've had!

A young white fellow, he happened our way,
Short red beard, pretty, blond face you see,
Smooth hair too and a watch on display,
He is the cause of what happened to me!

That Choucoune's a beauty he soon can tell.
He speaks French . . . Choucoune—she loves him
    well. . . .
I'd like to forget it, it makes me so sad,
She left me, since then in chains my two feet I've had!

But the saddest is this
And surprise you it will
Despite things amiss
Choucoune I love still.

Soon a baby mulatto there will be found,
Little Birds, Little Birds, look, see she's grown round.
Shut your mouths! Keep still . . . because I'm so sad,
In chains since that day both Pierre's feet he's had!

                                        E. W. U.

THE BLACK MAN'S SON[30]
by Oswald Durand

As Lise however my mother was white,
    Her eyes were blue where sleeping tears gleamed,
Whenever she blushed or in fear or delight,
    Pomegranates burst into bloom it seemed.

Her hair was gold too! In wind and the light
    It covered her forehead where pale griefs dreamed.
My father was blacker than I. Yet deemed
    Sacred their union the Church and right.

Behold, strange contrast, on her white breast
    A child as golden and brown as the maize,
Ardent too as the sun in our land always.
    I, orphan, loved Lise at youth's intensest,
But her face grew pale at such words from me,
    The Black Man's son held a terror you see.

                                        E. W. U.

[30]From *Poets of Haiti,* translated from the original by Edna Worthley Underwood; copyright, 1934.

IF[31]
by Oswald Durand

If ever I'd known Italy
   Or Florence where men grief forget,
Where Raphael painted grandly,
   Or Venice where the sails shine yet
And gaily they can sing a song,
   As soon as evening came along
I would call to some one dear:
   Come, dream in my gondola here
While these rare mansions slip along!

But 'tis only our sad mountains I know
   Where bend and sway the banana trees,
Our skies, horizons without bound,
   And forests sweet and springtime breeze.
At dusk when winds strut with such pride,
   Gay curling fields of rice are found,
Marianne I call unto my side:
   Come to the Savane let us go,
To love where blossoms the mango!

              E. W. U.

FAREWELL[32]
by Isaac Toussaint-L'Ouverture

Shores of my native land
   What tears I have shed for you
When the winds with cruel command
   Called the hour of my adieu!
Borne by the ship, swift, light,
   Far from love, from the joys I knew,

[31,32]From *Poets of Haiti*, translated from the original by Edna Worthley Underwood; copyright, 1934.

The little thatched-roof vanished from sight
Of the one love my heart knew.

Strange the stars, all this other world,
   Strange the cities, the people I view,
This longing which my soul suffers
   'Mid sailors where fires blew,
And the sea—this supreme barrier,
   All tell my grief again too—
How far, how far the little thatched-roof
Of the one love my heart knew!

I have braved both storm and war,
   Strange lands with their stranger ways!
But nothing has dimmed your face for me
   Whether safe in port or at sea's mercy,
I kept on saying of you:
When shall I see the little thatched-roof
Of the one love my soul knew!

E. W. U.

TO MADAME LA DUCHESSE DE BAUFFREMONT[33]
by Louis Morpeau

Your park's like a Gothic Cathedral to me,
   Your chestnut trees tower like antique marbles grandly.
The pallid hues under your opaline sky
   Delight me. Yet my homesick heart must sob and still cry.

Now the twilight is bleeding and the wind sweeps the grain,
   All my great sun-land at my throat leaps again—
Chestnut trees of Brienne, flower covered and old,
   Ah! Mangoes of Haiti—rich green and so gold!

E. W. U.

[33]From *Poets of Haiti,* translated from the original by Edna Worthley Underwood; copyright, 1934.

BELLE-DE-NUIT*, ³⁴
by Ignace Nau

Oh My Beauty of Night!—close, close quick your robe
    For the moon has grown pale on the edge of the dusk,
Waste not the rich sweetness of your censer so pure,
    The morning blooms soon and Dawn's eyes are wide!

The light of the sun is too bitter for you.
    Hide, hide humble flower, where the branches are thick
'Til night comes along with its breezes, its balm,
    And the moon's timid crescent comes back to the sky.

Your rare shaded purple again you can wear,
    Again among lovers you'll see round you glow
The wingéd night-moths with be-diamonded eyes.
    What kisses, what sighs—Oh! sweet, sweet fiancée!—
When disputing your heart in the fury of love
    They'll swarm tonight bee-like—love's manifold charms!

                   E. W. U.

AMITIÉ AMOUREUSE³⁵
by Luc Grimard

Look, look! Day dies and the evening has come!
    The dusk once again has surprised us here;
The light grew pale, fainted, too weary alas,
    Leaving memory only as its perfume.

The dusk once again has surprised us here,
    In front of the sea, the wall, the old tree,
Soon will vanish horizons for us less clear,
    Since something within is released, set free.

*Botanical name, *Mirabilis Jalapa,* the West Indian Four O'Clock.

³⁴,³⁵From *Poets of Haiti,* translated from the original by Edna Worthley Underwood; copyright, 1934.

> The last breeze of summer shivers over the palm
> Whose lower branches are yellowing some,
> Late hours of September are like this and calm!
> Look!—day dies now and the night has come.

E. W. U.

ELEGIES[36]
by Philippe Thoby-Marcelin

> *J'ai une alliance*
> *avec des pierres veinées bleu,*
> *et vous melaissez, également, assis,*
> *dans l'amitié de mes genoux.*

SAINT-LÉGER LEGER

I

Outside—wind heavy and wet
Plucks at the mango trees.

They keep on dropping—the stars
Without any wishing at all.

Night beckons back a cloud
To fling around one shoulder

Where I fain would stretch me out
For rest that's sweet.

II

Faiths washed away
As with sponge.

[36]From *Poets of Haiti,* translated from the original by Edna Worthley Underwood; copyright, 1934.

Yet children still hunt the sun
With pebbles flung, and with cries.

Mosquitoes circling warn me
Night will be long, long,

If there were not anything left to love
Or hate . . .

III

'Twas Summer I recall—
Summer, wet, heavy, unchaste,
With floating vapors,—and hot.

A shadow—in agony,
That crawls toward a far fountain.

Trees which keep grieving aloud
The echoes of pain grown great . . .

A woman I'd longed to love
Waited for me till the night.

IV

The season of love
Will it come back?

The season of love
When you loved me not?

My heart was rotting and sad
Like a leaf of Autumn that's dead.

My song lifted pure and high
The perfume of my land

Where wasps buzz and sting
Around mangoes ripe, rotting . . .

V

The morning's moist and fog-veiled,
The hills pasture like the cows
Belly-deep in grass bathing.

Sea Swallows last night's dusk knew,
Then burned in the late sunset,
Leap alive from their ashes anew . . .

Today is the day that I love you
My Beauty . . . my sweet regret.

E. W. U.

POET OF FAREWELL[37]
by Christian Werleigh

Partir c'est mourir un peu

TOSTI

My verses dream-rich and tender you've read,
    All my songs, old now and forgotten as well,
Like a black palm-trunk whose top's severed,
    And you have called me the poet of farewell.

The poet of farewell! It is true, as you tell,
    I have always sung of what fades and then dies,
My poor heart's been merely a kind of chapel
    Where Grief came to dry her beautiful eyes.

[37]From *Poets of Haiti*, translated from the original by Edna Worthley Underwood; copyright, 1934.

I have often known in that instant's brief gleam
  Just what broke in the heart at the fateful word,
Eternities seen with their hope, with their dream,
  Expand in one sob sent to God who heard.

E. W. U.

A NEGRO SINGS[38]
by Normil Sylvain

Oh! Little Girl!
  Do not try to love me.
  Beware black abysses that sleep in my eyes!
  In the deeps of my eyes dwells laughter that slays,
  Go away!

Little Girl, Little Girl!
  Do not pause,
  Not even to hear me sing
  In my songs are too many sobs.

  From the wind and the rain I stole my songs.
  They gave words.
  The rain . . . it knows tales and tales . . .
  And wind knows grief of the world,—
  That traveller everywhere.

  Songs I sing for self.
  They cradle thought and my grief.
  I am drunk on solitude,
  Like my ancestors the slaves.

  My despairing soul sings despair.
  Keep away from this black midnight!
  The labyrinth's ways are not yours.

[38]From *Poets of Haiti,* translated from the original by Edna Worthley Underwood; copyright, 1934.

Roads of silence I know,
Mystery's paths,
Grief's secret places, and dim.

Little Girl, you are wrong!
You could not love me,
I am sad,
Love lives on joy.

I am sadder than tears,
Than good-byes,
Than sadness.
I know Golgotha, Gethsemane,

Little Girl, Little Girl! . . .
Let me go,
Let me carry my own sorrow.

I am sad tonight—
The vast sadness
Of a martyred race.

E. W. U.

THE MANGOES[39]
by Duracine Vaval

To intoxicate you with the wine of things,
Might I not offer you a pale bouquet where roses fail?
A poem pleasing in its even rhythms?
I send you then a basket full of mangoes.

Desire clings to their yellow tawny flesh.
The savour of the soil lies deep within them.
Their dusky tang of camphor or of muscatel
Filters scent-borne into the very soul.

[39]From *An Anthology of Contemporary Latin-American Poetry*, edited by Dudley Fitts. Reprinted by permission of New Directions.

And these mangoes, honey-sweet, that decked the hedge,
They are fragrant with black shadow, with the sun,
Fragrant with a true and love-provoking breath.

In the orchard that bleeds in its vermilion cloak
The golden mango surpasses in prime sweetness
Our royal fruits swollen with juice and light!

D. D. W.

THE PEASANT DECLARES HIS LOVE[40]
by Emile Roumer

HIGH-YELLOW of my heart, with breasts like tangerines,
you taste better to me than eggplant stuffed with crab,
you are the tripe in my pepper-pot,
the dumpling in my peas, my tea of aromatic herbs.
You are the corned beef whose customhouse is my heart,
my mush with syrup that trickles down the throat.
You are a steaming dish, mushroom cooked with rice,
crisp potato fries, and little fish fried brown . . .
My hankering for love follows you wherever you go.
Your bum is a gorgeous basket brimming with fruits and meat.

J. P. B.

LA MAMBO DANS LE HOUNFORT[41]
by Charles F. Pressoir

Above a rough altar, coarse cement all,
  Beside wine bottles a candle glows
At the feet of Christ, a red flame shows,
  Shadows dance on the mortar wall.

But what can be done with a goat without horns?

[40]From *An Anthology of Contemporary Latin-American Poetry,* edited by Dudley Fitts. Reprinted by permission of New Directions.

[41]From *Poets of Haiti,* translated from the original by Edna Worthley Underwood; copyright, 1934.

On the whitewashed wall in bright colored paint,
  Obscure vague symbols and cabalistic,
Some simple old male forms hieratic
  Which edge the engravings of a saint.

But what can be done with a goat without horns?

One peasant plays the part of Legba,
  And like our country women here,
Comes from Ouédo the black one dear,
  In a short jacket, sweet Ayida.

But what can be done with a goat without horns?

Next Agoué, the Barkentine,
  Lord of the Tempests, Master of Seas
Who cuts off heads, Ogou precedes,
  A murderous general, menacing, mean.

But what can be done with a goat without horns?

In a corner they roll, they roar,—the big drums
  Covered with hairy wild-ass hide,
Monstrous black devils and side by side,—
  Mama, Papa, then *Cata* comes.

But what can be done with a goat without horns?

Now the old witch waves her *tiatia,*
  Strange, strange canticles kneeling sings,
In 'midst of the mystical hymning rings
  Over and over the name Maria.

But what can be done with a goat without horns?

But when Mambo ceases behold—*voilà*
  Something that moves on the ground is spread
Uplifting two shining points fiery red,
  This is the serpent of Damballa.

But what can be done with a goat without horns?

On the altar of this dim temple fall
  The flames of the candles, they tremble and shake,
While mysterious and horrible shadows make
  The old hag's dances along the wall.

Tonight the wind cries over the Mornes . . .

But what can be done with a goat without horns?

E. W. U.

COUNTRY GRAVEYARD[42]
by Charles F. Pressoir

> *"C'est le lent chemin de Guinée."*
>
> JACQUES ROUMAIN

In the high, high grass of Guinée
  The little houses hide,
Gray stone, moss-grown and thickly,
  Like dun hair that floats beside.

Sometimes the ground curves slightly
  In a long, vague, pebbly wave
Which the weeds veil but lightly—
  Some poor wretch's fresh-made grave.

At foot of the Cross suspended,
  Lest the dead should know *grangou*,
A tiny grain, some fish, foods blended
  At feet of Christ you find voodoo.

[42]From *Poets of Haiti*, translated from the original by Edna Worthley Underwood; copyright, 1934.

So they follow the two faiths ever—
The white, the bone-bred deeply.
Do the dead go then forever,
To Heaven or to Guinée?

E. W. U.

WHEN THE TOM-TOM BEATS . . .[43]
by Jacques Roumain

Your heart trembles in the shadows, like a face
    reflected in troubled water
The old mirage rises from the pit of the night
You sense the sweet sorcery of the past:
A river carries you far away from the banks,
Carries you toward the ancestral landscape.
Listen to those voices singing the sadness of love
And in the mountain, hear that tom-tom
    panting like the breast of a young black girl

Your soul is this image in the whispering water where
    your fathers bent their dark faces
Its hidden movements blend you with the waves
And the white that made you a mulatto is this bit
    of foam cast up, like spit, upon the shore.

L. H.

LANGSTON HUGHES[44]
by Jacques Roumain

At Lagos you knew sad faced girls.
Silver circled their ankles.
They offered themselves to you naked as the night
Gold-circled by the moon.

[43]From *An Anthology of Contemporary Latin-American Poetry*, edited by Dudley Fitts. Reprinted by permission of New Directions.

[44]From *Poets of Haiti*, translated from the original by Edna Worthley Underwood; copyright, 1934.

You saw France without uttering a worn, shop-made phrase;
            Here we are, Lafayette!
The Seine seemed less lovely than the Congo.

Venice. You sought the shade of Desdemona.
Her name was Paola.
You said: *Sweet, sweet Love!*

And sometimes
Babe! Baby!
Then she wept and asked for twenty *lire*.

Like a Baedeker your nomad heart wandered
From Harlem to Dakar.
The Sea sounded on in your songs—sweet, rhythmic,
      wild. . . .
And its bitter tears
Of white foam blossom-born.

Now here in this cabaret as the dawn draws near you
      murmur . . .
Play the blues again for me!
O! for me again play the blues!

Are you dreaming tonight, perhaps, of the palm trees, of
      Black Men there who paddled you down the dusks?

                                        E. W. U

GUINEA[45]
by Jacques Roumain

            It's the long road to Guinea
            Death takes you down
            Here are the boughs, the trees, the forest
            Listen to the sound of the wind in its long hair
                of eternal night

[45]From *An Anthology of Contemporary Latin-American Poetry*, edited by Dudley
Fitts. Reprinted by permission of New Directions.

It's the long road to Guinea
Where your fathers await you without impatience
Along the way, they talk
They wait
This is the hour when the streams rattle
    like beads of bone

It's the long road to Guinea
No bright welcome will be made for you
In the dark land of dark men:
Under a smoky sky pierced by the cry of birds
Around the eye of the river
    the eyelashes of the trees open on decaying light
There, there awaits you beside the water a quiet village,
And the hut of your fathers, and the hard ancestral stone
    where your head will rest at last.

                                        L. H.

NEDJÉ[46]
by Roussan Camille

Not quite sixteen,
you said you came from Danakil,
you whom vicious white men
crammed with anisette and whiskey
in that smoke-filled cafe
in Casablanca.

Through the narrow window
the dusk was dripping blood
on the burnous of the Spahis
leaning against the bar
and tracing above the desert outside
epic visions
of clashes, pursuits,
defeats and glory.

[46]Reprinted by permission of author and Mercer Cook, translator. First appeared in *The American Anthology*, Port-au-Prince, 1944.

One bloody evening
which was but a minute
in the eternal bloody night of Africa,
so sad a night
your dance became imbued with it
and made me sick at heart
like your song,
like your glance
blending with my soul.

Your eyes were full of countries
so many countries
that when I looked at you
I saw anew
in their wild light
the dark suburbs of London,
the brothels of Tripoli,
Montmartre, Harlem,
every pseudo paradise
where Negroes dance and sing
for others.

The nearby call
of your mutilated Danakil,
the call of black fraternal hands
infused into your dance of love
a virginal purity
and echoed in your heart
great familiar songs.

Your frail arms
through the smoke
yearned to embrace
centuries of pride,
kilometers of landscape,
while your steps
on the waxed mosaic
sought the highlands and the lowlands
of your childhood.

The window opened on the anxious East.
One hundred times your heart returned there.
One hundred times the red rose brandished
in your delicate finger-tips
adorned the mirage
of the gates of your village.

Your sorrow and nostalgia
were known to all the débauchés
sailors on manoeuvres
soldiers on leave
the idling tourists
crushing your brown breasts
with the vast boredom of travellers.
The missionaries and the fearful
sometimes tried to console you.

But you alone know
little girl from Danakil
lost in the smoke-filled cafés of Casablanca,
that your heart
will find its happiness when
in the new dawns
that bathe your native desert
you return to dance
for your living heroes,
your heroes yet unborn.

Then each step,
each gesture,
each glance,
each song
will show the sun
your land belongs to you!

                                        M. C.

HARLEM[47]
by Jean Brierre

I have seen you suffer in the midst of winters,
and your shadow erect amidst the street lamps
has told me often of its hunger at the doors
    of the eating houses.
I have seen you bleed at times on the sidewalks,
and I have not heard your agony make complaint.
I have seen you adorned in the springtime,
    bedecked in laughter and joy,
    dressed in sunshine and silk,
    singing and dancing,
    singing strange songs,
the heavy songs of sirens,
    of voyaging,
    of calls and of silence on forgotten seas,
    of bitter songs,
    ending with outbursts of laughter
    like mighty cymbals.
I have seen you dancing in whirlwinds
    like the frenzied,
    celebrating some god hidden in the
    depths of you.
Where, O Harlem, do you sleep?
Perhaps you pluck the leaves of the last star
in your fragile cup
and find again at the portals of the dawn
    the trouble,
    the toil,
    the weariness,
    the poverty,
    the hour which sounds like a knell
and your heart, weary and alone
on the road, hostile and black.

J. F. M.

[47]Translated by John F. Matheus, from *Ebony Rhythm*, edited by Beatrice M. Murphy. The Exposition Press, New York.

MARTINIQUE

TRANSLATED FROM THE FRENCH

Passages from:
MEMORANDUM ON MY MARTINIQUE
by Aimé Césaire

Neither the teacher of the class nor the priest with his catechism can get a word out of this sleepy Negro lad, although they drum energetically on his shorn skull, for his voice is engulfed in the swamps of hunger   (say-a-single-word-just-one-and-the-Queen-of-Castile-will-be-forgotten, say-a-single-word-just-one, look-at-the-boy-who-doesn't-know-a-single-of-the-ten-laws-of-the-Lord)

For his voice sinks in the swamps of hunger,
And there is really nothing to be drawn from this good-for-nothing,
nothing but the hunger which can no longer climb to the rigging of
his voice,
a heavy and slack hunger,
a hunger buried in the depths of the Hunger of this starveling hill.

.   .   .

Also mine: a little cell in the Jura mountains, a little cell, the snow adds white bars, the snow a white jailer guarding my prison cell
What is mine
A single man imprisoned in white
A single man defying the white cries of white death
(TOUSSAINT, TOUSSAINT LOUVERTURE)
A single man who fascinates the white hawk of white death
A man alone in the sterile sea of white sand
An old Negro facing the waters of the sky
Death describes a white circle above this man
Death gently stars his head
Death breathes in the ripe sugar-cane of his arms
Death gallops in the prison like a white horse

Death shines in the shadow like cats' eyes
Death hiccups like water under the Keys
Death is a hurt bird
Death wanes
Death vacillates
Death is an easily offended patyura
Death expires in a white swamp of silence.

L. A. & I. G.

FRENCH GUIANA
TRANSLATED FROM THE FRENCH

POEMS
by Léon Damas

REALLY I KNOW
nothing sadder
or more hateful
or more frightening
or more lugubrious in the world
than to hear love at the end of the day
repeating itself like a low mass
once upon a time
a woman happened to pass
whose arms were full of roses

.   .   .

TRITE WITHOUT DOUBT
but before giving over
entirely beautiful and black
to the whorl-flowered grass
on the path which leads
to the mountains
where a bamboo flute

cries in the night
the girl with the calabash
of indifference on her head
should pray three times each
to Lord Jesus
the Virgin
Saint Joseph

. . .

SHE LEFT HERSELF ONE EVENING
to prowl around
my misery
like a mad dog
like a naked dog
like a doggish dog
quite mad
quite naked
quite doggishly
dog

thus simply
the drama began

L. H.

CUBA

TRANSLATED FROM THE SPANISH

OPINIONS OF THE NEW CHINESE STUDENT
by Regino Pedroso

Until yesterday I was polite and peaceful . . .

Last year I drank the yellow-leaved Yunnan tea
in fine cups of porcelain,
and deciphered the sacred texts of Lao-Tze,
of Mang-tze,
and the wisest of the wise, Kung-fu-Tseu.

Deep in the shade of the pagodas
my life ran on, harmonious and serene,
white as the lilies in the pools,
gentle as a poem by Li Tai Po,
watching the loop-the-loop
of white storks at eve
against the screen of an alabaster sky.

But I have been awakened by the echo of foreign voices
booming from the mouths of mechanical instruments:
dragons setting ablaze with howls of grapeshot—
to the horror of my brothers
murdered in the night—
my bamboo houses
and my ancient pagodas.

And now, from the airplane of my new conscience,
I watch over the green plains of Europe,
and her magnificent cities
blossoming in stone and iron.

Before my eyes the western world is naked.
With the long pipe of the centuries
in my pale hands,
I am no longer enticed by the opium of barbarism.
Today I march toward the progress of the people,
training my fingers on the trigger of a Mauser.

Over the flame of today
impatiently I cook the drug of tomorrow.
I would breathe deep of the new era
in my great pipe of jade.
A strange restlessness
has taken all sleep from my slanting eyes.
To gain a deeper view of the horizon
I leap up on the old wall of the past . . .

Until yesterday I was polite and peaceful . . .

                              L. H.

CANE
by Nicolas Guillén

Negro
in the cane fields.

White man
above the cane fields.

Earth
beneath the cane fields.

Blood
that flows from us.

L. H.

SIGHTSEERS IN A COURTYARD
by Nicolás Guillén

Tourists in the courtyard
of an Havana tenement.
Cantaliso sings a song
not made for dancing.

Rather than your fine hotels,
stop in the courtyard of this tenement.
Here you'll see plenty of local color
you'll never find in your hotels.
Gentlemen, allow me to present to you
   Juan Concinero!
He owns one table and he owns one chair,
he owns one chair and he owns one table,
   and one oil stove.

The oil stove won't burn
and hasn't kissed a pot for ages.
But see how jolly and gay,
how well-fed and happy
    Juan Concinero
    is today!

JUAN CONCINERO INTERRUPTS:

With what one Yankee
drinks down
in steins of beer,
anybody could live
a whole year!

THE SONG CONTINUES:

Folks, this is Louis, the candy-maker.
And this is Carlos from the Canaries.
And that Negro there is called Pedro Martinez.
And that other, Norberto Soto.
And that dark girl over there, Petra Sarda.
All of them live in the same room—
No doubt because that's not so dear.
What people! What high-class people live here!

ALL IN CHORUS:

With what one tourist
spends on brandy in a day,
a month's room rent
anybody could pay.

THE SONG GOES ON:

That woman coughing over there,
folks, by name of Juana:

tuberculosis in an advanced stage.
Nobody looked after her
so, like a dunce,
she went all day
without eating. A funny idea—
with so much food to waste!

ALL IN CHORUS:

What one Yankee
drinks up with ease
Might've cured
Juana's disease.

THE SONG ENDS:

Oh, but tourists, stay here,
and have a good time!
This is your chance!
Tourists, stay here!
Have a good time!
This is your chance!
I'll sing you songs
Nobody can dance!

L. H.

DEAD SOLDIER
by Nicolás Guillén

What bullet killed him?
Nobody knows.
Where was he born?
In Jovellanos, they say.

Why did they pick him up?
He was lying dead in the road
And some other soldiers saw him.
What bullet killed him?

His sweetheart comes and kisses him.
His mother comes and cries.
When the Captain gets there
All he says is:
Bury him!

Rat-ta-tat-tat!
THERE GOES THE DEAD SOLDIER.

Rat-ta-tat-tat!
THEY PICKED HIM UP IN THE ROAD.

Rat-ta-tat-tat!
A SOLDIER AIN'T NOTHING.

Rat-ta-tat-tat!
THERE'RE PLENTY OF SOLDIERS.

                                          L. H.

WAKE FOR PAPA MONTERO
by Nicolás Guillén

You burned the dawn
with the fire of your guitar:
juice of the cane
in the gourd of your dark warm flesh
under a cold white moon.

Music poured from you
round and mulatto as a plum.

Steady drinker
with the throat of tin,
boat cut loose in a sea of rum,
horseman of the wild party,
what will you do with the night
now that you can no longer drink it,
and what vein
will give you back the blood
you've lost down the black drain
of a knife wound?

Tonight they got you,
Papa Montero!

They waited for you at your flat,
but they brought you home dead.
It was a good fight,
but they brought you home dead.
They say he was your pal,
but they brought you home dead.
Nobody could find the knife,
but they brought you home dead.

Now Baldemero's done for,
a devil, a dog, and a dancer!

Only two candles
burn away the shadows.
For your two-bit death
two candles are too many.
But the red shirt
that once lit up your songs
and the brownskin laughter of your music
and your gleaming straightened hair,
makes more light for you now
than any candles.

Tonight they got you,
Papa Montero!

Today the moon rose
in the courtyard of my house.
It fell blade-wise to earth
and stuck there.

Some kids picked it up
to wash its face,
so I bought it tonight
to be your pillow.

L. H.

TWO WEEKS
by Nicolás Guillén

She was a little girl who smelled
of nice cologne and castile soap.
I loved her with a simple passion
that some love poems and a look had given hope.

I remember when I told her that I loved her
a blush made red each pallid little cheek.
She put her stubby hands upon a chair back,
looked at her shoes, and did not speak.

That useless little girl could tell me
nothing new, so I began to see
her love as quite too young for lovers' ways.

Facts are, scarcely did we smile or pine.
We spoke five times and looked nine.
It lasted only fourteen days.

L. H.

PROPOSITION
by Nicolás Guillén

Tonight
when the moon comes out
I shall change it
into money.

But I'd be sorry
if people knew about it,
for the moon
is an old family treasure.

L. H.

BARREN STONE
by Nicolás Guillén

You will come back to me
when the road has given you all its secrets,
whispered its dusty voice in your ear—
when, like a barren stone,
your true self is worn away,
your mouth is bitter
and the hours,
with folded arms,
have nothing more to say.

I cannot talk to you then—
for you will be more unresponsive than ever.
Your presence will pass through mine
like a rolling stone
tumbling into the depths of myself,
falling into my past,
I shall see you sinking.
I shall hear the hollow sound.

I shall wait for the last echo,
the ultimate vibration
in the depths,
far down—
a barren stone,
your true self
worn away.

L. H.

FEDERICO
by Nicolás Guillén

*An excerpt concerning Federico García Lorca,
from "ESPAÑA, Poema en Cuatro Angustias
y Una Esperanza."*

I knock at the door of a romance.
"Is Federico not here?"
A parrot answers:
"No, he has gone."

I knock at the door of crystal.
"Is Federico not here?"
There comes a hand to answer:
"He is at the river."

I knock at the door of a gypsy.
"Is Federico not here?"
No one answers, no one speaks . . .
"Federico! Federico!"

Dark and empty is the house,
black moss on the walls,
rim of a bucketless well
and garden of green lizards.

On the spongy earth
snails that move,

and the red wind of July
sways among the ruins.

Federico! Federico!
Where does the gypsy die?
Where do his eyes grow cold?
Where is he, that he doesn't come?
Federico! Federico!

A SONG

He left on Sunday at nine,
he left on Sunday, at night,
He left on Sunday, and never came back!
In his hand was an iris,
in his eyes a fever,
the iris became blood,
the blood became death.

ANOTHER SONG

Where are you, Federico?
Where are you, that you don't come!
Federico! Federico!
Where are you, that you don't come!
Where are you, that you don't come!

MOMENT WITH GARCÍA LORCA

Federico dreamed of spikenard and wax
and olive and carnation and cold moon.
Federico, his Granada, and the springtime lax.

He slept alone in solitude's abode,
stretched out beneath ambiguous lemon trees
as songs passed down the lonely road.

Vast, the night with blazing starlight gleams.
In its transparent train it pulls along
over paths and cart-roads shining beams.

Passing slowly by, a gypsy crowd,
with unprotesting hands tied fast,
called "Federico!" suddenly aloud.

What voice is that of all their bloodless veins!
What softness in their steps, their steps!
And what benumbèd ardors cloak their pains!

Darkened by night, and olive-green they took
the harsh, the hard invertebrated road
Where senses used to walk barefoot.

Federico arose bathèd in shining light,
Federico, his Granada, and the springtime lax,
And with his moon, carnation, spikenard, wax
over the perfumed mountain followed them that night.

B. F. C.

FAREWELL TO MY MOTHER[48]
by Placido

(*Written in the Chapel
of the Hospital de Santa Cristina
on the night before his execution*)

If the unfortunate fate engulfing me,
The ending of my history of grief,
The closing of my span of years so brief,
Mother, should wake a single pang in thee,

[48]Translated by James Weldon Johnson from the Spanish of Placido; from *Saint Peter Relates an Incident*, copyright, 1935, by James Weldon Johnson. Reprinted bv permission of The Viking Press, Inc.

Weep not. No saddening thought to me devote;
I calmly go to a death that is glory-filled;
My lyre before it is forever stilled
Breathes out to thee its last and dying note.

A note scarce more than a burden-easing sigh
Tender and sacred, innocent, sincere—
Spontaneous and instinctive as the cry
I gave at birth— And now the hour is here—
O God, thy mantle of mercy o'er my sins!
Mother, farewell! The pilgrimage begins.

J. W. J.

AFRICA

NATIVITY[49]
by Aquah Laluah

Within a native hut, ere stirred the dawn,
Unto the Pure one was an Infant born;
Wrapped in blue lappah that His mother dyed,
Laid on His father's home-tanned deerskin hide,
The Babe still slept, by all things glorified.
Spirits of black bards burst their bonds and sang
'Peace upon earth' until the heavens rang.
All the black babies who from earth had fled
Peeped through the clouds—then gathered round His head.
Telling of things a baby needs to do,
When first he opes his eyes on wonders new;
Telling Him that to sleep was sweetest rest,
All comfort came from His black mother's breast.

[49]Reprinted by permission of The Atlantic Monthly.

Their gift was Love, caught from the springing sod,
Whilst tears and laughter were the gifts of God.
Then all the Wise Men of the past stood forth,
Filling the air, East, West, and South and North;
And told Him of the joy that wisdom brings
To mortals in their earthly wanderings.
The children of the past shook down each bough,
Wreathed frangipani blossoms for His brow;
They put pink lilies in His mother's hand,
And heaped for both the first fruits of the land.
His father cut some palm fronds, that the air
Be coaxed to zephyrs while He rested there.
Birds trilled their hallelujahs; all the dew
Trembled with laughter, till the Babe laughed too.
All the black women brought their love so wise,
And kissed their motherhood into His mother's eyes.

THE SERVING GIRL[50]
by Aquah Laluah

The calabash wherein she served my food,
Was smooth and polished as sandalwood:
Fish, as white as the foam of the sea,
Peppered, and golden-fried for me.
She brought palm wine that carelessly slips
From the sleeping palm tree's honeyed lips.
But who can guess, or even surmise
The countless things she served with her eyes?

THE SOULS OF BLACK AND WHITE[51]
by Aquah Laluah

The souls of black and white were made
By the selfsame God of the selfsame shade.

[50],[51]Reprinted by permission of *The Atlantic Monthly*.

God made both pure, and He left one white;
God laughed o'er the other, and wrapped it in night.

Said He, "I've a flower, and none can unfold it;
I've a breath of great mystery, nothing can hold it.
Spirit so illusive the wind cannot sway it,
A force of such might even death cannot slay it."

But so that He might conceal its glow
He wrapped it in darkness, that men might not know.
Oh, the wonderful souls of both black and white
Were made by one God, of one sod, on one night.

BIOGRAPHICAL NOTES

LEWIS ALEXANDER (Washington, D.C., 1900–   ) was educated in the public schools in Washington and at Howard University. He studied further at the University of Pennsylvania.

SIDNEY ALEXANDER (Brooklyn, New York, 1912–   )

HERVEY ALLEN (Pittsburgh, Pennsylvania, 1889–   )

RUSSELL ATKINS (Cleveland, Ohio, 1926–   ) attended public schools and later studied at the Cleveland School of Art and at the Cleveland Institute of Music. His poems have appeared in *View, Experiment,* and in several newspapers.

RAYMOND BARROW (British Honduras) (Belize, 1920–   ), the son of a district judge, was educated at St. John's College in Belize. His poems have appeared in magazines in the British West Indies. From 1942 to 1945 he was editor of the *Civil Service Chronicle* in Honduras.

STEPHEN VINCENT BENÉT (Bethlehem, Pennsylvania, 1898–1943)

WILLIAM ROSE BENÉT (Fort Hamilton, New York Harbor, N.Y., 1886–   )

GWENDOLYN B. BENNETT (Giddings, Texas, 1902–   ) received her elementary education in the schools of Washington, D.C., and was graduated in 1921 from the Girls' High School of Brooklyn, New York. She then studied at Columbia University and at Pratt Institute in Brooklyn. An early interest in the fine arts led to a year's study in Paris at the Académie Julian and the École de Panthéon and to an instructorship in Art at Howard University. She served for a time as a member of the editorial staff of *Opportunity.*

ELIZABETH BISHOP (Worcester, Massachusetts, 1911–   )

WILLIAM BLAKE (England) (London, 1757–1827)

MAXWELL BODENHEIM (Natchez, Mississippi, 1892–   )

ARNA BONTEMPS (Alexandria, Louisiana, 1902–   ) was educated in elementary schools in Los Angeles, at San Fernando Academy, at Pacific Union College in Angwin, California, and at the University of Chicago. He has held teaching posts in New York City, in Alabama, and in Chicago. In 1943 he became chief librarian of Fisk University in Nashville, Tennessee. His poetry first appeared in *The Crisis* magazine in 1924. In 1926 his "Golgotha Is a Mountain" won the Alexander Pushkin Award for Poetry offered by *Opportunity.* The following year his "The Return" was given the same award. His "Nocturne at Bethesda" won a first prize in the poetry contest sponsored by *The Crisis* in 1927. Since then his writing has been mainly in prose, as represented by the novels *God Sends Sunday,* 1931, *Black Thunder,* 1936, and *Drums at Dusk,* 1939; by biographical and historical books like *They Seek a City* (with Jack Conroy, 1945), *We Have Tomorrow,* 1945, and *Story of the Negro,* 1948; and the following stories for young people: *Popo and Fifina* (with Langston Hughes, 1932), *You Can't Pet a Possum,* 1934, *Sad-Faced Boy,* 1937, and *The Fast Sooner Hound* and *Slappy Hooper* (with Jack Conroy, 1942 and 1946). *St. Louis Woman,* a musical play based on his novel *God Sends Sunday,* was produced at the Martin Beck Theatre in New York City in 1946. Bontemps is the editor of *Golden Slippers,* an anthology of Negro poetry for young people.

KAY BOYLE (St. Paul, Minnesota, 1903–   )

WILLIAM STANLEY BRAITHWAITE (Boston, Massachusetts, 1878–   ) was born of West Indian parents. His career as a poet began in 1904, with the publication of *Lyrics of Life and Love*. A second volume, *The House of Falling Leaves*, followed in 1908, and in 1948 Coward-McCann, Inc., issued his *Selected Poems*. Braithwaite is best known, perhaps, for his *Anthologies of Magazine Verse*, begun in 1913 and continued until 1929. Edgar Lee Masters's Spoon River poems, Vachel Lindsay's chants, Carl Sandburg's free verse, and the early work of many other important American poets were included in the Braithwaite anthologies before they appeared in other books. Other anthologies by Braithwaite include *The Book of Elizabethan Verse*, 1906, *The Book of Georgian Verse*, 1908, and *The Book of Restoration Verse*, 1909. For several years he worked on the editorial staff of the Boston *Transcript*, and in 1918 he was awarded the Spingarn medal for high achievement by an American Negro. In the same year honorary degrees were conferred on him by Atlanta University and by Talledega College. Later he became a Professor of Creative Literature at Atlanta University, a position he held until his retirement in 1945. Since then he has been engaged in a biographical and literary study of the Brontës.

BENJAMIN GRIFFITH BRAWLEY (Columbia, South Carolina, 1882–1939) was educated at Morehouse College, the University of Chicago, and at Harvard. He taught English at Morehouse and at Shaw and Howard universities. His books were mainly works of literary and social history, such as *A Short History of the American Negro*, 1918, *A Short History of English Drama*, 1921, *A New Survey of English Literature*, 1925, *The Negro Genius*, 1937, and *Negro Builders and Heroes*, 1937. But he also wrote poems and short stories which had not been collected at the time of his death.

JEAN F. BRIERRE (Haiti) (Jérémie, 1909–   ) was educated by the Frères de l'Instruction Chrétienne and at the Lycée. Then he went to France to study political science and later to Columbia University in New York City. He is the secretary general of the Union of Haitian Writers and Artists and the director of cultural affairs in the Department of Foreign Relations. His *L'Adieu à la Marseillaise*, three verse tableaux on the life of Toussaint L'Ouverture, was produced in 1939 and again in 1947. His publications include *Le Petit Soldat*, 1933, *Nous Garderons le Dieu*, poems in memory of Jacques Roumain, 1945, and *Black Soul*, a poem, 1947. He is the editor of *Province*, an anthology in three volumes.

GWENDOLYN BROOKS (Topeka, Kansas, 1917–   ) has lived in Chicago nearly all her life. Public schools, Englewood High, and Wilson Junior College, from which she was graduated in June 1936, contributed to her education. Her poems, which first appeared in magazines, achieved book publication in 1945 in *A Street in Bronzebille*. Miss Brooks's early poems won prizes in the Midwestern Writer Conference competition and at Northwestern University, but her published volume quickly gained more important recognition. *Mademoiselle* selected her as one of the ten women of the year in 1945. The following year she was given an American Academy of Arts and Letters award. In 1946 she won a Guggenheim Fellowship which was renewed the following year.

JONATHAN HENDERSON BROOKS (near Lexington, Mississippi, 1904–45) was born on a farm. When his parents separated during his childhood, he remained with his mother, and together they worked the fields on "half shares" until he was fourteen. Then began the struggle for an education. Intervals in school were broken frequently by periods of farm work and teaching, but Brooks eventually made his way through high school at Jefferson City, Missouri, and then went to college at Tougaloo, Mississippi. Later he did graduate work at Columbia University. At the time of his death he was working in the post office at Corinth, Mississippi, where he had made his home since 1935. A posthumous book, *The Resurrection and Other Poems,* achieved publication as co-winner in the Eighteenth Book Publication Contest of Kaleidograph, Dallas, Texas, 1948.

STERLING A. BROWN (Washington, D.C., 1901–   ) was educated in the Washington schools and at Williams College and Harvard University. He started his teaching career at Virginia Seminary. Short periods at Fisk University and at Lincoln in Missouri followed. Then began his long and distinguished association with Howard University, where he holds a professorship in English. At intervals he has been visiting professor of English at Vassar College and at the University of Minnesota and a visiting lecturer at New York's New School. He served as editor on Negro affairs for the Federal Writers' Project and was a staff member of the Carnegie-Myrdal Study of the Negro. In 1937 he was given a Guggenheim Fellowship. His published books include *Southern Road,* 1932, a volume of poetry; *The Negro in American Fiction,* 1938; and *Negro Poetry and Drama,* 1938. He was an editor of the *Negro Caravan,* 1941.

ELIZABETH BARRETT BROWNING (England) (Carlton Hall, Durham, 1806–61)

WITTER BYNNER (Brooklyn, New York, 1881–   )

ROUSSAN CAMILLE (Haiti) (Jacmel, 1915–   ) began his education in his home town and continued it at the Tippenhauer Institute and at the Lycée National Alexandre Petion in Port-au-Prince. In 1935 he joined the staff of the Haiti *Journal.* Two years later he was appointed first secretary of the Haitian Legation in Paris. In 1940 he returned to Port-au-Prince, where he was appointed to an important post in the Department of National Education. Then followed periods as editor in chief of the Haiti *Journal* and an appointment to the post of vice-consul in the Haitian Consulate in New York. He has traveled widely and represented his country frequently as a cultural envoy. A collection of his poems, *Assaut a la Nuit,* was published in Port-au-Prince in 1940.

GEORGE CAMPBELL (Jamaica) (Panama, 1917–   ) attended local schools before entering St. George's College. He worked as a newspaper reporter on the *Daily Gleaner* of Kingston and later migrated to New York City.

DAVID WADSWORTH CANNON, JR. (New Brunswick, New Jersey, 1910–38) was educated in public schools, at Hillsdale College in Michigan, from which he graduated in 1931, and at the University of Michigan, where he was awarded a master's degree the following year. He was then appointed to the faculty of Virginia State College at Petersburg. In 1937 he was granted a Rosenwald Fellowship for further study at Columbia University.

H. D. CARBERRY (Jamaica, B.W.I.) (Montreal, Canada, 1922–   ) was educated in Jamaica at high schools in Spanish Town and Mandeville, at Jamaica College in St. Andrew, and at St. Catherine's College, Oxford University (England), where he received a degree in law.

CATHERINE CATER (New Orleans, Louisiana, 1917–   ) earned her first college degree at Talladega in Alabama and later joined the staff of the Fisk University library. From the University of Michigan she received a professional degree in Library Science and a doctorate in Language and Literature. She has held a Rosenwald Fellowship and is now connected with Olivet College in Michigan as a librarian-instructor.

AIMÉ CÉSAIRE (Martinique) (Basse-Pointe, 1913–   ) attended the Ecole Normale Supérieure de Paris and graduated as one of the youngest *agrégés* of France. Returning to his native island, he became a professor of literature at the Scholcher College of Martinique. He has served as representative to two national legislative assemblies of France, as mayor of Fort-de-France, and as Consul General. He is at present a Representative from Martinique in the French Assembly. His published works include *Cahier d'un Retour au Pays Natal*, Paris, 1939, (published in translation in the United States in 1947), *L'appel au magicien*, 1944, *Les Amies Miraculeuses*, 1946, *Soliel Coup Congé*, 1948.

MARCUS B. CHRISTIAN (Houma, Louisiana, 1900–   ) was mainly self-educated. He served as supervisor of the Dillard University Negro History Unit of the Federal Writers' Project and was later given a Julius Rosenwald Fellowship to complete a history begun on the project. He was appointed an assistant in the Dillard Library. His poems and articles have appeared in anthologies and periodicals.

MASSILLON COICOU (Haiti) (Port-au-Prince, 1865–1908) was educated by the Frères de l'Instruction Chrétienne and at the Lycée Pétion. He had an active political career, serving at one time as a member of the cabinet of President Thirésias S. Sam and as Haitian minister to Paris. Prior to his death before a firing squad in 1908, he also held a chair of philosophy in Port-au-Prince. He was the founder of the revue *L'Oeuvre* and the author of two collections of poetry: *Les Poésies Nationales*, 1891, and *Impression et Passion*, 1902. He wrote several works for the theater, among them *Dessalines Liberté*, performed in Paris in 1904 in celebration of the one hundredth anniversary of Haitian independence.

HELEN JOHNSON COLLINS (Hampton, Virginia, 1918–   ) is the daughter of schoolteacher parents. After several preliminary moves, her family reached Cleveland, where she attended Central High. Her undergraduate college work was done at Oberlin College (on a scholarship) and at Flora Stone Mather College, from which she received an A.B. in 1938. At Western Reserve University she studied library science, in which she earned a B.L.S. in 1944. She is an assistant in the Quincy branch of the Cleveland Public Library.

LESLIE MORGAN COLLINS (Alexandria, Louisiana, 1914–   ) is indebted to the Sisters of St. James at Alexandria for his elementary education. He went on to Straight College and Dillard University in New Orleans, however, graduating from the latter in 1936. Then followed graduate work at Fisk, teaching posts in several Southern schools, and more graduate study leading to a doctor's degree from Western Reserve University in 1945. He became a member of the English faculty at Fisk in the fall of 1945. His poems have appeared in *Poet Lore* and other little magazines.

FRANK A. COLLYMORE (Barbados, B.W.I.) (St. Michael, 1893–   ) was educated at the Combemere School, at which he has been teaching since 1910. Recently he went to England on a British Council scholarship. His verses have been collected in *Thirty Poems*, 1944, and *Beneath the Casuarinas*, 1945. He is co-editor of the local magazine *Bim*, in which his short stories and poems frequently appear with his own illustrations.

ALICE CORBIN (St. Louis, Missouri, 1881–   )

JAMES DAVID CORROTHERS (Cass County, Michigan, 1869–1919) was a neglected orphan. Later he worked in sawmills and lumber camps in Michigan, on the Great Lakes as a sailor, and elsewhere as a coachman, janitor, and barbershop bootblack. Then friends encouraged his efforts to get an education, and he became a minister and continued in that profession the rest of his life. His poems, first published in the *Century* magazine, attracted wide attention, partly for their resemblance to those of Paul Laurence Dunbar's. His verses were collected in 1907 in *Selected Poems* and later in *The Dream and the Song*, 1914.

JOSEPH SEAMON COTTER, JR. (Louisville, Kentucky, 1895–1919) was the precocious son of a well-known father. His health was frail from childhood, and he had to end his college work at Fisk University in his second year as a result of tuberculosis. A year before he died he published a small volume of poems called *The Band of Gideon*.

JOSEPH SEAMON COTTER, SR. (Bardstown, Kentucky, 1861–   ) was forced by circumstances to leave school when he was in the third grade, and he was twenty-two before he resumed his formal education. During the interval he worked as a ragpicker, tobacco stemmer, brickyard hand, whisky distiller, teamster, and prize fighter. When he finally completed his education, he became a schoolteacher in Louisville, Kentucky.

HART CRANE (Garrettsville, Ohio, 1899–1932)

COUNTEE CULLEN (New York, N.Y., 1903–46) was educated in the public schools of New York City. His recognition as a poet began when he was still in high school. As a student at New York University he won the Witter Bynner Poetry Prize, open to all undergraduates in American colleges. He received a master's degree from Harvard in 1926. He later became a teacher in the public schools of New York City, the work in which he continued till his death. *Color*, Cullen's first volume of poetry, appeared in 1925, when the poet was only twenty-two years old. This book won him the Harmon Gold Award for literature as well as notable critical approval. It was followed in 1927 by *The Ballad of the Brown Girl* and *Copper Sun*. Then came *The Black Christ*, 1929, written on a Guggenheim Fellowship; *One Way to Heaven*, 1932, a novel; *The Medea and other Poems*, 1935; *The Lost Zoo*, 1940; *My Nine Lives and How I Lost Them*, 1942; and *On These I Stand*, published posthumously in 1947. Cullen edited *Caroling Dusk*, 1927, an anthology of Negro American poetry, and collaborated with Arna Bontemps in the dramatization of *St. Louis Woman* from the latter's novel.

WARING CUNEY (Washington, D.C., 1906–   ) was educated in the public schools of Washington, at Howard University, at Lincoln (Pennsylvania), at the New England Conservatory of Music in Boston, and in Rome, where he studied singing. While he was still a student at Lincoln Cuney's poem "No Images" won a first prize in an *Opportunity* poetry contest This was in 1926. Since then his lyrics have appeared in magazines and anthologies, and some of them have been set to music and recorded. He served three and one half years in the Army as a technical sergeant in the South Pacific, receiving the Asiatic Pacific Theater Ribbon with three Bronze Battle Stars.

WESLEY CURTRIGHT (Brunswick, Georgia, 1910–   ) was educated in New York City and at Pacific Union College, Angwin, California. For a number of years he was employed by the New York State Civil Service. He now lives on a farm in Cass County, Michigan.

PIERRE DALCOUR (New Orleans, Louisiana,) was the son of wealthy parents who sent him to France in the early 1800s to be educated. A member of the free colored group in Louisiana, he elected to spend much of his adult life abroad. He returned to New Orleans after completing his education, but by then he was unable to accept the injustices of racial discrimination. He returned to France, though not before he had written a number of poems, several of which were included in the anthology *Les Genelles,* compiled by Armand Lanusse in 1845.

LÉON DAMAS (French Guiana) was born about the turn of the century. In his youth he went to Paris where he became a protégé of André Gide and a friend of the surrealist, André Breton. After World War I he returned to his native land and in 1917 was elected a deputy to the French National Assembly.

FRANK MARSHALL DAVIS (Arkansas City, Kansas, 1905–   ) attended school in Arkansas City until he was ready for Kansas State College. There he studied journalism, part of the time on a Sigma Delta Chi scholarship. During the summers he worked on farms and with street-construction gangs. In 1931 he went to Georgia to help start the Atlanta *Daily World.* He remained as editor of the *World* until 1934. The following year he became feature editor of the *Associated Negro Press* in Chicago, of which he later became executive editor. Meanwhile he has been a Rosenwald Fellow in Poetry, 1937, a lecturer on the History of Jazz Music at the Abraham Lincoln School in Chicago, and a member of the National Board of the Civil Rights Congress. Davis is the author of *Black Man's Verse,* 1935, *I Am the American Negro,* 1937, and of *47th Street,* 1948.

CLARISSA SCOTT DELANY (Tuskegee Institute, Alabama, 1901–27) was the daughter of Emmett J. Scott, the distinguished secretary of Booker T. Washington. After a childhood at Tuskegee she went to Bradford Academy in New England and then to Wellesley College. Three years of teaching in Dunbar High School in Washington, D.C., followed. She was married to Hubert Delany in 1926.

H. BINGA DISMOND (Richmond, Virginia, 1891–   ) was educated at public schools, at Howard University Academy, and at the University of Chicago, where he became a celebrated track star. He entered Rush Medical College before World War I and later specialized in physical therapy. He is the director of this department in the Harlem Hospital in New York City. A book of his poems, published in 1943, is called *We Who Would Die.*

OWEN DODSON (Brooklyn, New York, 1914–   ) was educated at public schools and at Bates College. He took graduate studies leading to a Master of Fine Arts degree at Yale. Two of his plays, *Divine Comedy* and *Garden of Time,* were produced at Yale, and others have been performed by little-theater groups at various colleges. Talladega College commissioned him to write a play on the Amistad mutiny. He has taught drama at Spelman College in Atlanta, Georgia, and at Howard University in Washington, D.C., where he is now a member of the faculty. His first published book, *Powerful Long Ladder,* 1946, was a collection of poems. He has contributed poetry and prose to a number of magazines and received a Rosenwald Fellowship for Creative Writing.

WILLIAM EDWARD BURGHARDT DuBOIS (Great Barrington, Massachusetts, 1868–   ) began his education in Great Barrington, Massachusetts. He went to Fisk University and continued his studies at Harvard and the University of Berlin. Best known as a scholar and a spokesman for the dark peoples of Africa and the world, he has always been a poet at heart. The poetic prose of books like *The Souls of Black Folk* has already inspired generations of Negro artists and writers. His first published book, *The Suppression of the African Slave Trade,* appeared in 1896. A long list of scholarly volumes has followed. Occasionally, however, in the course of his work as college professor, editor, and founder of *The Crisis* magazine, director of research and publicity for the National Association for the Advancement of Colored People and champion of human rights, he has written poetry as such. His verses are scattered through periodicals and miscellanies.

ALFRED DUCKETT (Brooklyn, New York, 1918–   ) attended the Boys' High School in Brooklyn. He was a newspaperman for a while and worked on the Amsterdam *News,* the New York *Age,* and the Pittsburgh *Courier.* He was attached to Special Services overseas during World War II. His poems have appeared in *Twice a Year,* and a piece by him was included in *This Is Our War.*

PAUL LAURENCE DUNBAR (Dayton, Ohio, 1872–1906) was the son of former slaves, one of whom, the father, had escaped by way of the Underground Railroad. Young Dunbar attended the public schools of Dayton and graduated from high school in 1891. When he was unable to attend college, he went to work as an elevator operator. He was employed in this capacity in 1893 when his first book, *Oak and Ivy,* was privately printed. A second volume, *Majors and Minors,* followed in 1895. Neither of these attracted wide attention but they won enough approval to assure the success of his *Lyrics of Lowly Life,* which came out in 1896. This book soon gained for Dunbar a national reputation and enabled him to pursue a literary career. In spite of the declining health which resulted in his early death, Dunbar produced a large quantity of work. He wrote much prose, and his other books of verse include *Lyrics of Love and Laughter,* 1903, *Lyrics of Sunshine and Shadow,* 1905. His *Complete Poems* was issued in 1913.

OSWALD DURAND (Haiti) (Cap Haitien, 1840–1906) was one of the best-loved poets of his country. A prose writer, dramatist, and editor as well as poet, he held important government offices and traveled abroad. He is remembered as "an ardent Nationalist" and as a "man of merry and tempestuous living, who, in his later days, bore resemblance to Dumas, *père*, with his leonine head of unruly hair, gay flowered shirts, flowing ties." He worked best in the Creole idiom, and it was in this dialect that his widely popular "Choucoune," 1884, was written.

JESSIE REDMOND FAUSET (Philadelphia, Pennsylvania) was educated in the public schools of Philadelphia and at Cornell University. She received an A.B. from Cornell in 1905 and was elected to Phi Beta Kappa. Graduate study, leading to the M.A. degree, was taken at the University of Pennsylvania, and further work at the Alliance Française, Paris, earned her a certificate. For several years she was literary editor of *The Crisis*, but mainly her work has been teaching. Her poems have appeared in numerous magazines and anthologies. She is also the author of four novels: *There Is Confusion*, 1924, *Plum Bun*, 1929, *The Chinaberry Tree*, 1931, *Comedy: American Style*, 1933.

JOHN GOULD FLETCHER (Little Rock, Arkansas, 1886–   )

LUC GRIMARD (Haiti) (Cap Haitien, 1886–   ) received an elementary education from the Sisters of St. Joseph de Cluny in Cap Haitien before going on to the secondary l'Ecole Moderne de Saindoux and then to the Lycée National Philippe-Guerrier. He has since had a notable career as a professor and then as a director of this institution. His work has also included the practice of law, a professorship in law in Cap Haitien, service as Consul General of Haiti in Havre, France (1922–26), and a period as curator of the National Museum in Port-au-Prince. His poems have been collected in *Sur ma Flûte de Bambous* and *Ritournelles*, both published in Paris, 1927. He collaborated in the preparation of the volumes *Quelques Poèmes, Quelques Poètes*, Port-au-Prince, 1934, and *La Corbeille*, Port-au-Prince, 1942, and a book of short stories, *Du Sable entre les Doigts*, Port-au-Prince, 1941.

ANGELINA WELD GRIMKÉ (Boston, Massachusetts, 1880–   ) was educated at various northern schools, including the Girls' Latin School and the Boston Normal School of Gymnastics. She became a teacher in the Armstrong Manual Training School of Washington, D.C., in 1902. Beginning in 1916 she taught English for a number of years at Dunbar High School in the same city. Later she moved to New York City. *Rachel*, a three-act play by Miss Grimké, was published in 1921.

NICOLÁS GUILLÉN (Cuba) (Camaguey, 1904–   ) graduated from the Institute of Camaguey in 1920 and the following year entered University of Havana's School of Law. He soon dropped this course, however, for a career in journalism, politics, and poetry. His books of verse, which began appearing in 1930, soon won him a place among the foremost poets of Latin America. In 1947 *El Son Entero*, a collected edition of his poetical works, was issued by Pleamar of Buenos Aires. In 1948, *Cuba Libre*, a volume of his poems translated into English appeared in the United States.

JUPITER HAMMON (Queens Village, Long Island, 1720?–1806?) was the slave of one Henry Lloyd. The dates of his birth and death are obscure, but the earliest reference to him is found in a letter dated May 19, 1730, when Hammon was perhaps a little more than ten years old. He probably did not die before 1806. Hammon was an intelligent and privileged slave, respected by his master for his skill with tools and by his fellow slaves for his power as a preacher. His first published work, sometimes called the first literary effort by any Negro in the United States, was "An Evening Thought: Salvation by Christ, with Penitential Cries." It appeared as a broadside in 1760. His next known work, "A Poetical Address to Phillis Wheatley," appeared eighteen years later. His "An Essay on the Ten Virgins," of which no extant copy has been found, was printed in 1779. "A Winter Piece," including also "A Poem for Children with Thoughts on Death," "An Evening's Improvement," and a rhymed dialogue entitled "The Kind Master and Dutiful Servant" appeared in 1782. Hammon's "An Address to Negroes in the State of New York," his most substantial literary work, was issued in 1787. It went into three editions.

FRANCES E. W. HARPER (Baltimore, Maryland, 1825–1911) was educated in Baltimore and later moved to Ohio, where she taught for a while at Union Seminary in Columbus, but by 1853 she was in Little York, Pennsylvania, working in the interest of the Underground Railroad. A year later, as a result of her growing reputation, Mrs. Harper was engaged by the Anti-Slavery Society of Maine as a lecturer. After the Civil War she traveled extensively as a representative of the Women's Christian Temperance Union. Her first book, *Poems on Miscellaneous Subjects,* was published in 1854. Another, *Poems,* followed in 1871, and a third, *Sketches of Southern Life,* in 1872.

ROBERT HAYDEN (Detroit, Michigan, 1913–   ) was educated in Michigan. He went to college at Wayne University in Detroit and then to the University of Michigan for graduate work. From 1944–46 he held a teaching assistantship in the department of English at Michigan. He left to accept a position on the faculty of Fisk University. He is a member of Phi Kappa Phi, scholastic honors society. The first collection of his poetry, *Heartshape in the Dust,* 1940, was published by the Falcon Press of Detroit. Hayden received Hopwood awards for poetry in 1938 and 1942. He was granted a Fellowship in Creative Writing by Special Services Committee of Ann Arbor in 1946. In 1947 he received a Julius Rosenwald Fellowship for Creative Writing. His poems have appeared in *Poetry, Atlantic Monthly, Cross Section,* 1945 and 1947, and other periodicals and anthologies. A brochure, *The Lion and the Archer,* 1948, presented a group of his poems with some by Myron O'Higgins.

DONALD JEFFREY HAYES (Raleigh, North Carolina, 1904–   ). Beyond high school Hayes's education was gained entirely through private study. His interest was music, and he studied singing and directing with distinguished teachers. As a member of singing choruses he appeared in several Broadway productions in the twenties and thirties. Many of his poems have appeared in such magazines as *Harper's Bazaar, Good Housekeeping,* and *This Week.* They have also been in anthologies. He is employed as a counselor for the mentally and physically handicapped with the New Jersey State Employment Service.

DU BOSE HEYWARD (Charleston, South Carolina, 1885–1940)

LESLIE PINCKNEY HILL (Lynchburg, Virginia, 1880–   ) was educated in the public schools of his home town and at Harvard University. He taught at Tuskegee Institute and later became the principal of the Cheyney Training School for Teachers in Pennsylvania. He published two volumes of poetry: *The Wings of Oppression,* 1922, and *Toussaint L'Ouverture—A Dramatic History,* 1928.

CONSTANCE HOLLAR (Jamaica, B.W.I.) (Port Royal, 1880–1945) spent most of her life on the island where she was born. After completing her education she traveled in Great Britain and returned to Kingston to conduct a private kindergarten school. A collection of her poems appeared in 1941 under the title *Flaming June*. Her last years were marked by frail health and retirement.

JOHN WESLEY HOLLOWAY (Augusta, Georgia, 1865–1935) was the son of an ex-slave who had become by his own efforts one of the first Negro schoolteachers in Georgia. Holloway was educated at Clark in Atlanta and at Fisk University, where he was a member of the famous Jubilee Singers. He became a teacher and then entered the ministry.

LUCY ARIEL WILLIAMS HOLLOWAY (Mobile, Alabama, 1905–   ) received her early education at the Emerson Institute of Mobile and in the high school department of Talladega College. She went to Fisk and then to Oberlin Conservatory to study music. She was for a while the director of music at the North Carolina College, Durham. Since 1945 she has been supervisor of music in the Negro public schools of Mobile. Her first recognition as a poet came in 1926 while she was still a senior at Fisk University. Her "Northboun' " was selected as one of the winning poems in the *Opportunity* contest that year.

MOSES CARL HOLMAN (Minter City, Mississippi, 1919–   ) was educated in the public schools of St. Louis, Missouri. He attended Lincoln University in Jefferson City, majoring in English. Following his graduation he taught school for a year and then went on to the University of Chicago, where he received an M.A. in 1944. At Chicago he won a Fiske Poetry Prize. A year later a Julius Rosenwald Fellowship was awarded to him for further study and creative writing. He later joined the English faculty at Hampton Institute in Virginia.

FRANK HORNE (New York, N.Y., 1899–   ) was educated in the public schools and at the College of the City of New York. His professional and graduate studies were continued at the Northern Illinois College of Ophthalmology, at Columbia University, and at the University of Southern California. A member of his college's track team, Frank Horne's first poems reflected his athletic interest and achievements. After college he became a Doctor of Optometry and practiced in Chicago and New York, but he returned to the academic field and taught at Fort Valley Normal and Industrial School before entering governmental service in Washington with the U.S. Housing Authority. His poems have been published in magazines and anthologies. The first of his writings to attract attention, perhaps, was the series called "Letters Found Near a Suicide," which won a *Crisis* poetry award in 1925.

GEORGE MOSES HORTON (North Carolina, 1797–1883) was a slave of the Horton family of Northampton County, North Carolina. During most of his life he served one member or another of that family. At Chapel Hill he was permitted to hire himself out, and it was in this way that he gained employment in the home of the president of the university. Here he learned to read and write. He also discovered a way to earn pocket change: by composing love poems for the students at the rate of twenty-five to fifty cents each. In 1829 a volume of his poems was published in Raleigh under the title *The Hope of Liberty*. Horton hoped that the sale of this work would earn enough money to enable him to purchase his freedom, but, like many another poet, he was disappointed. When the Northern troops occupied Raleigh in 1865, Horton was an old man, but he escaped to their lines and to freedom, and the same year his second work, *Naked Genius,* appeared. The remainder of his life, one gathers, was spent in Philadelphia.

LANGSTON HUGHES (Joplin, Missouri, 1902–   ) attended the public schools of Lawrence, Kansas, but moved with his mother to Cleveland at the age of fourteen. There he attended Central High and graduated with the class of 1920, which he served as class poet and editor of the yearbook. A year in Mexico followed, and Hughes returned to enter Columbia University in 1921. A break with his father ended this phase of his education, however, and he went to work at odd jobs around New York. Then followed two years of sea-faring, with voyages along the African coast and to Europe. During this period his poetry, which had already been appearing in *The Crisis* and other maga-zines, began to attract the attention which resulted in the publication of his first volume. He then entered Lincoln University in Pennsylvania and gradu-ated in 1929. He has pursued a literary career ever since. Meanwhile awards and honors accumulated. There was a first prize in the *Opportunity* poetry contest in 1925, and another in 1926 in the Witter Bynner undergraduate poetry competition. He won a Harmon Award in 1931 and later received Guggenheim and Rosenwald fellowships and a grant from the American Academy of Arts and Letters. His published works include *Not Without Laughter,* 1930, a novel; *The Ways of White Folks,* 1934, short stories; and *The Big Sea,* 1940, an autobiography; in addition to the following collections of poetry: *The Weary Blues,* 1926, *The Dream Keeper,* 1932, *Shakespeare in Harlem,* 1942, *Fields of Wonder,* 1947, and *One Way Ticket,* 1949. He has had broad experience as journalist, song lyricist, dramatist, and lecturer, as represented by a column called "Here to Yonder" in the Chicago *Defender,* the lyrics for the Broadway musical version of Elmer Rice's *Street Scene* and the libretto for the William Grant Still opera *Troubled Island,* the Broadway play *Mulatto,* and six coast-to-coast poetry-reading tours.

DOROTHY VENA JOHNSON (Los Angeles, California) received her early education in a convent. She attended the University of California at Los Angeles and the University of Southern California, earning degrees from each. She is a junior high school teacher in Los Angeles. Her poems have appeared in periodicals and anthologies.

FENTON JOHNSON (Chicago, Illinois, 1888–   ) was educated in Chicago in the public schools and at the University of Chicago. At nineteen he produced original plays at the historically interesting Pekin Theatre of the same city. *A Little Dreaming,* his first volume of poetry, appeared in 1914, and in the two following years came *Visions of the Dusk* and *Songs of the Soil. Tales of Darkest America,* 1920, was a book of short stories. Johnson edited and pub-lished several small literary magazines.

GEORGIA DOUGLAS JOHNSON (Atlanta, Georgia, 1886–   ) was educated in the elementary schools of Atlanta, at Atlanta University, and at Oberlin Con-servatory in Ohio. She prepared herself for a career as a composer but soon felt that the road to this goal was obstructed. Instead, she became a schoolteacher. When her husband was appointed Recorder of Deeds under President William Howard Taft, she moved to Washington, D.C. Later she herself was employed in government agencies in the capital. The hope of becoming a composer was replaced by an interest in poetry. The published volumes of her lyrics include *The Heart of a Woman*, 1918, *Bronze*, 1922, and *An Autumn Love Cycle*, 1928.

HELENE JOHNSON (Boston, Massachusetts, 1907–   ) was educated in public schools and at Boston University. In 1926 she went to New York to attend the extension division of Columbia University. She remained long enough to see her poems published in such magazines as *Opportunity* and *Vanity Fair* and reprinted in a number of anthologies.

HERBERT CLARK JOHNSON (Mattoax, Amelia County, Virginia, 1911–   ) was educated in Virginia and at the Cheyney Training School for Teachers in Pennsylvania. His poems have been published in magazines and collected in the volume *Poems from Flat Creek*, 1943.

JAMES WELDON JOHNSON (Jacksonville, Florida, 1871–1938) received his early education in Jacksonville, and then attended Atlanta University. A subsequent career as public school principal, lawyer, diplomat, executive secretary of the National Association for the Advancement of Colored People and Professor of Creative Literature at Fisk University paralleled his growth and maturity as a poet and man of letters. In 1900, with his brother J. Rosamond Johnson, he wrote "Lift Every Voice and Sing," a song that has become a kind of national anthem for the Negro people in the United States. His long list of published works include the following books of poetry: *Fifty Years and Other Poems*, 1917, *God's Trombones*, 1927, *St. Peter Relates an Incident of the Resurrection Day*, 1930, and *Book of American Negro Poetry*, first issued in 1922. Johnson wrote the lyrics for several musical shows and put his name on a number of hit songs in his early writing days. At the time of his death in an automobile accident in 1938 he was regarded as one of the foremost Negro Americans of his generation.

AQUAH LALUAH [Gladys May Casely Hayford] (African Gold Coast) (Axim, 1904–   ) is a Fanti by birth, but she attended college at Colwyn Bay in Wales. Returning to Africa after five years in England, she became a teacher in the Girls' Vocational School of Sierra Leone. Her poems, first published in the *Atlantic Monthly*, have also appeared in American anthologies.

ARMAND LANUSSE (New Orleans, Louisiana, 1812–67) was one of the most distinguished members of a social group in New Orleans known as free men of color. He received an excellent education, but it is not clear at this date whether or not he studied in France, as did so many of the talented colored youths of his group at that time. Lanusse was best known during his lifetime as the principal of the Catholic School for Indigent Orphans of color, a position he held from 1852 to 1866. Earlier than this, however, he was the leader of a group of young poets writing in French whose work he compiled in a significant little volume published in 1845 under the title *Les Cenelles*.

BETTE DARCIE LATIMER (Rochester, New York, 1927–   ) was educated in Rochester schools and at Fisk University, from which she graduated in 1948. She was then given a tuition fellowship for graduate study at the University of Michigan, mainly on the strength of her creative writing. As an undergraduate she was an assistant editor and a frequent contributor to the *Fisk Herald*. Her poems have also appeared in *Phylon* and *The Crisis*.

WILLIAM ELLERY LEONARD (Plainfield, New Jersey, 1876–1944)

VACHEL LINDSAY (Springfield, Illinois, 1879–1931)

HENRY WADSWORTH LONGFELLOW (Portland, Maine, 1807–82)

JAMES RUSSELL LOWELL (Cambridge, Massachusetts, 1819–91)

GEORGE MARION McCLELLAN (Belfast, Tennessee, 1860–1934) was educated at Fisk University and at Hartford Theological Seminary. *The Path of Dreams,* the volume that contains his best poems, was published in 1916.

BASIL McFARLANE (Jamaica, B.W.I.) (Kingston, 1922–   ) is the son of J. E. Clare McFarlane. He attended briefly Jamaica College and Calabar College before joining the Royal Air Force in 1944, but is mainly self-educated. He served in England for two years but returned to Jamaica to be demobilized after the war. He has since been a clerk in the government service of the island. His poems have appeared in the London *Mercury* and in *Life and Letters*.

J. E. CLARE McFARLANE (Jamaica, B.W.I.) (Spanish Town, 1896–   ) was educated privately and at Cornwall College. He has had a long and distinguished career in the island's civil service and now holds one of the most important government posts filled by a Jamaican. He is the deputy financial secretary and treasurer, and president of the Civil Service Association. Even more important, in the opinion of some, has been his contribution to the cultural life of the West Indies. He founded the Poetry League of Jamaica a quarter of a century ago and is the editor of *Voices from Summerland,* the first anthology of Jamaican poetry. Among other honors bestowed upon him, he has been named a Fellow of the Royal Society of Arts and an officer of the Order of the British Empire.

CLAUDE McKAY (Jamaica, B.W.I.) (Clarendon, 1891–1948) was the youngest of eleven children. His father was a farmer, his older brother the schoolmaster of the village. McKay received his elementary education in his brother's school, and at the age of seventeen he won a Jamaica Trade Scholarship and was apprenticed to a cabinetmaker and wheelwright. At nineteen he joined the Jamaica constabulary, and a year later he published his first book of poems, *Songs of Jamaica*. These dialect verses became popular locally and earned McKay an award from the Institute of Arts and Sciences. A year later he came to the United States to attend Tuskegee Institute in Alabama. After a few months at Tuskegee he went to Kansas State University, where he remained two years as a student in the Department of Agriculture. He then went to New York City and began contributing poetry to American magazines. In 1919 he went to Europe. During a year in London he published *Spring in New Hampshire*, 1920, a volume of poetry. On his return to America he became associate editor of the *Liberator* under Max Eastman. *Harlem Shadows,* his widely known book of poetry, came out in 1922. McKay then went abroad again and remained on the continent of Europe for about a decade. During that time, and in the years immediately following, he wrote much prose, including such well-known books as *Home to Harlem,* 1928, *Banjo,* 1929, *Gin-*

gertown, 1932, *Banana Bottom*, 1933, *A Long Way from Home*, 1937, and *Harlem: Negro Metropolis*, 1940.

ST. CLAIR McKELWAY (Charlotte, North Carolina, 1905–   )

A. B. MAGIL (Philadelphia, Pennsylvania, 1905–   )

ROGER MAIS (Jamaica, B.W.I.) (Kingston, 1905–   ) has had a varied and sometimes stormy career in his native Jamaica. His activities have included planting, clerkship, photography, painting, newspaper reporting, magazine editing, and several other occupations. One of his articles, "Now We Know," provoked a bitter political controversy and resulted in his internment for eighteen months. He is the author of *Face and Other Stories*, 1942, and of *And Most of All Man*, 1943, in which a group of his stories are collected with some of his poems.

UNA M. MARSON (Jamaica, B.W.I.) (Santa Cruz, St. Elizabeth, 1905–   ) has had a brilliant career as a journalist, lecturer, and poet. After serving in several secretarial and editorial posts on her native island, she went to London and worked with the League of Colored Peoples from 1933 to 1935. She was a delegate to the 12th Congress of the International Alliance of Women, Istanbul. She was given an assignment in connection with the League of Nations in Geneva the same year, and a year later she was attached to the staff of the Ethiopian Legation in London. She accompanied H. M. Haile Selassie to the meeting of the League of Nations at which he undertook to deal with the Italo-Ethiopian problem. She lectured widely in England and served as editor and broadcaster in the West Indies Program of the BBC, London, from 1941 to 1946, when she returned to Jamaica. Her published books include *Tropic Reveries*, 1930, *Heights and Depths*, 1931, *The Moth and the Star*, 1937, and *Towards the Stars*, 1945. She has also written plays, one of which was produced at the Scala Theatre in London in 1934. Her plays have had three Kingston productions.

AGNES MAXWELL-HALL (Jamaica, B.W.I.) (Montego Bay, 1894–   ) was educated in London, Boston, and in New York City, where she studied short-story writing at Columbia University. Her stories and poems have appeared in little magazines in the United States and in England. She owns and operates a dairy in the Jamaica mountains at Kempshot, the site of the observatory of her father, the late Maxwell Hall, F.R.A.S., F.R.M. et S.

HERMAN MELVILLE (New York, N.Y., 1819–91)

CATULLE MENDES (France) (Bordeaux, 1841–1909)

JOSEPHINE MILES (Chicago, Illinois, 1911–   )

LOUIS MORPEAU (Haiti) (Aux Cayes, 1895–1926) studied at the College of St. Martial and at the Lycée National in Port-au-Prince. Later he became a teacher in the Lycée National and an influential figure in Haitian literature. He has represented Haiti at various conferences in Paris and elsewhere and contributed many articles on his country to French periodicals. His publications include *Pages de Jeunesse et de Foi*, 1919, *Une Oeuvre de Pitie Sociale*, a brochure, *Anthologie Haitienne des Poètes Contemporains, 1904–1920*, 1920, and *L'Enterrement de la Merlasse*, Paris, 1924.

BEATRICE M. MURPHY (Harrisburg, Pennsylvania) has spent most of her life in Washington, D.C., where she is now a stenographer in the Veterans' Administration.

She also writes for newspapers and has edited two anthologies: *Negro Voices*, 1938, and *Ebony Rhythm*, 1948.

PAULI MURRAY (Baltimore, Maryland, 1910–   ) began her education in the public schools of Durham, North Carolina, and continued it in the high school at Richmond Hill, New York, at Hunter College in New York City, in the Howard University School of Law in Washington, D.C., and at the University of California School of Jurisprudence, which conferred on her the degree of LL.M. in 1945. She also attended Brookwood Labor College. She is a member of the bar of California and of New York, where she is now practicing. She has held academic fellowships, including one from the Julius Rosenwald Fund, and won prizes and awards from Howard University, the National Council of Negro Women, and the magazine *Mademoiselle*. She has written articles and pamphlets, and her poems have appeared in such magazines as *Common Ground, South Today, Opportunity, The Crisis,* and the *Saturday Review of Literature.*

IGNACE NAU (Haiti) (Port-au-Prince, 1812–45) studied in Haiti at L'Institution Jonathas Granville and then in New York at L'Institut Catholique. On returning to Haiti he was made officer détaché of the arsenal but was later discharged from his post. An eloquent nationalist orator, he became an authority on colonial life and traveled in France. But he soon retired from the political arena and withdrew to his country home to write and study at leisure. Earlier he had a hand in the publication of *Revue des Colonies,* Paris, 1837.

ALICE DUNBAR NELSON (New Orleans, Louisiana, 1875–1935) was the wife of Paul Laurence Dunbar. She was educated in the public schools of New Orleans and at Straight College. Later she attended several Northern universities. She taught school in New Orleans and in Brooklyn prior to her marriage to Dunbar in 1898. She published several volumes of prose.

EFFIE LEE NEWSOME (Philadelphia, Pennsylvania, 1885–   ) has lived much of her life at Wilberforce, Ohio. Most of her writing is for children and deals with nature lore. She is the author of *Gladiola Garden,* 1940.

MYRON O'HIGGINS (Chicago, Illinois, 1918–   ) was born on Chicago's south side, where he attended both public and parochial schools. He went to Howard University for his college work, studying under the guidance of Sterling A. Brown. As an undergraduate, his literary efforts won him a Lucy Moten Fellowship for travel and study in Mexico and Cuba. O'Higgins remained at Howard to take the master's degree and then served briefly as an instructor in English before entering the Army. He was awarded a Julius Rosenwald Fellowship upon his discharge from the Army. His poems have appeared in magazines and in a limited collection called *The Lion and the Archer,* 1948, issued in collaboration with Robert Hayden.

BARBARA STEPHANIE ORMSBY (Jamaica, B.W.I.) (Savanna-la-Mar, 1899–   ) was educated at Colonial High School in Kingston and at Whitelands College, Putney, England. She has been writing poetry since childhood.

KENNETH PATCHEN (Niles, Ohio, 1911–   )

REGINO PEDROSO (Cuba) (Union de Reyes, 1896–   ) is of Chinese and Negro ancestry. His youth was marked by heavy labor in the sugar, railroad, and steel industries, but later he was employed in the Ministry of Education. He is children's librarian at Parque Marti in Havana. He published several volumes of poetry, including *Nostros*, 1933, *Mas Alla Canta el Mar*, 1939, which received the National Literary Prize; and *Bolivar: Sinfonia de Libertad*, 1945.

PLACIDO [Gabriel de la Concepción Valdes] (Cuba) (Havana, 1809–44) is one of Cuba's national heroes. The illegitimate son of a colored father and a white Spanish dancer, he started life in an orphanage in Havana. Later he was rescued from this institution by his father and brought up by his paternal grandmother. At seventeen Plácido left Havana and made Matanzas his home. He was apprenticed to a tortoise-shell craftsman, an occupation which fostered in him the contemplation of nature. Poetry was the next step. At the age of thirty-five Plácido was executed by the Spanish rulers of the island, a martyr in Cuba's struggle for liberty.

KENNETH PORTER (Sterling, Kansas, 1905–   )

CHARLES FERNAND PRESSOIR (Haiti) (Paris, France, 1910–   ) was educated in France and England up to and including his baccalaureate in Paris in 1928. He took a law degree in Port-au-Prince in 1931, studied philology in Haiti, and then went to Columbia University in New York for studies in economics. He is now attached to the Internal Revenue Service in Haiti. He is also president of the Creole Academy. He is the author of *Au Rythme des Coumbites*, 1933, and *Debats sur le Créole et le Folklore*, 1947.

TOM REDCAM [Thomas Henry McDermot] (Jamaica) (Clarendon, 1870–1933) was educated at Falmouth Academy and at the Church of England Grammar School at Kingston. He started his career as a schoolmaster and gradually moved into journalism and literature. His patriotic songs have earned him a high place in the esteem of the island, where his countrymen sometimes called him "The Uncrowned Laureate of Jamaica."

WALTER ADOLPHE ROBERTS (Jamaica) (Kingston, 1886–   ) grew up in the town of Mandeville and became a reporter on the *Daily Gleaner* at the age of sixteen. Two years later he arrived in the United States and began a journalistic career that has since included work on newspapers and magazines from New York to San Francisco. When World War I broke out, Roberts was sent to France as a war correspondent by the Brooklyn *Daily Eagle*. Between 1918 and 1921 he served as editor of *Ainslee's Magazine*. A year later he became associate editor of *Hearst's International Magazine*, and this was followed by other editorships. His books include novels, biographies, and such vivid historical works as *The Caribbean*, and *The French in the West Indies*. His books of verse are *Pierrot Wounded and Other Poems*, 1919, and *Pan and Peacocks*, 1928.

EDWIN ARLINGTON ROBINSON (Head Tide, Maine, 1869–1935)

SELDEN RODMAN (New York, N.Y., 1909–   )

JACQUES ROUMAIN (Haiti) (Port-au-Prince, 1907–44) was educated largely in Europe. He was a prominent member of the group of young Haitian writers who founded the influential *Revue Indigène* in the late twenties, and he contributed some of its most distinguished poems. The first of his published works was a volume of short stories, *La Proie et L'Ombre*. It was followed in 1931 by *La Montagne Ensorcelee* and *Les Fantoches*. *Gouverneurs de la Rosée* appeared in 1944. Roumain's name became widely known internationally as a result of his political imprisonment and exile and his subsequent return to his native land and a post in the foreign service of the government. He died soon afterward, but the posthumous publication in English of his novel *Masters of the Dew*, New York, 1947, added to his literary stature.

EMILE ROUMER (Haiti) (Jérémie, 1903–   ) attended the Institute of St. Louis de Gonzague and later studied in France and England before entering the practice of law. He was one of the group that founded the *Revue Indigène*. His publications include *Poèmes d'Haiti et de France*, 1925, and *Nouveaux Poèmes*, 1945.

MURIEL RUKEYSER (New York, N.Y., 1913–   )

CARL SANDBURG (Galesburg, Illinois, 1878–   )

A. J. SEYMOUR (British Guiana) (1914–   ) was educated at Queen's College, Georgetown, and is now an assistant public information officer for British Guiana. He also edits *Kykoveral*, a twice-a-year literary and critical magazine, and serves the British Guiana Writers' Association and the British Guiana Union of Cultural Clubs as president and home secretary respectively. His published works include *Verse*, 1937, *More Poems*, 1940, *Over Guiana Clouds*, 1944, *Sun's in My Blood*, 1945, and *Six Songs*, 1946. He is, moreover, married and the father of six children.

KARL SHAPIRO (Baltimore, Maryland, 1913–   )

PHILLIP M. SHERLOCK (Jamaica) (Portland, 1902–   ) was educated at Calabar High School on the island and in London, where he received his college degree. He has had a long career as schoolmaster, librarian, and education officer in Jamaica. He has written and published a number of books for use in schools and is considered an authority on Jamaican folklore.

EDWARD S. SILVERA (Jacksonville, Florida, 1906–37) was graduated from the Orange High School in 1924 and then went on to Lincoln University in Pennsylvania. At Lincoln he participated in athletics and wrote poems, some of which were included in a pamphlet called *Four Lincoln Poets*, 1930. His verses also appeared in magazines and anthologies before his early death.

LOUIS SIMPSON (Kingston, Jamaica) (1923–   ) came to the United States to enter Columbia University. During the war he served in Europe with distinction. His studies, interrupted at Columbia, were resumed in Paris at the end of the hostilities.

ANNE SPENCER (Bramwell, West Virginia, 1882–   ) was educated in the Virginia Seminary in Lynchburg, Virginia, the city in which she has spent most of her life. She is the librarian of the Dunbar High School there. Recently she developed a pink candy-striped Chinese peony, eight years from seed. This fact, perhaps, tells as much about her life as anything—with the exception of her poems. Though these have appeared in magazines and anthologies for a number of years, they have not been collected in a book.

EDMOND CLARENCE STEDMAN (Hartford, Connecticut, 1883–1908)

NORMIL G. SYLVAIN (Haiti) (Port-au-Prince, 1901–29) was educated first in Paris at l'Institution Ste. Marie de Monceau and then at the Collège St. Martial in Port-au-Prince. He studied medicine in Haiti and entered the medical profession in 1926. He was associated with the group of young writers who founded the *Revue Indigène* in their search for an idiom native to their own

Haitian background. He was equally interested in medical affairs of the island, and he was among the founders of l'Association de Médecine Haitienne. He founded the *Annales de la Médecine Haitienne*.

HAROLD MILTON TELEMAQUE (Trinidad, B.W.I.) (Plymouth, Tobago, 1911–   ) is the son of a captain of a sailing schooner which operated among the islands of the West Indies. He was educated by Moravian ministers at Bethesda, at Bishop's High School at Scarborough, and at the Government Training College for Teachers. His work as a schoolteacher on the island led finally to the head mastership of the large Fyzabad Intermediate E. C. School, his present position. *Burnt Bush*, 1947, presents the first published collection of his poems.

LUCY TERRY (Eighteenth century) was the slave of Ensign Ebenezer Wells of Deerfield, Massachusetts. Her "Bars Fight" recounts the events of a bloody Indian raid on the settlers of that town on August 25, 1746. George A. Sheldon, historian of Deerfield and student of the Indian wars in the Connecticut Valley, says that her description of that episode during King George's War is the best and most colorful version extant.

PHILIPPE THOBY-MARCELLIN (Haiti) (Port-au-Prince, 1904–   ) was educated in the Petit Séminaire and the Collège of St. Martial. He is a professional journalist, but from the first his interest has been in the literary reviews and newer kinds of writing. He was associated with *La Nouvelle Ronde* (1925–26), the *Revue Indigène* (1927–28), *La Revue Européene* (1928), *La Revue Caraïre* (1931), *La Relève* (1932–1940), *Les Criots* (1938–39), *France-Amérique* (1934), and *Gaceta del Caribe* (1944), *Conjonction* (1947–48). He was in charge of "Studio No. 3," bulletin of the *Centre D'Art* (1945–46). He has published several books of poems, including *La Négresse Adolescente*, 1932, *Dialogue avec la Femme Endormie*, 1941, and *Lago-Lago*, 1943. Two novels by him, written in collaboration with Pierre Marcellin, are known in the United States. *Canapé Vert*, New York, 1944, won the Farrar & Rinehart prize for a Latin-American novel. *La Bête de Musseau* was brought out in New York by the same publishers in 1946 under the title *The Beast of the Haitian Hills*.

MELVIN BEAUNEARUS TOLSON (Moberly, Missouri, 1898–   ) completed undergraduate college work at Lincoln University and then went to Columbia for an M.A. For twenty-two years he was a member of the faculty of Wiley College in Marshall, Texas, where he became widely known for his debating teams and his work with the drama club and the English department. His poem, "Dark Symphony," won a prize at the Negro American Exposition in Chicago and later appeared in the *Atlantic Monthly*, before being included in a collected volume of his poetry, *Rendezvous With America*, 1944. From Wiley he went to Langston University as professor of English.

JEAN TOOMER (Washington, D.C., 1894–   ) was educated at the University of Wisconsin and the College of the City of New York. In 1918 he decided on a literary career, and his poems, short stories, and sketches began appearing in magazines. These were collected in 1923 in the book *Cane*.

RIDGELY TORRENCE (Xenia, Ohio, 1875–   )

ISAAC TOUSSAINT L'OUVERTURE (Haiti) (Ennery, 1782–1854) was the son of the Haitian liberator and governor of Santo Domingo. He was educated in a military school in France. An eloquent prose writer as well as poet, Isaac Toussaint L'Ouverture left memoirs unpublished in Bordeaux at the time of his death. He is sometimes credited with authorship of *L'Haitiade,* a poem in the epic tradition, published in Paris in 1828. He was one of those unusual individuals who combine the qualities of charm, bravery, good looks, and physical prowess with the ability to write well.

PERIENT TROTT (McKeesport, Pennsylvania, 1910–   )

H. A. VAUGHAN (Barbados, B.W.I.) (1901–   ) continued his education in England, where he studied law. He has been a member of the Barbados House of Assembly, but is now a district magistrate on the island. His special interest is the history of Barbados, in which connection he is working on a biography of Sir Conrad Reeves. He published *Sandy Land and Other Poems* in 1945.

DURACINE VAVAL (Haiti) (Aux Cayes, 1879–   ) studied in Paris and went on to qualify for the practice of law. He has been a teacher as well as a civil judge in his home city and in Port-au-Prince. He was at one time the chief of the Haitian Legation in London. His publications include *L'art Dans la Vie,* 1900; *Conferences Historiques,* 1907; *Coup d'Oeil sur l'Etat Financier de la République,* a brochure, 1907; *Litterature Haitienne,* critical essays, Paris, 1911; *Les Stances Haitiennes,* Paris, 1912; and *L'Ame Noire,* 1933, also published in Paris.

VIVIAN L. VIRTUE (Jamaica, B.W.I.) (Kingston, 1911–   ) was educated at Kingston College. The first collection of his poems appeared in 1938 under the title *Wings of the Morning.* He has contributed to such British magazines as *Life and Letters* and the London *Mercury.* He is an officer of the Poetry League of Jamaica and a member of the Royal Society of Literature of England.

MARGARET ABIGAIL WALKER (Birmingham, Alabama, 1915–   ). A minister's daughter, Margaret Walker attended Methodist church schools in Mississippi and Alabama before enrolling at Gilbert Academy in New Orleans, from which she graduated in 1930. She graduated from Northwestern University in 1935. In 1940 she received a master's degree from the State University of Iowa and two years later became an instructor in English at Livingstone College, Salisbury, North Carolina. From 1942–43 she taught English at West Virginia State College. Her first book of poems, *For My People,* was published in 1942 after winning the Yale University Younger Poets competition. A Rosenwald Fellowship for creative writing followed in 1944.

IRMA WASSAL (Amarillo, Texas, 1909–   )

CHRISTIAN WERLEIGH (Haiti) (Cap Haitien, 1895–1945) was educated by the Frères de l'Instruction Chretienne and at the Lycée National Philippe Guerrier in Cap Haitien. He later became a professor of rhetoric in the same institution and remained in this post the rest of his life. His best-known work, perhaps, is *Le Palmiste Dans l'Ouragan,* Cap Haitien, 1930 (but two earlier collections of his verse were *Contre la Balustrade,* published in France, and *La Halte au Bord du Fleuve*). Later came *Le Palmiste Dans la Lumière,* 1934, publication of which was sponsored by President Stenio Vincent of Haiti, and finally *Ma Ville, Mon Pays,* Port-au-Prince, 1944. For the theatre Werleigh wrote two verse plays, *La Fleu du Sacrifice* and *Tout Pour le Roi.* He left in manuscript a five-act drama dedicated to Toussaint L'Ouverture, *La Mort Couronne.*

DON WEST (Ellijay, Georgia, 1909–   )

PHILLIS WHEATLEY (Senegal, West Africa, 1753–84) was captured and sold into slavery in early childhood and brought to Boston in 1761. She became the property of John Wheatley of Boston whose wife and daughter soon noted the alert sensitivity of the young African girl and encouraged Phillis's efforts to acquire learning. Within a few years she was completely at home in the language and literature of her captors. She began writing poetry, and in 1770, at the age of seventeen, published "A Poem, by Phillis, A Negro Girl in Boston, on the Death of the Reverend George Whitefield." When her health began to fail, Phillis was advised by doctors to take a sea voyage. This was arranged by the kindly mistress, who also gave the girl her freedom before she sailed for England. In London, Phillis was a success. It was there that her only collected volume of verse was first issued under the title *Poems on Various Subjects, Religious and Moral,* 1773. Then one by one the patrons of this talented ex-slave girl died and she returned to Boston. Her marriage was unhappy, and she died as a servant in a cheap lodging house at the age of thirty-one.

CHARLES ENOCH WHEELER (Augusta, Georgia, 1909–   ) attended private schools in Augusta and the Henry George School in New York. He has been published in *The Crisis* and other periodicals, and a book of his poems, *Prelude,* was privately issued in 1943.

WALT WHITMAN (near Huntington, Long Island, N.Y., 1819–92)

JOHN GREENLEAF WHITTIER (Haverhill, Massachusetts, 1807–92)

NAOMI LONG WITHERSPOON (Norfolk, Virginia, 1923–   ) is the youngest of three children of a Baptist minister. She attended elementary school in East Orange, New Jersey, and high school in St. Louis, Missouri. She graduated from Virginia State College in 1945 and in the following year enrolled at New York University. A brochure of her poems was issued in 1941 under the title *Songs to a Phantom Nightingale.* Her work has also appeared in magazines.

WILLIAM WORDSWORTH (England) (Cockermouth, Cumberland, 1770–1850)

BRUCE McM. WRIGHT (Princeton, New Jersey, 1918–   ) attended college at Lincoln University in Pennsylvania. After a period of army service overseas during World War II, he entered Fordham University's School of Law. While he was abroad, a collection of his poems achieved publication in Wales under the title *From the Shaken Tower,* 1944.

RICHARD WRIGHT (near Natchez, Mississippi, 1908–   ) was born on a plantation. His family moved frequently and his education didn't get far. At fifteen he left home to work as a porter and messenger in Memphis. It was there he began to read and educate himself. The urge to write followed quickly. He made his way to Chicago, and in 1935 got on the Federal Writer's Project. By this time he had published poetry, articles, and stories in the little magazines. He then began working on the stories which finally went into his first book, *Uncle Tom's Children,* 1938. This book won a contest open to all WPA writers and led to a Guggenheim Fellowship for its author. Wright was thus enabled to quit the project and complete his first novel. *Native Son,* 1940, was not only a Book-of-the-Month Club selection but an outstanding critical and popular success. From the point of view of the Negro in American literature it became a significant milepost. It was followed by *Twelve Million Black Voices,* 1941, a folk history, and by *Black Boy,* 1945, an autobiographical book which repeated in nearly every way the success of Wright's *Native Son.* A dramatization of *Native Son* by Wright and Paul Green was produced in 1940 and later included among the best plays of the year.

TRANSLATORS

L. A.	Lionel Able
J. P. B.	John Peale Bishop
B. F. C.	Ben F. Carruthers
M. C.	Mercer Cook
I. G.	Ivan Goll
L. H.	Langston Hughes
J. W. J.	James Weldon Johnson
J. F. M.	John F. Matheus
E. W. U.	Edna Worthley Underwood
D. D. W.	Donald Devenish Walsh

AUTHOR INDEX

AUTHOR INDEX

FIRST LINE INDEX

FIRST LINE INDEX

DATE DUE